Putting the *Luxe* Back in Luxury

D0931601

Putting the *Luxe* Back in Luxury

How New Consumer Values are Redefining the Way We Market Luxury

PAMELA N. DANZIGER

Paramount Market Publishing, Inc.

Paramount Market Publishing, Inc.
950 Danby Road, Suite 136
Ithaca, NY 14850
www.paramountbooks.com
Voice: 607-275-8100; 888-787-8100
Fax: 607-275-8101

Publisher: James Madden
Editorial Director: Doris Walsh

Copyright © 2011 Pamela N. Danziger
Printed in USA

All rights reserved. No part of this book may be reproduced,
stored in a retrieval system, or transmitted in any form or by
any means, electronic, mechanical, photocopying, recording, or
otherwise, without the prior written permission of the publisher. Further
information may be obtained from Paramount Market Publishing, Inc.,
950 Danby Road, Suite 136, Ithaca, NY 14850.

This publication is designed to provide accurate and authoritative
information in regard to the subject matter covered. It is sold with
the understanding that the publisher is not engaged in rendering
legal, accounting, or other professional services. If legal advice or
other expert assistance is required, the services of a competent
professional should be sought.

All trademarks are the property of their respective companies.
Cataloging in Publication Data available
ISBN-10: 0-9819869-4-3 | ISBN-13: 978-0-9819869-4-4 paper

for Greg

Contents

Part 4 Rainmaking in the Luxury Drought

The Future for Luxury Marketers Depends on Putting the Luxe Back In Luxury

Nothing will be the same again. It would be illusory to think it will be the same again.
—Bernard Arnault, chairman, LVMH Moët Hennessy Louis Vuitton

"Gleam Returns to Luxury-Goods Sales" proclaimed the *Wall Street Journal* on October 18, 2010, based on a new study by Bain & Company and its partner Altagamma, the Italian trade association for luxury goods. What a huge disservice this headline did to marketers trying in earnest to get a handle on what is really going on in the luxury market today. The danger is that marketers dependent upon the indulgent spending of affluent consumers will heave a sigh of relief and go back to luxury business as usual. That course, unfortunately, will be a big mistake because the luxury market has changed, and changed dramatically, from the go-go years prior to 2007.

What's wrong with this overly-optimistic and very simplistic report on the luxury market is that it measures the wrong things. The Bain assessment of consumers' return to luxury is founded on the results of about 220 luxury goods companies' sales reports. A sizeable portion of the revenues measured by the Bain study include LVMH and PPR, two giant multinational luxury brand conglomerates with exposure in developing markets, like China, India, and Brazil, where luxury is hot and growing. Without question these companies are doing very well, but their growth in revenues says more about their success at managing their businesses than it does about the affluent consumer market. The boom in luxury goods sales that Bain reports is based on a couple of core factors that have nothing to do with rising consumer sales in the U.S. and everything to do with economic trends and management practices. First, the companies have very weak comparables to work against, so 10 percent overall growth isn't particularly hard to achieve given the low starting point. Second, the euro suffered significant depreciation from the previous year, accounting for "40 percent of the sales revenue increase," as the Bain's press release reports. Third, luxury marketers have been successful at shifting a significant portion of their distribution from department stores and other third party retailers to company-owned stores. The end result is that in the current year these companies are booking 100 percent of the retail price of goods, rather than a lowly wholesale percentage. Take away these three factors that have nothing to do with the consumer market and the gleam turns to gloom for the luxury marketers that don't have these key factors going for them.

Just days following the Bain bit of mis-information came another story out of the American Affluence Research Center that also did no favors to luxury marketers. In a survey about plans for future spending among 439 high-net-worth households ($800,000+ net worth) which the study sponsors claim are representative of the wealthiest 10 percent of American households, they find "for the most part [the wealthiest 1 percent] are going to continue to spend," while everyone else is very much on the ropes. The AARC's primary advice for luxury marketers looking to grow is simple, and in my view, foolish. "Luxury brands and luxury marketers should be focused on the wealthiest one percent because they are the least likely to be cutting back and are the most knowledgeable about the price points and brands that are true high-end luxury."

If everybody takes this advice and goes after the top 1 percent of the wealthiest customers with household incomes of $500,000 and above, which is actually just a tiny, highly unrepresentative segment of the affluent market (what I call outliers because that is what they are—far, far outside the norm of households at the top 20 percent of incomes), a lot of brands are going to crash and burn on their rush of competition to the top. And we also have to face the fact that a lot of luxury marketers and their brands are really not equipped to compete in the rarified air of the super rich.

There is a lot more oxygen to sustain growth at lower income levels.

With the turn of the new year and positive reports out of the luxury retailing sector for the fourth quarter 2010, more headlines proclaimed that the luxury shopper was back. Among the typical headlines is this one from the *Dallas Morning News*, "Neiman Marcus holiday quarter profit rose as luxury spenders returned." Similar stories have reported long-overdue positive results for Saks and Nordstrom. Frankly, these luxury retailers' reports are a far better barometer than the luxury brands' of what is going on with the luxury consumer sector since they are much closer to the actual customers and their transactions. But what is missing from these glowing news stories out of the retail sector is that the luxury retailing giants—Neiman Marcus, Saks, and Nordstrom—are very different today than they were pre-2007, before the recession. These companies have made dramatic adjustments in their businesses starting with more realistic pricing and greater focus on delivering product and services to online shoppers. They aren't selling the same stuff the same way they did before the recession and now they are being rewarded for making those changes. While luxury shoppers haven't returned to what they were before, they are starting to come back, but with new ideas, new demands, and new expectations.

We need to get real about luxury consumers and the potential in the luxury market

Make no mistake: The luxury consumer market has changed and will continue to morph through the next decade. Rather than wishing and hoping and praying for the good old days when luxury was hot and affluents as well as upper-middle-income folks couldn't get enough luxury, marketers' only hope is to face the reality that much of the luxe has gone out of their brands and their marketing. Using their old tricks, luxury brands aren't pulling in enough shoppers and enough dollars to sustain the past levels of business. People who used to be able to afford luxury brands aren't willing to pony up anymore, or only very occasionally. Customers are fundamentally different than they were just two or three years ago and there are fewer luxury customers coming to build a bridge to the future.

This is the reality of the luxury market through the next decade, until about 2020. This period of low levels of growth for luxury marketers, the luxury drought, is caused by fundamental shifts in the demographics of the consumer market, as well as changes to affluent consumers' purchase behavior and psychology. Taken together, these three factors—demographics, purchase behavior, and psychographics—will work synergistically to slow down the growth in the U.S. luxury market through the next decade. The way for marketers to succeed in this increasingly hostile low-growth environment is to integrate their understanding of the negative forces with innovative new products and inspiring new marketing and sales strategies.

Putting the Luxe Back in Luxury is intended to strip away the illusions and fantasies many marketers hold about the luxury consumer marketplace. In my many years of consumer research, I have never faced a business segment so under- and mis-informed about the customers served. Marketers' fantasies about how the luxury consumer lives and behaves cloud their judgments. In this book you will learn who the luxury consumers are, what they really want, and how marketers that depend upon reaching them can tap their potential.

At its core, this book is about *aspiration* or creating desire in the minds of consumers for luxury. An aspiration is "a strong desire to achieve something high or great or an object of such desire." I often find marketers attribute motives to the aspirations of their customers when they really are projecting their own aspirations onto the customer. As marketers, we can't build consumer aspiration if we are caught up in our own personal aspirations. We must strip away the aspirational to get to the fundamentals of marketing luxury to customers who have different desires than they had just a few short years ago.

Why luxury and the affluent consumers matter

In a time of economic upheaval where unemployment is at record highs, and government debt has reached unimaginable proportions, the middle class is getting squeezed. Middle class incomes actually declined in real terms from 1999 to 2009; the average income of the average U.S. household dropped 3.5 percent in current dollars from $70,462 to $67,976. The obvious question is how important are luxury and the affluent anyway? As a culture, don't we have bigger problems to deal with than indulging the privileged few with more luxuries? Not true. In the future, affluent consumers are going to become even more important to marketers at every step up the pricing ladder—from discount to middle-market to ultra-high end—simply because the American economy is so highly dependent on consumer spending, which makes up roughly 70 percent of the GDP.

Affluent households at the top 20 percent of the income scale do far more than their fair share in propping up the nation's economy and GDP. This 20 percent of households accounts for:

- more than 50 percent of all income and earnings, and
- more than 40 percent of all consumer spending.

The households in the 20 percent are truly the heavy-lifters in the U.S. consumer economy.

Luxury marketers' new challenge: To put the luxe back in luxury

Luxury marketers must change the old way of doing business. They must embrace the values of today's affluent consumers' and deliver products and services that have meaning and value given the consumers' new enlightened, increasingly post-materialistic perspective. It is no surprise that Merriam-Webster named *austerity* word of the year for 2010. The old luxury model based on image, status, conspicuous consumption, and spendthrift indulgence is now tarnished and dull. Marketers and brand managers have to find new ways of marketing and communicating that will put the luxe back in their luxury brands, products, and services.

Marketing starts with understanding the customer

Today's luxury marketers face a marketing challenge: how to build connections with a new type of customer with new values and new priorities. To meet that challenge, luxury marketers must integrate new learning about the consumer into their marketing, advertising, communications, and product-development strategies.

Understanding the new consumer market for luxury will take a three-pronged strategy:

Demographics

If marketing starts with understanding the consumer, then understanding the consumer starts with demographics. Demographics are the facts and figures that define the people who are the target market for luxury now and in the future. The 2010 Census data reveal the changing demographics of affluence and how those demographics will shift during the next decade.

Purchase behavior

Luxury marketers have to understand how their customers change product and brand preferences, where they shop, how much they spend, and their basic shopping strategies. The latest findings from Unity Marketing's exclusive luxury tracking study allows us to examine in detail the shifts, turns, and transitions of luxury customers over time.

Psychographics or why people buy

The underlying psychology of the consumer is without a doubt the most important piece of the puzzle. Psychology is where consumers' values lie, what guides and directs their purchase behavior. To put the luxe back in their luxury marketing efforts, marketers must tap deeply into the psychology of the consumer.

You can use these three key understandings of the consumer—demographics, purchase behavior, and psychographics—as a springboard to new marketing and branding strategies.

This requires three more steps:

Integrate

As a luxury marketer you need to integrate consumer insights (i.e., understandings from the study of demographics, purchase behavior, and psychology) into your business and strategic planning. This book presents the most relevant insights that you need to integrate into your new business models.

Innovate

You must discover unique and original ways to innovate your brands, your products, and your marketing messages to find new ways of connecting with your consumers. Innovation is particularly challenging for luxury brands. The long-standing heritage of many of these brands is crucial to their marketing and branding proposition. Yet innovation is critical for luxury brands to remain relevant to consumers empowered by the internet and who employ new strategies for shopping. Use the consumer insights presented in this book as a springboard for innovation and to reinvent your marketing messages and brands for a new kind of luxury customer.

Inspire

Ultimately, luxury products and services must inspire consumers to spend their time, money, and personal resources to forge a relationship with your brand. Luxury executives must be inspired to manage their brands carefully and honestly. They must find inspiration to create better products, more meaningful services, and more value for the customer. Retail sales executives and associates must be inspired when dealing with customers. The time when luxury and high-end items could be sold without sales skill has passed. Inspiring the people who connect with customers is crucial to the entire luxury consumer experience. Luxury marketers should forget about *aspiration*. The new challenge is to give customers *inspiration* for your brands and your products.

Companies that use the formula above to put the luxe back in luxury will grow sales, build market share, and create a sustainable business model for the future.

My personal goal in writing *Putting the Luxe Back in Luxury* is to inspire you to grab hold of a bright future. I will highlight inspiring examples of companies and brands who are putting the luxe back, and are tapping the new consumer psychology to more effectively market luxury goods and services to affluent consumers.

Putting the Luxe Back in Luxury concludes with steps that luxury brands must take now to put the luxe back into their brands. I hope it will provide inspiration for you as a luxury marketer or branding executive, to create a new business model for the 21st-century luxury consumer. Your challenge for the future is to sell luxury goods and services that will ultimately transform the individual. This book will show you how.

The Luxury Market Has Changed — and It's Never Going Back to the Way It Was Before

I have the feeling the luxury market has hit bottom and will slowly—not like it was in the Eighties—but slowly, grow again.

—Yves Carcelle, chairman and CEO, Louis Vuitton

From boom to bust—that is the story of the luxury market in the past decade. Not too long ago, luxury was the "it" word in marketing circles. Luxury was hot; luxury was what everyone wanted a piece of; luxury was on a never-ending upward spiral of prosperity; luxury was relevant; luxury was meaningful; luxury was attainable. Until it wasn't.

Somehow in luxury's rise to the top it faltered, lost its way, grew complacent, grew out of touch with reality. It ignored the warning shots over the bow as the overheated housing market started to cool. It was indifferent to the earth tremors that preceded the fall of AIG, Lehman Brothers, and Bear Stearns and the nearly $7 billion collateral damage done to the stock market by the financial crisis. With the first inklings of recession headed in our direction, luxury kept on its merry way; conventional wisdom told us the affluent remain unaffected by the economic ups and downs that afflict the middle class. That is, until the affluent closed up their wallets and pocket books, put their credit cards on hold, and instituted new spending rules to live by. The luxury drought had set in as the bottom fell out of the global economy—the result of all that borrowing and spending at the micro (i.e., household) and macro (i.e., corporate and government deficits) levels.

Before the recession, people, corporations, and governments spent against their *perceived* wealth, which was on the rise. But in the recession of 2008, all of that wealth vanished. People were forced to go back to spending what they really earned, not what they could beg or borrow, or even steal from their future.

In the economic and cultural turmoil brought on by too much valueless spending, luxury lost its luster, as Dana Thomas wrote in her exposé of the luxury industry in *Deluxe*. Thomas chronicles how many luxury brands crossed over to the dark side of mass marketing while riding the wave of the luxury market boom. These brands were making money hand-over-fist, as middle-class consumers traded up to luxury brands they couldn't really afford. In going down-market and losing their luxury allure, many luxury brands lost touch with true luxury—their entire reason for being—and affluent consumers' reason for buying.

From boom to bust in luxury

The luxury market was poised for a fall, and fall it did. Luxury consumers started to cut back their spending on luxuries in the second half of 2007. They continued to reduce their spending through 2008 and into early 2009, though spending on luxury has started to rise slightly since then, as measured by Unity Marketing's Luxury Tracking Study. Conducted every three months, it is an in-depth luxury tracking survey of 1,200+ affluent luxury consumers. It records details about the luxury goods and services purchased (up to 22 different categories of luxury products and services are tracked), place of purchase, amount spent, and brands favored. The study results show that growth in luxury consumer spending reached its peak in 2006, then spending on luxury started to decline. Spending on luxury started to decline rapidly beginning in the middle of 2007 and continued its rapid decline until hitting bottom in 2008.

As I write, most economists agree that the recession is history and that the U.S. economy is in recovery mode. Consumer spending, the ultimate measure of economic vitality in the U.S., is posting growth in fits and starts. Retail sales are beginning to lift, but much of that growth can be attributed to the dramatic adjustments retailers made through the course of the recession.

Luxury market optimists are trying to revive the fortunes of their brands by boasting of the return of the luxury shopper, as *Forbes* announced with its juicy March 30, 2010 headline, "The millionaires are back." Only thing is, the brands that the *Forbes* writer advised investing in—Coach and Nordstrom—are not those normally associated with millionaire spending. These brands are described in luxury circles pejoratively as *aspirational brands,* "aspirational" in this case referring not to their target market, but to themselves—brands that aspire to true luxury brand status on a par with Louis Vuitton, Gucci, Hermès, and Chanel, or Saks Fifth Avenue, Neiman Marcus, and Bergdorf Goodman. While U.S. luxury brands are beginning to make a comeback after their fall from grace in 2008, they have a long way to go to get back to the exuberant growth of 2005, 2006, and 2007.

 Figure 1.1 U.S. Luxury Brand Revenues, 2005–2009

in thousands

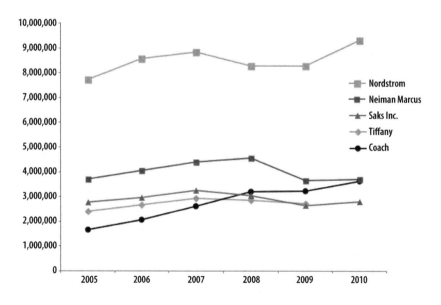

Source: Unity Marketing and company annual reports

The luxury brands that are hot in the U.S. market today are no longer the "true" luxury brands, but the more affordable "up-starts." The U.S. market can't boast the fastest-growing affluent population—the Asian markets of Hong Kong and India win that honor, according to the *21st Annual World Wealth Report* compiled by Capgemini and Merrill Lynch. However, the U.S. leads the world with the largest number of high-net-worth individuals, 2.87 million in total, way ahead of number two–ranked Japan with 1.65 million, and third-ranked Germany with 861,500. Short of walking away from the U.S. market in search of quick growth out of Asia, luxury marketers can't ignore the U.S. luxury market. It is, without question, the world's richest consumer market. But the U.S. luxury market is not what it used to be and luxury marketers here have got to change or languish.

What makes Coach and Nordstrom hot and the others not?

In a word: value. Each brand works hard at understanding its customer, what she values, how she shops, and what she wants to spend. Each brand puts that understanding of the good-value equation for its customer into its unique marketing strategy. We are going to take a closer look at the Coach brand shortly. But recent issues of Nordstrom's monthly catalogs provide a powerful lesson in how a brand delivers what today's post-recession affluent shopper wants. The catalogs are chock full of fashion-forward styles that look like they should cost 25 to 50 percent more than they actually do. That is a winning strategy in today's post-recession luxury market—give the consumer more luxury for less.

If giving the consumer more for less is the ticket for success in the luxury drought, then brands only need to lower their prices to increase perceived value, and *voilà*, sales dollars result. But that makes no sense and indeed proved disastrous after the rush to the pricing bottom that came during the 2008 Christmas shopping season. Many brands and retailers that jumped on the discounting bandwagon suffered long-term damage to their profit margins and their brand reputations. Even worse, it got harder for retailers and brands to command full prices again, as they tried to get back to business as usual after the excess inventory was moved out.

Rather than just reducing prices, luxury brands and marketers need to focus on the *good* part of the *good value* equation. That is, they have to figure out how to up the ante on the good—or as I prefer to say, to put more luxe into the consumer equation. The problem is the luxe or the good, like beauty, is in the eye of the beholder. To understand the good, you have to understand how customers assign value to a purchase they are considering and what specific parts of the value equation gives them justification to spend more. And that takes a deep understanding of the consumer's mindset.

• • • • •

Coach Gives a Lesson in
Doing Consumer Centricity Right

Founded in 1941, Coach became known for its high-quality leather goods and handbags. Now after nearly 70 years, the company operates 330 Coach retail stores, plus 111 factory outlet stores. These sell both factory store–exclusive and discontinued and irregular product, discounted from 10 to 50 percent below list price. The brand is also featured in over 900 department store locations in the U.S. In addition, it maintains an active international presence in 159 department stores, retail shops, and duty-free locations in over 20 countries. Further, Coach has a wholly owned subsidiary in Japan that operates 155 locations, plus 28 company-operated locations in China.

The company has been at the forefront of multi-channel marketing, with its Coach.com website attracting 51 million unique visits in 2009 and blasting 94 million emails as part of the company's electronic outreach program. Its direct-marketing division maintains a database of 13 million households in North America as well as 3.5 million in Japan and it mails five million catalogs to targets in the U.S., Japan, Canada, Hong Kong, Macau, and China.

Coach also is cutting edge in social media. Its 800,000 friends on Facebook and 270,000 followers on Twitter all receive updates from the company. What is truly impressive is how Coach puts its connections with brand customers, loyalists, and potential customers to work to guide product development and design, and innovations in marketing programs. As a luxury marketer, it is way out in front of its competitors in understanding its customer, as shown in the company's numbers.

As the recession started to take hold in late 2007 and early 2008, Coach CEO Lew Frankfort was asked about the economy by fashion trade magazine *Women's Wear Daily*. "I thought it would likely be a serious, prolonged downturn. And that Coach would need to create even more compelling reasons for consumers to shop," he told the magazine. That led the company to put in place plans to launch a new lower-priced product line aimed to inspire the more youthful and price-conscious shopper. At its official release June 26, 2009, that product line, Poppy, emerged with an average price point of $260, 20 percent lower than the typical Coach handbag.

Another move inspired by consumer insights focused on lowering the prices for the regular line of Coach handbags, which during the boom times had crept up to an average of $330. By July 2008 the company recognized it had reached its pricing limit and it was time to back pedal. It set a new goal to offer half of the company's handbags under $300, the optimum price point in 2007 when it sold the most purses ever, rather than selling only 30 percent of its stock at the under-$300 price point as it did in 2008.

Understanding how its customers were looking at its prices led the company to institute a strategy that it called "price rebalancing," designed to generate more volume to offset lost revenues due to shifts in consumers' willingness to spend not just in the short term, but over the long haul. Frankfort said, "We took the view that the world will forever be different and we need to acclimate ourselves."

Coach's laser-focus on its customers alerted the company early to the shift in consumer sentiment as the recession gained strength. It was then able to develop strategies in anticipation of worse to come, and didn't wait around like other brands until panic set in.

On a daily and weekly basis company executives are given a blow-by-blow detail of store operations, including number of customer visits per store, percentage of visitors who made purchases, what they bought, and how much was spent. According to a June 25, 2009 article in *BusinessWeek*, Coach's consumer insights are supported by a budget of $5 million. Lead designer Reed Krakoff, who just launched a separate high-end apparel brand under his own name, said, "relentless consumer research keeps the company aware of what customers want."

What sets Coach apart from the rest is not only the investment it makes in market research, but more importantly the way the company uses consumer insights to direct strategy. Market research isn't used after the fact to reassure executives or reinforce decisions already made; rather it is used to drive decisions, change strategy, and set a new course. One notable example of using research to direct strategy was the discovery through research that the typical Coach customer regularly visits a Coach store once every month or so. That led to the directive that every Coach store change the floor layout and displays every 30 days to provide returning customers with something new to browse. It also resulted in new product introductions timed on a 30-day cycle to catch the repeat shopper's roving eye.

To the detriment of fashion brands, the idea of consumer research— listening to the consumer and actually changing styles and offerings based upon what customers say—is anathema to many designers. The culture of the fashion world centers on the designer as inspired visionary who leads, rather than follows, the consumer market. However, signs are that other designers are starting to get customer-centric "religion" thanks to the growing power of social media.

Marc Jacobs will be expanding its offerings of plus sizes due to Twitter feedback from customers in need of more accommodating sizing. Facebook fans commented that Ann Taylor LOFT's new pants line, modeled by a size-zero "glamazon," were only wearable by the super-skinny, not the normal curvy woman. This led the company to post new photos showing the same pants on company employees from sizes 2 to 12. Social media–fed input also resulted in Ann Taylor expanding its petite offering and its shoe collection. The success of the Ann Taylor company in listening to its customers is written in the numbers: a 16 percent increase in second-quarter 2010 same-store sales, a 55 percent uptick in LOFT e-commerce revenues, and a 29 percent boost to Ann Taylor brand online sales.

Coach, and brands like Marc Jacobs and Ann Taylor, are using research not to *dictate* design and strategy, but to *inform decisions* about design and strategy. Research gives direction and provides point-counterpoint to executives who need to make decisions on more than just a whim or a hope and a prayer.

Frankfort describes the yin-yang of design inspiration and consumer research, "One of the ways we think at Coach is as a company that is run as a blend of logic and magic. Magic is the touch and feel and instinct of good product, good looking product, and understanding trends, and logic is using all the knowledge that is available to you, so you can really understand where the consumers are today and where they're going tomorrow."

• • • • •

Shifting demographics

As luxury consumer spending declined during the recession, Unity Marketing's Luxury Tracking Study also documented a shift in the demographic makeup of the luxury consumer market. Previously, more than half of the luxury consumers responding to the tracking survey fell into the "HENRY" (High Earners Not Rich Yet: an acronym coined by *Fortune* writer Shawn Tully) segment of upper-middle-class consumers with incomes of $100,000-$249.999 But in the 2009 and 2010 surveys, the luxury consumer sample has increasingly skewed away from lower-income toward higher-income affluents. In effect, the ultra-affluent segment (households with incomes at the top 2 percent of all incomes, or $250,000 and above) are playing a more important role in the overall luxury market, while many of those at the HENRY affluent income levels from $100,000 to $249,999 have dropped out of the luxury market.

A luxury drought has set in with the recession

This is the "luxury drought," a dry period following the luxury market boom of the last decade. The luxury drought is characterized by affluents sharply reducing their spending on luxury as they reevaluate, reprioritize, and reassess their lifestyles.

The new economy post-recession will be a dry spell for luxury marketers overall. They face an environment where many with high incomes are sharply curtailing their purchases of luxury products and many others with lower incomes who used to trade up to luxury, have simply dropped out of the luxury market. As mentioned above, the luxury-consumer market that remains is a much smaller and more concentrated segment made up primarily of the highest-income ultra-affluents. Where luxury spending used to be spread across a much wider array of consumers with a broader range of incomes, in the new environment a much smaller segment of consumers accounts for the bulk of luxury marketers' revenues.

This trend is not good news for many companies who historically have drawn a significant share of revenue growth from a much bigger playing field of consumers. There are ten HENRY (High Earner Not Rich Yet) households (21 million households with incomes from $100,000–$249,999) to every ultra-affluent one (2.5 million at the ultra-affluent level). The simple fact is that the U.S. post-recession economy can no longer support the large number of stores and retail outlets that resulted from the boom in luxury. The next decade will mark a period of necessary contraction of the luxury space in the United States.

Confronting the effects of luxury drought, some esteemed luxury brands went under—Escada and Christian Lacroix among the most prominent. Other brands faced the realities of the post-recession new normal by sharply curtailing operating expenses. In 2010, Saks Fifth Avenue shuttered seven stores in secondary markets and Bulgari closed three, while Versace announced it was leaving Japan for good with the closing of its three high-end boutiques. And that doesn't even take into account the scores of independent high-end boutiques that have been casualties of dramatically reduced consumer spending. Other companies laid off legions of staffers in an effort to adjust. Burberry and Cartier recently announced company-wide layoffs, while Chanel eliminated 200 positions, Versace 350, and Neiman Marcus slashed 825 staffers from its payroll while forcing salaried employees to take a pay cut.

Across the entire luxury industry, companies have been cutting back, cutting out, and revising strategic plans downward by 10 to 20 percent. That figure is suggested by Bain & Company's *Luxury Goods Worldwide Market,* a study based on the financial performance of 220 of the world's leading luxury goods companies. Bain reported a net decline in the global luxury market of 8 percent in 2009, with 8 percent declines expected for Europe and 10 percent in Japan. The Americas experienced the sharpest drop in luxury revenues, down 16 percent from 2008 to 2009. For 2010, prospects for luxury brands were improved, but even if luxury company revenues grew as expected, sales would still be way off the luxury industry's peak year of €170 billion.

Affluent consumers' values are shifting toward meaningful consumption, away from indulgence

While the global recession has taken a lot of the wind out of luxury brands' sails, the recession alone does not account for all the pain. People at all income levels were no longer assigning a premium to luxury. It wasn't something worth striving for any more. In a June 2010 consumer sentiment survey from Boston Consulting Group, one-half of the Americans surveyed said luxury is less important to them now compared with two years ago, putting luxury at the bottom of their list of important values. By contrast, saving, stability, family, home, and ethics rose to the top as the most important values for Americans today.

As people shifted away from valuing luxury, it is not surprising that luxury brand marketers lost touch with what their target customers really wanted—the dreams and aspirations that attracted consumers to these brands in the first place. Luxury brands lost their *mojo*—their luxe. The challenge for luxury marketers in the next decade will be to get their luxe back.

The luxury drought was inevitable; the recession simply brought it on faster and more intensely than otherwise would have happened

At its root, the current dry spell in the luxury market was not *caused* by the global recession. However the recession acted as the tipping point that accelerated the impact of underlying trends already at work in the luxury consumer mindset. Prior to the recession, those trends were underground, quietly and slowly transforming the luxury market. These trends include shifts in the demographics of luxury, especially the aging of the Baby Boom generation, and the resulting changes in consumer attitudes and psychology that come about naturally as people mature. Then the recession hit in 2008 and the luxury drought came on fast and furiously.

At its core, the American culture started to turn away from luxury. People started to look for something more out of life than just having and getting more "stuff." Richard Florida, the futurist author of *The Great Reset,* views the pursuit of material for materialism's sake, "For a time I saw too many people like this, the whole L.A. gossip-blog, L.A.-style magazines where people without purpose or meaning were literally buying their identity off a rack. What a horrifying thing."

Luxury became tainted by excesses and overindulgence, and in some widely publicized cases like the Bernie Madoff scandal, outright corruption. As a result, many Americans now view the word "luxury" and the visual imagery of the luxury lifestyle in a negative light. In a move reflecting the *zeitgeist,* Time Inc. has ceased publication of its quarterly *Time Style & Design* magazine, its paean to yesterday's luxury lifestyle. Luxury indulgence is no longer the American ideal nor is it the fulfillment of the American Dream.

The new American Dream is about quality of life, not quantity of stuff

> *Luxury today is not about something expensive. . . . Luxury is an experience that will enrich you. After having had this, you as a person are richer spiritually and intellectually.*
>
> —Thierry Samuel, chairman, Relais & Chateaux
> (an association of fine hotels and gourmet restaurants)

A new age of post-materialism, which shouldn't be confused with asceticism or an overall denial of consumption, will ultimately transform the individual and our society. Post-materialism springs not from scarcity, but from an abundance of material possessions or resources. When everyone has as many possessions as Americans have, riches can no longer be the measure of their status or social position. We see post-materialism emerging with new non-materialistic ways to display and measure personal success, including how a person contributes to society and makes the world a better place.

Many people with means are rejecting a lifestyle of material wealth and luxury as the fulfillment of the American dream in favor of the goal of achieving personal happiness and fulfillment. That doesn't mean they necessarily want to live without, but simply accumulating material wealth isn't enough. They recognize that personal happiness and fulfillment are not defined by their accumulated assets or a high income, or by what brands they buy or how much you own. Unfortunately for marketers selling the material expression of the American dream, people at all income levels, especially the affluent, are discovering that getting more "stuff" is not the way to achieve personal happiness. As the values of Americans change, so does their shopping behavior.

Having spent the last twenty years in acquisition mode, today's affluent customers, out of both necessity and desire, are redefining their lives and their value systems. They are committing to a new responsible consumerism where luxury is not a birthright, but a special privilege; where indulgence is not an everyday affair, but something best enjoyed occasionally and selectively. Affluents are turning from shopping for fun to shopping primarily for the things they need, and those needs are dramatically reduced after they take stock of their overfilled closets.

Luxury consumers' desire to "do good and give back" signals a cultural shift

The luxury consumer market is shifting away from conspicuous consumption where "he who dies with the most toys wins" to a new enlightened mindset of caring, sharing, and conserving. More and more, the affluent consumer's goal is a drive to enhance the quality of life, not to acquire more stuff.

Unity Marketing's on-going research of the mindset of the affluent consumer has found that affluent Americans (the top 20 percent of U.S. households based upon income) have a new perspective on their luxury lifestyle and the responsibilities that go with it. This new perspective will bring significant challenges for luxury marketers over the next decade. In the future, marketers won't find the same indulgent, free-spending customers they had before the recession. They will have to work harder to give shoppers new and more compelling reasons to buy.

We see evidence of this cultural shift from a consuming to a caring and sharing society in the extent of affluents' charitable contributions. *Giving USA 2010,* a yearbook on philanthropy, reports that charitable giving in the United States reach $303.75 billion in 2009, exceeding $300 billion for the second year in a row. In keeping with historical precedent, individual giving accounts for some 75 percent of all charitable contributions. And, affluents with incomes of $100,000 or more make up an estimated one-half of all individual giving. We also see evidence of the cultural shift in the way affluents are adopting a green lifestyle. Affluent consumers are concerned about the way companies do business and manufacture and deliver products. They expect the companies, brands, and retailers they support to be good stewards of the environment by implementing green practices and to be good citizens of the world by giving back and donating to charities. In a recent Unity Marketing survey among over 1,000 affluents, three-fourths of those surveyed said that a company or brand's concern with the environment influences which products they buy and over two-thirds said a company's green practices influence where they decide to shop.

We see evidence of the cultural shift in what affluents really value. When we asked more than 1,000 affluents where they gain the greatest happiness and satisfaction in their luxury lifestyles, we found that the majority find their happiness comes from the things they do, rather than from the things they own. By a wide margin, affluent consumers chose experiences, such as travel, dining, and entertainment as the luxury purchases that give them the most satisfaction, with over half (52 percent) naming experiences as their most satisfying luxury purchases. This compares with 25 percent who derive the greatest satisfaction from their luxury home, and 15 percent who find the most happiness and satisfaction in personal luxuries, such as fashion and jewelry. Thus in valuing the things they do, over the things they own, affluent consumers are best expressing this new trend toward post-materialism.

And we see evidence in the fact that luxury shoppers, at all income levels, are no longer willing to pay exorbitant retail prices for luxury goods and services. Neiman Marcus and Saks Fifth Avenue put luxury brands on notice in early 2009 when they demanded that marketers offer their shoppers lower "opening" price points. That was a polite way to say "cut your prices or we won't stock your brand anymore."

Ever since the recession began and retailers were forced to dramatically cut prices to move luxury merchandise, luxury marketers have been wringing their hands over the fact that they have lost their ability to control what people will pay. They believe that once their brands are marked down, people will refuse to go back to paying full retail price because the brand has lost its exclusivity and its brand image is irreparably damaged.

They are correct in assuming people with means won't go back to paying the high retail prices that were common prior to the recession, but not for the reason they believe. Affluents won't pay retail simply because in many cases the price isn't worth it any longer—the *value* is no longer there. During the boom years, luxury brands inflated their prices season after season, and the affluent shoppers who felt flush, paid. But no longer. Affluents demand a new kind of value for the prices they pay, and today many luxury consumers are refusing to pay the asking price because it just isn't worth it to them.

When the recession is over, the luxury consumer market will be very different

As the economy continues its slow recovery out of the recession, we will find the luxury consumer market different from the way it was before the current crisis during the boom time. These changes in how people look at luxury and their new value system that rejects rampant materialism will be lasting. The emerging consumers are thinking about their future in new ways. They are learning that conspicuous consumption is not the way to grow wealth, to achieve happiness, or to make their lives more meaningful. Many of today's affluents who have much are giving back, doing good, and taking concrete steps to make the world a better place.

In the new-normal economy after the recession, luxury brands must strive to build a deeper, more personal relationship with their customers, one that goes beyond a mere commercial, customer relationship. By aligning their brands with the new values that are so important to affluents, such as green marketing, fair-trade, corporate philanthropy, and support for causes, as well as offering their luxury goods and services at more realistic prices, luxury marketers can build a platform for a deeper customer relationship. Luxury marketers will find that doing good is good business.

As this new age dawns, luxury doesn't mean the same thing it once did. People with money will always want the best quality, best workmanship, best style and design, but they want the emphasis on concrete attributes and values that are measurable and defined by facts and figures, not image or status. And they are no longer willing to pay ten times, twenty times, fifty times more than the ordinary mass market price for a luxury brand. They demand more value today in exchange for their hard-earned money.

Luxury is turning inward. It is no longer about an external or outward show of status or wealth, but an inner state of being defined by personal happiness and an outstanding quality of life. The challenge for marketers and retailers that sell luxury goods is to get inside the minds of these new post-materialistic, value-driven, affluent consumers and demonstrate in a measurable way how the things they sell improve consumers' quality of life. They must develop a new language of value to communicate with their potential customers. This new language must reflect emerging cultural trends and resonate deeply and honestly with the emotions and feelings of affluent consumers.

To put the luxe back in luxury, we need to understand our customers

As luxury marketers, our future path is clear. We need to focus first on a deep understanding of the customers for our goods and services to learn how to deliver the luxe values that luxury consumers crave. To put the luxe back in luxury, marketers must be vigilant to align the attributes, values, and qualities of their products and brands with their target consumers' true desires. That takes identifying the unique segments within the customer base and researching what they value about the brand.

Steven Dennis on Consumer Centricity

Consumer centricity is key to putting the luxe back in the brand. It's "an approach to doing business that starts with the needs and wants of target customers and aligns all major business processes to improve the customer experience and maximize long-term customer value," as defined by Steven Dennis. Dennis, the founder of SageBerry Consulting, was formerly the Senior Vice President of Strategy, Business Development & Marketing for the Neiman Marcus Group.

Steve and I share a commitment to consumer centricity as the driver for marketing and business strategy. This is contrasted with product-centric or channel-centric strategies that once may have worked, but today are old fashioned, out-moded, and just plain backwards.

What sets Steve above others offering consumer-centric consulting (Google lists over 250,000 hits on the term) is that he helps his clients put the principles of consumer and relationship management to work not just in marketing, but from a corporate strategic and operations perspective. Steve explains, "Consumer centricity is not such a new idea, but a lot of companies struggle with it. Retailers struggle with it because they are mostly run by merchants, and the way most retailers organize their businesses is by product. Retailers have a long-standing tradition of organizing to be product centric. But by being consumer centric, retailers are challenged to look at their businesses in new ways, not how many handbags were sold this quarter, but how much each customer segment spent."

Steve continues, "Consumer centricity all comes down to how you orient your business, looking holistically at your consumers and their behavior. For example, today many retailers are moving toward channel-centric strategies, as they venture into the internet, and organizing their businesses around separate sales channels. This is not to say that product isn't important or channel isn't important, but it is all about where you start. You have got to come at it from the customer first; otherwise you are going to miss a lot of what is really going on in your business."

Steve points to Best Buy as a company that is setting the standard in consumer centricity. The success of its customer-centered approach can't be ignored; it was instrumental in putting its firmly product-centric chief competitor Circuit City out of business. He says, "The most important thing that Best Buy did was create customer segment managers on par with the merchandise managers. In that one step they were able to overcome the biggest problem I see with organizations, which is to convince the merchants to change. I ask my clients to give me their 'customer score card,' which tracks their performance with different customer segments. Nine out of ten times people don't know what I am talking about. But if I asked them to give me data on handbag sales or jeans by style and price point, they have that broken down every way you can imagine. But their data isn't organized around customers and different segments, and that is the challenge, that is the mistake, that is what is missing."

When it comes to implementing consumer-centric strategies for luxury brands, the challenge is often that the luxury customer base is narrower and brands have limited direct contact with their customers. But Steve says every company, every brand, every retailer can put consumer centricity to work because it all starts with understanding what really motivates your customers, why they choose your brand over the competition, what your customers come to you for. However, he warns that a lot of luxury brands confuse customer service with being consumer centric. "Customer service is taking care of customers in the store and solving their problems. Consumer centricity goes way beyond that into the whole way your brand and your organization delivers on the promise to the customer."

From talking about consumer centricity at the company level, Steve turns to talking about what his consumer-centric approach to business has taught him about the future luxury consumer market. "Ultimately sales growth is a function of three things: 1) capacity for the consumer to spend; 2) willingness to spend, assuming they have the capacity; and 3) how they allocate the spending that they do. Obviously we have come through a recession where the capacity and the willingness to spend have been constrained as people have worried about their jobs and what the future looks like. Now as things start to recover, people are somewhat more willing to spend, but revenues for most brands are still running way below 2007 levels. People keep talking about how the luxury market is back, but one quarter's 10 percent increase in sales doesn't make up for the 30 percent decline that occurred over the last two years. Talk to me after two years of 18 percent increases and then we will know if the luxury market is really back, but I don't think that is likely to happen."

He points to two different consumer segments in the luxury market, what he calls the über-wealthy and the working affluent, as critical to understanding the fortunes of luxury brands over the next decade. "All the things that are going on in the economy are not making much of a difference to the über-wealthy. They can afford anything, but they are hardly the whole luxury market. There are plenty of people that are still quite affluent that historically were important contributors to the luxury market, but that have tempered their spending. They've lost their willingness to feel comfortable spending as liberally as they used to. Certain consumer segments will never, or at least not in the foreseeable future, get back to their past spending levels."

Steve explains the differences in luxury indulgence among affluents in their fifties versus those in their forties. He cautions, "Various demographic factors like age start to reduce the size of the wallet. At 50 or so people are looking to retirement and often have big college expenses to adjust for. It puts a damper on their willingness to spend for really expensive stuff. This is going to cause retailers and manufacturers to adjust their business model to deal with lower volumes or to try to get back market share in a different way to make the economics work."

He points to customers who grew out of the middle-class to reach affluence as not likely to bounce back after the recession because they retain their middle-class consumer orientation. Steve explains the change in the mindset of the luxury consumer, pre- and post-recession, "The price-value equation got really out of whack over the last several years. Luxury retailers and brands were virtually able to raise prices indiscriminately because there was so much demand. People weren't being thoughtful about their spending. But then all the outside economic forces hit and people realized how out of whack the price-value equation had become. Even for wealthy people focused on true luxury, the price-value relationship needs to improve."

Steve also finds luxury consumers trading down from the high end toward a more moderate price point in the wake of the recession, leaving luxury marketers with no clear-cut strategy for growth. "Customers are saying to themselves that it is crazy to spend over $1,000 for a handbag. They decided they just aren't going to do that anymore. Luxury brands have to adjust to find growth, since they can't increase the prices as they used to. They have to grow either customers or transactions. The challenge for luxury marketers in the new environment is how to grow share. You can't count on new stores or price increases. You are going to have to win customers away from the competition and that is something that is much harder to figure out. That is where you have to really go to your customer base and understand what drives your business."

Steve concludes, "It all comes down to understanding how your different customers buy and then using those insights to drive strategy. You need to understand the customer segments drawn to your brand and their way of spending. You need to understand the buying process for each segment: How customers get information, how they learn about your brand, how they decide to consider purchasing from you, where they are going to actually make the purchase. You need to understand the journey the customer goes through from first learning about your brand to trying you, and buying, and then growing sales with that customer. The more you really understand how that works, the better you can decide where to put your time and energy."

• • • • •

Now let's move on and examine the current and changing demographics of the luxury consumer market.

part 1

Marketing Begins with Understanding the Customer – Understanding the Customer Begins with Demographics

chapter 2

The Income Demographics of Affluence

The business of demographics is really the business of getting to know who your customers are, where they live, what they buy.

—Peter Francese, founder, *American Demographics*

The dictionary definition of demographics "the physical characteristics of a population such as age, sex, marital status, family size, education, geographic location, and occupation" makes it sound deadly dull and boring, but fairly straightforward. After all, how much complexity and nuance can there be in defining a population by age, sex, or marital status? An awful lot, as we will discover.

When the question of demographics comes up there are two authorities I immediately turn to: U.S. Census data and Peter Francese, known in marketing circles as "Mr. Demographics." Peter founded and published *American Demographics* magazine, a trade journal that was without peer in studying and explaining the trends in the consumer population. It was on the desk of every serious marketer and market researcher until the sad day it ceased publication in November 2004. While it is now part of the *Ad Age* family, but without its monthly delivery to our desks, we marketers have lost the one reliable source for the hidden mysteries in census data. Now companies like Ogilvy & Mather have to hire Peter to make sense of it all.

I sat down with Peter to talk about the role of demographics in marketing in general and the luxury market in particular. In answer to the overriding question of "Why do demographics matter?" Peter couldn't be clearer. "The American population, the number of consumers in America, is growing at 0.94 percent per year—less than 1 percent annually. No product manager, no business manager, no CEO is ever going to be satisfied with revenue growth of 0.9 percent per year.

"It is necessary for anyone who is marketing consumer products in America to figure out what are the faster-growing segments; what are the wealthier segments; what are the segments that buy more of my product than average; where are these people and what are they like? The business of demographics is really the business of getting to know who your customers are, where they live, what they buy. And the thing about it is that, in our rush to the digital world of Web 2.0, it's easy to get mired down in the technicalities and forget about the fact that real people have to go out and spend real money to buy what you are selling. And if you expect them to do more of that in future years, you've got to learn who they are. It's nothing more complicated than that."

Peter continues, "Demographics really matter. It has been proven over and over that companies who are market-focused, meaning they are customer-focused, have much better long-term survival rates than companies who are product-focused. It is the difference between a company coming up with a product then trying to sell it, and a company that finds out what a customer needs or wants, then develops something to serve those wants or needs. The first kind of company that just has a product and tries to get rid of it because the factories are running has a really grim future. It is not thinking about the customer or the demographics of the customer. It is thinking about the product, and that's a losing proposition."

To understand the luxury consumer, identify those with high levels of disposable income

Looking more closely at the luxury consumer market, I asked Peter how the luxury consumer is similar or different from the mass market. "First we need to redefine luxury, because luxury carries a lot of excess baggage. I prefer the term affluent," he said.

In demographic terms an "affluent" is a person who is financially well off. The term "luxury consumer" says nothing about an individual's financial well being, only about what they bought, i.e., a luxury. Many of us assume "luxury" means a product that is made for wealthy or affluent people. Michael Silverstein, in *Trading Up,* proved that wrong in a big way. He defines the trading up consumer as someone with modest income who selectively indulges in luxury consumption.

From Peter's perspective, the luxury market is made up of two types of people—those who can afford luxury and those who really can't afford it, but aspire to it. "There are two kinds of buyers of luxury brands. First, the people who can afford them. Take Rolex for instance. Some people with lots of money value what a Rolex offers. To these people spending $1,000 is like spending $50 to almost everybody else. They purchase a Rolex watch because they can afford it and they'd like it. The second part of that market is what I call aspirationals. These are people who can't afford $1,000 for a watch, but they will buy that watch because it is important to them to create the appearance of wealth. And so they will drive fancy cars, much fancier than they can afford, but they lease them. They will wear expensive suits because it creates the impression of affluence. And they aspire to be somebody who can easily afford that. They aspire to what affluence represents."

Then, to confound the efforts of marketers even more, there are those with lots of money, who can afford the Rolex, but don't necessarily want it. "There are people who could easily afford to spend $1,000 on a watch, but they don't. They don't think that it makes sense to spend $1,000 to put something on your wrist when you can buy an equally accurate time piece for $100," Peter explains. "These people who can afford it but don't buy it would be called affluents, but not luxury consumers."

Regardless of what we call them—luxury consumers or affluents, trading up, or aspirational consumers—the people who purchase luxury goods share one characteristic: high levels of disposable income. Luxuries are without question the extras in life and because nobody needs them, people spend their disposable income on them, as opposed to the money allocated toward taxes and daily needs like food, clothing, and shelter. Of course, there is a whole lot of discretionary spending that goes along with buying food (e.g., organic produce, meals out), clothing (e.g., designer brands), and shelter (who really needs a 6,000 square foot house?).

To differentiate the affluent consumer from the rest of the consumer market, Peter sees it not just in terms of income and wealth, but how affluent consumers relate to their wealth. As he reminds us, not all affluents with high incomes and lots of money in the bank feel the need to spend it on luxury goods. "There are people, and I have personal friends, who have assets in hundreds of millions of dollars who drive beat-up old cars or pick-up trucks, who would never buy a watch that cost more than 20 bucks, but who donate lavishly to their special causes or charities. They are obviously extraordinarily wealthy people who do not exhibit it in any way, shape, or form, except they give $10 million to this group and $5 million to that organization. They exhibit their wealth by engaging in charitable works that are really important to them."

chapter 3

Household Income Defines Demographics

The highest earners are able to save much of their incomes, whereas lower earners can't. That means high earners can accumulate more and more wealth as time goes on (assuming they don't blow it all, of course).

—Charlotte Rampell, economics reporter, *New York Times*

"Consumers with above-average disposable income available to purchase the extras in life" seems to be the best way to think about the people who luxury marketers need to attract to their goods and services. Income and wealth, sometimes together and sometimes separately, are the most popular ways to measure whether a person has more than the average amount of money to spend on the extras.

When asked whether high income or high net worth/wealth is the more important indicator of the target market for luxury in the future, demographics expert Peter Francese votes for income. "Income is the only thing that you can focus on because it is the only data you can get on a consistent basis. Wealth or assets are not something that can be obtained on any regular basis from anywhere. Most people who have a million dollars or more in assets have it someplace, in a 401(k) plan or money market account managed by Fidelity, Vanguard, or another investment firm. It never occurs to them to spend it on something.

"People live off income and they sometimes generate income by investments. They may invest income, but they are unlikely to buy something

like a car with their assets. Again, anybody with real affluence is going to
look at a car today that they want and finance it. They would finance it
because the cost of money is so cheap. And so they know that they can
make 8 or 10 percent a year on their investments and they can pay 3 or
4 or 5 percent to borrow money to buy a car. They know how to manage
money."

People don't usually use their wealth to buy consumer goods and services. But wealth does play a psychological role in how people spend. A
good deal of the consumer-spending boom the economy enjoyed from
2001 to 2008, which contributed mightily to the growth in the luxury
industry, resulted from people's confidence in their personal wealth. The
value of their homes was on the rise and their 401(k)s and other investments were going through the roof. They felt empowered to spend the extra
money that came in the door, rather than save it. With the recession, all
that perceived wealth vanished. People had to go back to spending their
real income again. And with the average American household income just
shy of $70,000, that doesn't leave a whole lot of money at the end of the
month to splurge on luxuries.

⮑ **Figure 3.1 Households by Income Quintile, U.S. Census 2009**

in thousands

Income quintiles	Number of households
Lowest quintile (0 to $20,453)	23,508
Second quintile ($20,454 to $38,550)	23,508
Third quintile ($38,551 to $61,801)	23,508
Fourth quintile ($61,802 to $99,999)	23,508
Fifth quintile – affluent	
Top 20 percent (starts at $100,000)	23,508
Top 5 percent ($180,001 to $249,999)	5,877
Top 2 percent ($250,000 and above)	2,372

Source: U.S. Census Bureau, Current Population Survey, 2010 Annual Social and Economic Supplement

Peter and I share a focus on *income* as the best indicator luxury marketers can use to identify their potential target customers. We define "affluent"
consumers as those in the top 20 percent of U.S. households, which, in

2010, started at about $100,000. There are about 23.5 million households in the top 20 percent, out of a total of 117.5 million American households.

From 1999 to 2009, the starting income for those in the top 20 percent of households rose 26 percent, from $79,232 in 1999 to $100,000. The starting income for those at the top 5 percent rose even faster, 26.8 percent from $142,000, to $180,001. By contrast, in the decade from 1999 to 2009, the average income of all households grew from $54,737 to $67,976, at the slower rate of 24 percent. This attests to the new economic fact of life that the rich are getting richer, while those at lower levels of income are on the decline, losing both income and spending power.

The top 20 percent are the heavy lifters in the U.S. consumer economy

Affluent households in the top 20 percent of all U.S. households take in half of all the nation's income, and they account for roughly 40 percent of all consumer spending. They are the consumer "heavy lifters." Peter Francese predicts that in the next decade these top 20 percent are going to become even more important to the consumer economy and marketers, both up and down the pricing spectrum. He writes in a recent *Advertising Age* white paper titled *2010: What the 2010 Census Means for Marketing and Advertising*, "We expect that in the next five to ten years an even higher fraction of total income is likely to accrue to the most affluent 20 percent of households. Their share of total consumer spending likely will rise above the present 40 percent and may very well approach 50 percent."

Based upon the current demographic trends, the disposable income among middle-class households will slow, which will "severely limit their ability to purchase goods and services in the near future. The widespread exuberant spending that took place between 2001 and 2008 at retail outlets and on housing is not likely to return anytime soon, except among high-income households." With this increasing concentration of income and resulting spending toward the affluent segment of the market, the top 20 percent will be a desirable target for not just luxury marketers. Attracting affluents' disposable income may be crucial for many mass brands and mass retailers as well in the next decade.

Only two segments in the affluent market really matter: HENRYs and Ultra-Affluents

For marketers tapping the high-end, clearly not all affluents are equal in spending power. There are only two affluent income segments that really matter: those above $250,000 income and those below.

⮑ Figure 3.2 Affluent Income Segments: HENRYs and Ultra-Affluents

Affluent households by income	Share of affluent market	Average income
HENRYs		
$100,000 – $149,999	59%	$119,749
$150,000 – $199,999	22%	$169,399
$200,000 – 249,999	9%	$219,666
Ultra-affluents		
$250,000 and above	10%	$425,226
Average income		$170,130

Source: Unity Marketing; U.S. Census Bureau, Current Population Survey, 2010 Annual Social and Economic Supplement

The nation's 23.5 million affluent households are divided into two segments. At the lower income range, from $100,000 to $249,999 and accounting for 21.2 million households, are the HENRYs—an acronym coined by *Fortune*-writer Shawn Tully that stands for *High Earner Not Rich Yet*. At the upper income range, representing some 2.4 million extremely high-income households are the ultra-affluents.

There is an intriguing aspect to the affluent income data. At each step up the income ladder below the ultra-affluents (incomes of $250,000+), the average income of each income group skews toward the *lower end* of the range. Households with incomes from $100,000 to $149,999 have an average income of $119,749. That means, more of these households clump at the bottom, rather than the top, of that income range. For households earning from $150,000 to $199,999, the average is $169,399. And for households with incomes of $200,000 to $249,999, the average is $219,666. Again, more households cluster toward the bottom of each range. However, for ultra-affluent households the average income is *way above* that range's starting point of $250,000. The ultra-affluents' average income is just shy of one-half million, or $425,226. This testifies to just how rich those at the top of the income ladder are. There really aren't a whole lot of households at the bottom of the ultra-affluent income scale around $250,000, but a whole lot with incomes up in the stratosphere.

⊃ **Figure 3.3 Affluent Household Segments**

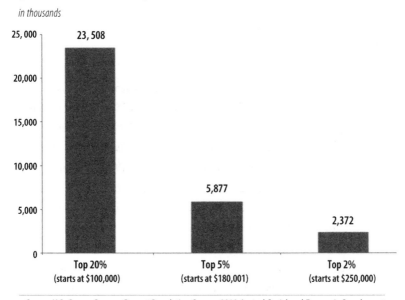

in thousands

Source: U.S. Census Bureau, Current Population Survey, 2010 Annual Social and Economic Supplement

The reasons why only two income segments matter in the affluent market are simply a function of spending power, into which we will delve more deeply in the next section. Ultra-affluent households with incomes of $250,000 typically spend three to four times more on luxury than typical HENRY households. Unity Marketing's tracking study of affluents has consistently found that households with incomes from $200,000 to $249,999 are far more similar in terms of luxury purchases and spending to those with incomes from $100,000 to $149,999 than they are those with incomes over $250,000.

Ten HENRYs to one ultra-affluent means more opportunity

The number of affluent households also reveals where marketers' real opportunity lies: there are ten HENRY households for every one ultra-affluent households. Ten HENRY households ultimately command more luxury spending power than a single ultra-affluent household. That is why HENRYs with incomes at the lower-range of the affluence income scale are ultimately so important for luxury marketers.

• • • • •

Fierce Competition for Affluents Coming from Mass Marketers

Given the long-term trends in the U.S. economy with middle-class consumers growing poorer as the affluent segment grows in numbers and relative spending power, mass marketers like Procter and Gamble aren't going to be satisfied selling brands like Tide, Comet, and Swiffer mops to middle-class homemakers. To assure a vibrant future, the P&Gs of the marketing world are going to have to go after the big bucks that the affluent represent. P&G has already staked its claim to the luxury consumer market. The company recently acquired two luxury-leaning brands: Zirh offers an upscale line of men's fragrance, and skin and hair care lines, and The Art of Shaving includes both a product and experiential component through its more than 40 shaving and spa boutiques. The Olay brand, especially the higher-priced Regenerist skin care line, is giving serious competition to super-luxury offerings from La Mer and La Prairie, with science to back up its claims. Further, the company has recently entered into a partnership with Dolce & Gabbana to develop a line of fragrances and cosmetics to be sold exclusively through Saks Fifth Avenue.

Another reality that luxury marketers will face in the future is this: The paradigm shifts that will define the future of the luxury industry are far more likely to come from unexpected places, like P&G, rather than from the luxury brands themselves. Luxury marketers need to get ready for a brave new world where competition comes not just from their peer group of luxury brands, but from powerful consumer goods companies with huge advertising budgets and legions of highly skilled and educated employees. Like P&G's high-end acquisitions, inroads into the luxury space are particularly strong in the beauty and cosmetic sector. Brands like L'Oréal Paris, Olay, Aveno, Maybelline, COVERGIRL, and Neutrogena have positioned themselves as what smart girls with money buy, rather than the overpriced luxury brands in fancy bottles that don't work any better, as actress Diane Lane reminds us in a Neutrogena commercial.

Mass-market competition is also coming on fast and furiously in the fashion, automotive, and home furnishings sectors. Don't make the mistake of saying, "But Procter & Gamble isn't my competition," or Liz Claiborne, or Target, or Hyundai. You had better wake up to the fact that there are only so many consumers and dollars to go around. More brands that didn't seriously target affluents in the past will take aim at them in the future out of necessity. As Peter Francese reminds us, organic growth in the consumer market is less than 1 percent per year, which explains the urgency of finding market segments that are growing and spending faster than that.

The next decade will see fierce competition from new and unexpected places for affluents' disposable income. Mass marketers and retailers are upping their game and learning how to gain traction with affluent consumers. They are positioning themselves as the products and brands that savvy, smart shoppers favor, because they offer value comparable to the high-end brands' at a more affordable price. Putting the luxe back in luxury will be a priority for the luxury brands in the next decade, as mass marketers get in on the luxury game.

• • • • •

How Lynda Resnick Found Rubies in an Orchard, and You Can, Too

I've always believed in giving people more than they expect. It compliments not only their taste, but their awareness and intelligence.

—Lynda Resnick

My last corporate job before setting out on my own through Unity Marketing was at The Franklin Mint (TFM), where I had the honor of working for Lynda Resnick, who at the time owned TFM with her husband Stewart. From 1986 to 1992, I worked in her marketing division, and I owe my launch into luxury market research to Lynda. She gave me my first up-close-and-personal look at true luxury, when she sent me to her Beverly

Hills mansion on Sunset Boulevard to catalog the Resnick's extensive art collection.

I also credit The Franklin Mint with the title of my first book. Someone in a meeting asked rhetorically about the collectible products we sold, "Why DO people buy things that they don't need?" Lynda, of course, didn't need to ask that question because she already knew. People buy stuff they don't need because they desire it and that desire springs from emotions that can be tapped through good and effective marketing communications. Lynda knows all about that.

No longer affiliated with The Franklin Mint, Lynda has moved on to a new stage as the marketing inspiration and brand champion behind the success of such brands as FIJI Water, POM Wonderful, Teleflora, Paramount Farms and its Wonderful Pistachios brand, and Paramount Citrus, which markets clementines under the brand name Cuties. These brands and more are owned by the Resnick's privately-held Roll International Corporation. The story of how she created POM Wonderful and these other brands is in her recent book, *Rubies in the Orchard: How to Uncover the Hidden Gems in Your Business,* written with Francis Wilkinson. It's a rare look inside the mind of a marketing genius shared through stories and personal biography. Because I know Lynda, it was a special treat for me to read, but it is highly recommended to anyone who needs to understand marketing and branding and their role in transforming businesses. And unlike so many business books, it is neither dry nor dull, but as creative and witty as Lynda is herself.

While all of Lynda's brands are positioned at the luxury end of their respective markets, she makes no claims about marketing luxury brands, but she has lots to teach luxury marketers. I asked Lynda if there are any differences when marketing luxury brands.

"Marketing is marketing and creating a brand is creating a brand, the disciplines are the same. When one feels that because it's a luxury brand different disciplines take over, then we run into trouble. They don't," Lynda says. "You still have to have value. You still have to be unique in the marketplace. You have to have sustainability. And you still have to understand the consumer. I don't think there is any difference."

In her book, she says that the place to start in any marketing effort is to "think inside the box," her phrase for discovering the true value and unique selling proposition of whatever she is trying to sell. She writes, "Every marketing campaign begins with the same question: What is the intrinsic value of the product or service? I know that it [think outside the box] has become a fashionable cliché in recent years, but it's just about always wrong. The answers are not outside the box, they're *inside*. They're inherent in whatever task you've undertaken, whatever product you want to market."

With a brand's value found "inside the box," I asked Lynda about the values she associates with luxury. "I just had a very interesting experience. I have a lot of dresses that I put away and saved because they were great brands when I bought them in the 70s, 80s, and 90s. My Chanel clothes are just as good today as they were 30 years ago. They held up. Whatever I paid for that white bouclé Chanel jacket in 1980 was worth every dime. Brands like Chanel have a lasting quality. You buy a Chanel dress or jacket and it's going to last for 30 years."

Lynda's story says volumes about the true values inherent in luxury brands. It goes much further than that phrase I hear so frequently from marketers who define the essential value proposition for their luxury as "exceptional quality," as if that is enough. Rather than exceptional quality, true luxury brands have exceptional *qualities*, like classic, timeless design, impeccable workmanship, superior fabrication, and heritage that commands respect from the customer. Too many luxury marketers, I am afraid, stop at the surface and don't delve deeply "inside the box" as Lynda emphasizes. That takes hard work. An example is how she uncovered the value inherent in the POM Wonderful brand. "That's where research comes in. Before we squeezed our first pomegranate into a bottle, I wanted to know everything there was to know about this fruit, and then some."

Every luxury marketer and brand manager should be as determined to explore the full depth, breadth, and dimension of value inherent in their brand. As Lynda explains, you have to "look within the brand itself for creative solutions to marketing challenges." And for those who fail to do their inside-the-box due diligence, she warns, "Value is rewarded, while the absence of value, sooner or later, is always exposed and penalized." Another key to successful marketing is understanding the customer, and Lynda has a rare form of ESP common to great marketers. Understanding the customer goes far beyond traditional consumer research, though she does plenty of that as well. Lynda describes it, "Marketing is all about listening. If you don't listen and you don't care, you'll never be a good marketer. You want to be the equivalent of a good friend, someone who cares, someone who listens carefully, someone who tries to anticipate another's needs and to meet them or indeed exceed them."

At their core, luxury brands have to respect the customer and understand their value proposition from the customer's point of view. For most people buying a luxury brand is not an impulse purchase, but one that is carefully thought out due to the price. Lynda reminds luxury marketers to deliver more than what the customer expects. "When you buy an expensive product that touches you emotionally, and that product fails you, you experience that disappointment as betrayal. In addition to feeling used and hurt, you get angry. I've always believed in giving people more than they expect. It compliments not only their taste, but their awareness and intelligence."

In *Rubies in the Orchard*, Lynda writes about banishing the word "customer" from The Franklin Mint's vocabulary and replacing it with "collector." This step was pivotal in orienting the entire staff toward the right target: the ultimate collector. "By referring to the people who bought our products as *collectors*, we immediately elevated them in the minds of our employees. And we let our collectors know that we understood their passion and respected it."

I remember meeting one of those collectors at The Franklin Mint Museum one day who told me with pride that she "belonged" to The Franklin Mint. That perspective was commonly heard around The Mint among those with direct collector contact. Our collectors *belonged*. That belonging feeling, when its customers have ownership and a stake in the brand, is what every brand marketer aspires to achieve. Changing the way we think about these luxury customers could be a start to engendering deeper connections with our brands.

Lynda says, "Knowing your customer is the single most important thing that you can do. If you don't know that, you have no idea where you are going or how you are going to get there. Many girls I know collect Fendi handbag. They want the new one every season. They are collecting them because Fendi handbags never wear out. I've collected Fendi baguettes for years. It is the perfect handbag. It isn't too big, but big enough to hold your glasses, iPhone, makeup. It nestles right under your arm. I have the first one I ever bought and I've never thrown one away."

She gives sage advice to luxury brands, "I think that if they thought of their customers as collectors, they might have better ideas for what to do next—like Fendi. They hit it so they never left it. They keep designing the baguette over and over again by staying with a silhouette and changing the accouterments."

As Lynda looks to the future, she is as firmly committed to her personal values as she is to uncovering the brand values of the products she markets. Lynda and Stewart Resnick are generous philanthropists who live by the tenet of doing well by doing good. This extends to their customers, employees, and the communities where they do business.

As a final word on values, both personal and corporate, Lynda writes in the introduction to the paperback edition of her book, "In a brand, value is a defining trait. Like character, value endures in the good times, and it shines through the bad." She reminds us that this idea of value in the luxury market, which often was overlooked in the boom times that we came through, is now being rediscovered. On the value perspective lost in the boom, she says, "It comes roaring back as soon as the good times end. And end they have."

We all need to spend more time inside our products and services working to discover their true luxury value and then bring those luxe values out and communicate them to our customers.

• • • • •

With an Average Income of $170,130, There's Not a Lot Left Over for Luxury Spending

Ask the three key questions before parting with your cash. "Do I need this? Will it make my family better, smarter, more prepared? Can I even afford it?"

—Christine Romans, *Smart Is the New Rich*

The average income of all those who fall into the top 20 percent of U.S. households by income is roughly $170,000. The Bureau of Labor Statistics Consumer Expenditure Survey (CEX) reports that those in the top 20 percent pay around $8,000 or so in taxes, leaving $162,000 in disposable income. The CEX also tells us a lot about what affluents spend their money on. For example, in just about every product and service category tracked, those at the top spend nearly twice as much as the average U.S. household.

Unfortunately, the CEX doesn't give perspective on debt, so I turned to research that Christine Romans, a CNN business reporter and financial show host, did for her new book, *Smart Is the New Rich*. She found that the average U.S. household's debt totals $227,537. The high debt load is heavily weighted toward the affluent top 20 percent, since households in the lower income ranges are limited in the amount of debt they can incur.

⊃ **Figure 3.4 Average U.S. Household Debt**

Home mortgage	$177,186
Student loans	27,777
Auto	14,873
Credit card	7,701
Total	$227,537

Source: Christine Romans, *Smart Is the New Rich*

The affluent 20 percent by every measure are the economy's heavy lifters. But, after they pay their monthly mortgage and utilities, car loan, student loan or college tuition (depending on their age), and credit-card bills, not much is left to indulge in weekly shopping trips to Neiman Marcus or regular vacations in foreign destinations. The vast majority of affluents work, maybe not punching time clocks, but most definitely engaged and involved in meaningful, rewarding, and demanding work.

People's spending follows their values. A recent Unity Marketing exploration into the values of affluent luxury consumers (n = 1,364 respondents with average income $298,300) adds dimension to the underlying personal values that guide and direct the spending of the affluent. Affluents ranked *financial security* as number one among a listing of eight key values in the survey. Financial security was rated as extremely or very important (index 114 on 100-point scale, meaning 14 percent higher than average) by 92 percent of those surveyed. This compares with 68 percent who rate having enough money to buy nice things (index 85) as extremely or very important. The ultra-affluents and the high-net-worth affluents surveyed gave even higher ratings to the importance of maintaining their financial security. This should come as no surprise; these are people who are willing to work harder, or who have chosen specific highly-paid professions to earn more money.

• • • • •

⮑ **Figure 3.5 Priorities in Affluents' Lives**

Below are a list of things that some people look for or want out of life. Rate each on how important it is in your daily life, where 1 = Not At All Important and 5 = Extremely Important

importance index: 100 = average

Financial security	114
Security	111
Fun & enjoyment of life	109
Warm relationships with others	109
Self-fulfillment	107
Being well-respected	97
Sense of belonging	91
Having enough money to buy nice things	85
Excitement	76

Source: Unity Marketing

Smart shoppers view their spending as investments

In research, when I talk with affluents about their incomes, wealth and money, what stands out is that affluent customers want to maximize their investments when shopping for luxury goods and services. Therefore luxury marketers need to invest heavily in discovering the value in the luxuries they want to sell, and effectively communicate that value in ways that resonate and impact the consciousness of luxury customers. Luxury marketers have to justify every penny they are asking people to spend. That, in a nutshell, is critical to putting the luxe back into luxury.

On Paper, the Affluent Are Very Much Alike – But Not in the Store

Know where to find the information and how to use it. That's the secret of success.
                                                      —Albert Einstein

Demographic expert Peter Francese is famously quoted as saying, "The concept of an 'average American' is gone, probably forever. The average American has been replaced by a complex, multidimensional society that defies simplistic labeling."

While this may be true for the 300+ million Americans, it doesn't necessarily apply to the 23.4 million affluent households. Affluents are far more similar than different, at least on paper. As a consumer segment, affluents are one of the most demographically bound segments that most marketers will ever have the pleasure to target.

Besides being defined by income, they share extremely high levels of education. Whereas only 31 percent of all U.S. households are headed by an individual with a bachelor's degree or higher, 60 percent of affluent households are headed by someone with at a four-year college degree or higher. Peter explains, "The affluent market is a group of households that have extremely different characteristics than the rest of the marketplace, but unfortunately most of the managers of companies that sell to consumers don't understand the differences. They are clueless that college graduates are a minority of household heads in the United States. The luxury market is not just an affluent marketplace, it's an intelligent, well-educated segment.

It is a marketplace that understands how to calculate value."

Luxury marketers that target the affluent need to understand just how street smart, consumer smart, and shopping smart affluent consumers are and how it impacts all their shopping decisions.

In a recent research study with ultra-affluent luxury consumers, I was surprised to hear men talking about finding great products at deep discounts. For years I was used to hearing women brag about the items they snagged at discounted prices, but I've never heard men talking like that. Men typically have taken pride in how much they spend, or rather how much money they *have* to spend, as opposed to how much they saved in making a purchase. But in a recent series of focus groups with affluent men, it was as if the men had finally learned from their wives how to shop and find discounts. They were bragging about the great new electronic gadget they found on WOOT.com, even getting competitive in the group, happy to see that they saved more than the next guy on the exact same item.

Peter sees this new-found sophistication about discount shopping as another sign of today's super-smart shoppers and how they have learned new ways of discovering value. "What the affluent segment of our population has learned is that the concept of value is changing and that the perception of value is changing. The internet has gone a long way toward creating a situation where consumers, if they wish, can easily find out what the real price of something is, not the price at which the person down the street bought it, or the price at which a store is trying to sell it to them, but what the real price is. And so you've got companies on the web like Priceline, for example, where the price-to-value relationship has shifted completely toward the consumer's value, not the marketer's price."

Peter continues, "Consumers, particularly smarter, more affluent consumers, are getting better at ferreting out what they consider the real value of what they want to buy. For example, they see a sweater and it's got a price tag of $675. They look at that and they say, 'I can go on the web and buy that same sweater or one exactly like it for $220.' And virtually all of the individuals in this top 20 percent of income households are on the web. What you are observing is a society-wide shift in which the perception of value is altered by the information that those individuals have when they are making purchase decisions."

In essence, the change in discount-seeking affluent male shoppers that I observed is really a function of their new way of interpreting value. As Peter says, "When you see men going for the lower-priced options, it isn't the discount that they are concerned about, it is a shift in their perception of what the value-to-price relationship is. And I see this happening across the culture."

• • • • •

Smart Shoppers Call for Ever Smarter Marketers

Affluent shoppers are really smart about how they spend their money and how they determine value, and they are getting smarter all the time. The takeaway of this demographic finding is clear: Because affluent customers are smart, successful marketers in the future have got to be even smarter to succeed. They won't fall for stupid marketing tricks. You can't put one over on them—they are too smart.

Consider how a typical affluent shopper interprets the deep discounts offered on clothes in department stores. A wise affluent shopper in a focus group said, "When I go into a store and see a shirt for $70 one day, then it is marked down to $35 the next, I know that it was at least $35 overpriced the day before. You just can't believe the retail prices you see."

Another favorite retail ploy that smart shoppers see through is the buy-one-get-one offers. Either get one free, a 50 percent discount proposition that doesn't sound anywhere near as compelling as "free," or get each for half-off, an even worse deal of only 25 percent off the total price. Jos A. Bank Clothiers offers buy-one-suit-and-get-TWO-free. Just a minimal amount of thought shows that if they can give away two more suits and still keep their stores' doors open, the full list price of that first suit is way, way over its real value. Why would any smart shopper ever pay full retail price at Jos. A. Bank? I'm sure that isn't the way the company wants its customers to think. The smart affluent shoppers they ultimately want to attract are definitely in the know and have been trained by the company's own marketing efforts to shop there only when the discounts are on. Jos. A. Bank is a perfect example of a marketer not smart enough to meet the challenge of the really smart affluent shopper.

By contrast internet grocer FreshDirect is meeting the challenge of the affluent smart shopper and winning. Rick Braddock, the company's CEO, said in an *Advertising Age* article, "Early on we got into a view that we wanted to reinforce the idea that our customers were the smart ones. So our tag line is 'Our food is fresh. Our customers are spoiled.'"

This online retailer doesn't resort to lowest price to attract its shopper. Its prices are pretty hefty compared to do-it-yourself shopping at the grocery store—you pay not just for the food but also for the delivery. Yet, its business proposition has a powerful appeal to affluent customers who are time-challenged and value the restaurant-quality produce, meats, and seafood FreshDirect provides. It also offers ready-made meals, another premium-priced service that has strong appeal for the company's New York City–area clientele.

In developing the company's offerings, positioning its brand and its product, and refining its service, FreshDirect started with the customer and worked back to the business, rather than the other way around. That took deep understanding of the target customer. Braddock explains, "The needs that we are fulfilling—and certainly convenience is one, but there are several others—you have to understand what that means to your customer, how they define what those various attributes and benefits are, and then deliver on it and measure to be sure you're effectively doing it. You also need to marshal the voice of the customer in a way *that is very timely* and can be spread throughout the organization. Keeping the customer in front of us every single day gives us a chance to understand what we need to accomplish to do our job well."

Understanding the "voice of the customer" and their values proposition is achieved through a carefully managed program of intense consumer research to measure customer attitudes, intentions, and awareness. Braddock credits this research with the company's success, "The reality of this environment is that everyone is more value-conscious. There are two ways in a troubled economy for a company to do well. One is by aggressively selling values. But the other way is to be close to your customers and to use the information you have to create a tight bond with your customers. We're trying to use [customer] information in a troubled time to give our customers a feeling we're there for them and that we're giving them a better way."

The company disseminates consumer insights widely to all employees, as Braddock explains, "We promote ownership of the company throughout the company, because if the plant doesn't do its job or transportation doesn't do its job, we're not going to give our customers good service. [Customers] don't know the difference, they just know FreshDirect." And its understanding of their customers' value proposition is clearly explained point-by-point on the company's FreshDirect.com website under the "Ten Reasons Why" tab. FreshDirect gives its customers the detailed information they need to make a smart, informed decision. It's smart and helps its customers get smart, too.

• • • • •

Marvin Traub Ranks Among the Smartest in Luxury Retailing

Today's consumer is looking for different things. Luxury is still wonderful, unique products with limited distribution, but it extends into services, experiences.

—Marvin Traub

Marvin Traub's story has been told many times. First was the story of his greatest success, *Like No Other Store: The Bloomingdale's Legend and the Revolution in American Marketing*, published in 1994, and recently, his autobiography, *Marvin Traub: Like No Other Career,* written with Lisa Marsh. Since retiring as chief executive of Bloomingdale's in 1991 he has been anything but retired. He hung out his shingle, Marvin Traub and Associates, where he consults with all the greatest luxury brands, including Ralph Lauren, Lanvin, Harvey Nichols, Oscar de la Renta, and Karl Lagerfeld, among others. Marvin was instrumental in putting the Time Warner Center on the luxury map in New York City. He is exporting luxury to the world by advising similar supercenters that combine department stores and boutiques with hotels, restaurants, theaters, and sporting activities in Dubai and India. As if that isn't enough work for Marvin in his retirement, he recently founded TSM Capital, a private equity firm that has investments in designers Rachel Roy and Matthew Williamson. Another testament to Marvin's accomplishments is that some forty retailing leaders emerged from his corporate ranks while at Bloomingdale's, including Mickey Drexler (Gap and J.Crew), Andrea Jung (Avon Products), four CEOs for Saks, and two for Neiman Marcus.

With these accomplishments and a CVA that includes an undergraduate degree and MBA from Harvard, it's an understatement to call Marvin simply smart. And like the smart retailer that he is, Marvin started our interview asking me questions about my background, my business, and what I needed from him. Smart marketers and retailers always start by listening.

We started by talking about luxury then (he joined Bloomingdale's in 1950) and now, and while many things have changed, many more remain the same. "Luxury in the 80s and 90s had a great deal to do with price, narrowness in distribution, prestige, and what was in the product, as well as the image about luxury that you projected in the store. That is all still there, but today it extends beyond product to the services, including how the store is in touch with the environment, the issue of social responsibility, awareness of labor practices. Today's consumer is looking for different things. Luxury is still wonderful, unique products with limited distribution, but it extends into services, experiences," Marvin said.

Perhaps Marvin's greatest claim to fame in the retailing world is his focus on shopping as entertainment. Very early on in his career he promoted the idea of "retailing as theater" at Bloomingdale's and transformed the store into a destination for cool shoppers in the know. Bloomingdale's brand became famous for hosting special events. For the grand opening of the King of Prussia store, the company flew designers Ralph Lauren, Calvin Klein, Bill Blass, and others in a dozen helicopters from New York to Philadelphia to make a grand entrance landing in the parking lot. Another store opening featured the entire Big Apple Circus with Diane von Furstenberg riding the lead elephant.

As if that wasn't cool enough, I asked Marvin what else he did to make Bloomingdale's cool, or as he described it, "a cultural happening." Marvin explained, "What helped to make Bloomingdale's cool was recognizing the changing lifestyles of the shopper. If you are running a store or a brand, you have to be a step ahead of what the customer is interested in. Today it seems like customers are more interested in social responsibility, so it is being able to give back to society. For example, a shoe brand like TOMS Shoes, that for every pair you purchase gives a pair to child in a Third World country. Or the FEED Bags program* started by Laura Bush. Bergdorf Goodman, which is a rather traditional store, got involved with it. My guess is that young customers are pleased to find something like that at Bergdorf."

With the issue of social responsibility, luxury marketers and retailers like Bergdorf are able to create a platform for a new kind of relationship with their customers. It can include not just the joy and pleasure of shopping, but the ability to give back through buying a FEED Bag to also feed a child, or buying shoes from TOMS. Providing opportunities to exercise social responsibility will be increasingly important in the future, as Marvin explains, "The new generation is very concerned with responsibility in the world." It's no longer all about "me" but for young people especially, the new focus is on "we."

While the essential message of luxury, quality and value may still be the same, the way luxury marketers communicate today is vastly different. Marvin says, "Today you have to be able to communicate with the consumer differently, through internet and social networking. Many young people no longer read newspapers. Advertising in newspapers has to make way for new advertising media."

The overnight emergence of social media has also created confusion for many luxury brands. Marvin advises, "Through social media viral marketing is real 'today.' It often is marketing that originates from the consumer rather than the brand. It is all about pull, rather than push marketing. Take Puma—it suddenly discovered it had 1.8 million fans after four of its subscribers created Puma fan pages on Facebook. Puma had nothing to do with creating the 'buzz,' but now Puma can tailor special offerings for their fans and has created a clubhouse on Facebook for all its Puma fans. Companies have to give thought as to how they can build the image of

---

* FEED Bags are 100 percent organic cotton reusable bags sold in stores like Whole Foods and Trader Joe's to raise funds for the World Food Programme. The FOOD Project's pledge: Proceeds from the purchase of one bag, usually sold for about $30, feeds one child for a year.

their brand in social media. Most major companies are recognizing they have to be proactive in this area."

Technology is bringing change, not just in the way we advertise and market over the internet, but it is also impacting the in-store experience. "Take Bloomingdale's beauty department at the 59th Street store. It uses all manner of new presentation techniques, like internet and video, that change the whole way you shop," Marvin explains.

Another trend impacting the luxury market is globalization and exporting luxury to the world. "My consulting practice is heavily built on globalization," Marvin said. "Globalization is important because the United States is a mature economy. Even though we account for over 40 percent of the world's consumer goods, companies have to do business outside the United States to grow, which is why I helped with Harvey Nichols and Bill Blass. More and more companies are thinking about how to do business globally. But it is not one-size-fits-all. If you want to do business in the Middle East, the look and pace of customers is different from those in Europe, and different in Asia. You have to think of how to tailor the product to the needs of the market, and it is not just its size, but that is the obvious one."

In tailoring a product to the market, Marvin points to Hermès. It recently announced the launch of a lower-priced handbag collection specifically for China. "Here you have one of the world's great luxury brands looking at what is the fastest growing market in the world and saying they're going to do something different to go after that market."

As we closed I asked Marvin about the impact of price on people's perception of luxury and luxury brands. Is there a danger for luxury brands if they lower their price points? Or can they, or more correctly, *must* they be more sensitive to price? In short, price matters, even to the luxury market. Marvin explains, "Five or ten years ago the consumer equated luxury with price so Mercedes-Benz was luxury. Today, Starbucks is luxury. It is the qualities that go into the value of luxury, and a big part of that is the experience. Consumers are looking for the opportunity to acquire some of these brands at lower price points. I talked with the CEO of one of the major brand apparel-designer companies who commented that his business is much healthier than it was a year ago. Before, if he did five jackets, four would be $5,000 and one would be $1,000. Now he does four at $1,000 and one at $5,000 and the consumer is responding.

"The consumer today is looking to a much greater extent for more attractive pricing. That's not destructive to the brand," Marvin reiterates. "Similarly, when luxury brands do a secondary line, as long as they are fashionable and consistent, I don't think that tears away the brand. You have Emporio Armani, you have Lauren or DKNY. One of our designers, Matthew Williamson, did a one-shot collection for H&M—totally different prices. And the Matthew Williamson brand sold out completely in their stores."

Marvin gives a final word of advice for the future. "There has been a transformational shift in consumer sentiment as consumers reevaluate how and why they spend. They are changing their lifestyles accordingly. Value is the priority. Not necessarily inexpensive or sale products, but consumers will focus on products with superior quality and functionality at an accessible price. This new attitude extends to luxury products. In recent years luxury goods [prices] skyrocketed to levels that are no longer sustainable."

And he points to young people, the luxury customers of the future, as being keen for new ways to participate, express, and enjoy luxury. "The new Millennial generation is interested in so much more than product. They are looking beyond simply the product to everything that goes with it. I have always believed that retailing is about change. Great merchants will recognize this and have the courage to try new strategies. Now is not the time to shy away from innovation or uniqueness."

● ● ● ● ●

More demographics that define affluence

⮕ **Figure 4.1 Affluent Households by the Numbers**

	All households	Top 20% (starting at $100,000)	Top 5% (starting at $180,001)
Total number *(in thousands)*	117,540	23,508	5,877
Northeast	18%	22%	24%
Midwest	22	20	17
South	37	32	31
West	22	26	28
Inside principal cities	33	29	32
Outside principal cities	50	61	61
Outside metropolitan area	16	10	7
Family Households			
Married couple	51	79	84
Male householder, no wife	5	4	3
Female householder, no husband	12	5	2
Non-family Households			
Male householder	15	8	6
Female householder	18	5	4
Age of Householder			
24 years or less	5	2	1
25-to-34 years	16	13	10
35-to-44 years	19	25	25
45-to-54 years	21	29	31
55-to-64 years	17	21	24
65 years and over	21	10	10
Number of Earners			
No earners	21	3	2
One earner	37	21	24
Two or more	25	76	75
Home Ownership			
Owner occupied	67	88	91
Rent	31	12	9

Source: U.S. Census Bureau, Current Population Survey, 2010 Annual Social and Economic Supplement

Among affluents the vast majority are married, 79 percent for all affluents and an even higher percentage among the top 5 percent (84 percent). By comparison only 51 percent of all U.S. households are traditional married-couples. Peter Francese predicts that the share of households led by married couples will continue to decline in the population at large, in part, because of the growth in the number of single women heading households, especially young women. In 2008 an unprecedented 40 percent of children born in the U.S. were born to single mothers.

For the affluent households, marriage often means two people are bringing home the bacon. The average income of a one-income household is $57,045; that of a two-earner family is $96,766. In other words, average household income is 70 percent higher when a husband and wife both work. And the difference between one income and two can easily bump the household up to the threshold of affluence.

Further declining marriage rates among people aged 25 to 34 spells more bad news for luxury marketers. Since marital status is a key demographic of affluence, young people postponing marriage or even permanently rejecting the institution bodes ill for the future for luxury marketers. Single people live in less affluent households; less affluent households can afford fewer luxury indulgences.

This demographic finding presents an important opportunity for luxury marketers today. The best target customer is most likely to be living in a two-earner household whose average size of 2.5 people. These hard-working affluent householders lead increasingly complex and demanding lives, constantly juggling work-home-childcare obligations, with women in the home still feeling the tug of home and childcare responsibilities the most.

• • • • •

Busy People Need Time-saving, Time-efficient Solutions

Everyone is time pressured today, but no one more so than the typical married working woman in mid-life. In 2008, Unity Marketing conducted an in-depth issues and attitudes study with *Marie Claire* magazine, a Hearst publication targeting "women with a point of view . . . a woman who is never afraid to make intelligence a part of her wardrobe." Time, finding time to do it all, to meet responsibilities and juggle the many demands on her, is one of women's most critical challenges, according to our research.

A recent study by research firm JWT and reported in an *Ad Age Insights* white paper, "The Reality of the Working Woman," brings women's time management issues to light. Today's average working woman:

- works 4.9 days per week, starting at 9 a.m. and wrapping up at 3:50 p.m.;

- prepares dinner 3.5 nights per week, goes out to dinner 1.2 times, and brings home a prepared meal 1.3 times per week;

- watches television 2 hours and 12 minutes per day and spends 24 minutes reading a newspaper; and

- devotes 2 hours per day to the internet, and spends 84 minutes on the phone, 48 minutes reading a book, 48 minutes exercising, and 42 minutes shopping.

And that litany of activities doesn't include child-care demands, even though the average household in the JWT survey included 1.9 kids.

While women are doing all that work at home and in the office, they are also largely responsible for the household's shopping, and managing the checkbook to acquire the goods and services the household needs. The Boston Consulting Group estimates that women control or influence as much as 73 percent of household spending, or $4.3 trillion of the $5.9 trillion in U.S. consumer spending.

Today's working woman is busy, and she is likely to be more, not less, busy in the future. Women are moving from lower-paying service jobs into higher-paying management and executive jobs that demand more time and resources. Demographic trends are key, as Peter Francese explains, "For the first time in American history there are more women college graduates than men. You are going to see this reflected in affluent households with more women taking the lead, owning their own homes, being the bread-winners. That is going to bring more big changes to the way American families live."

As a result of their increasingly complicated and demanding lifestyles, affluents of both genders, but especially women, need solutions that save time. This trend has contributed to the phenomenal success of Rachel

Ray and her 30-Minute Meal brand. Rachel's brand encompasses a simple concept: "You can put a healthful and delicious meal on the table in thirty minutes from start to finish." This led to the entire multi-million dollar Rachel Ray empire of cookbooks, a daytime talk show, food and cooking products, and even a line of healthy dog food. Despite the criticism that she has endured from professional chefs, her brand totally resonates with her target market of ordinary home cooks who need a time-efficient way to make dinner happen at home.

The attraction of internet shopping is much the same. Shopping takes time; the internet lets you shop whenever you have a moment to spare. Lots of people think the internet attracts shoppers because of its ability to access discounts. While it also can be a money-saving tool, Unity Market's research shows time efficiency is its primary attraction for the affluent customer. A study Unity Marketing did with Google on how the ultra-affluents (incomes $250,000 and above) use the internet to shop showed the importance of its time efficiency.

Before we conducted the research, we interviewed a number of top executives of major luxury brands. A common thread voiced by these execs was that the internet didn't provide the kind of shopping experience they thought their customers wanted. The in-store shopping experience, from their point of view, was infinitely better—more luxurious—than what could be provided over the internet. Our research revealed quite the opposite. Affluent customers, who hold responsible and time-demanding jobs, value internet shopping largely because it respects their time. Going to the store, while it may be an experience, is also a time drain that must be planned for, managed, and executed. Internet shopping, on the other hand, provides the customer an experience that is most highly valued by the affluent.

Luxury brands that offer customers access to their brands over the internet, without forcing them to be window shoppers online, are providing real, substantive value to their customers. Sometimes the affluent have the time or the inclination for the in-store shopping experience. But much more often, I would argue, they prefer the speed, convenience, and efficiency of internet shopping.

Marketers need to understand the increasingly complex lives their highly paid, high-income customers lead. They need and are willing to pay for time-saving products and services, like internet shopping. Or even better, they want products and services that help them do more with the time they have available, like Rachel Ray's 30-Minute Meals, or the equally compelling Tony Horton's 10-Minute Trainer workout.

• • • • • •

Ethnic diversity at the affluent level lags that of the population at large

Perhaps the growing diversity of the American population is the single most important demographic trend for the future. In the *Advertising Age* white paper *2010 America*, Peter Francese writes, "We are a truly multicultural nation. In our two largest states (California and Texas) and all of our ten largest cities, no racial or ethnic category describes a majority of the population. Diversity varies greatly by age, with the younger population substantially more diverse than the old. By 2015 the traditional majority group—white, non-Hispanics—will account for fewer than half of births nationwide."

The widely anticipated "minority majority" is expected to occur about 2040 when the majority of the U.S. population will be classified ethnically as something other than white, non-Hispanic. It will take a bit longer before a minority majority comes to the affluent segment, but Peter warns we can't ignore the growing ethnic diversity of affluent consumers. He says, "It is a big, big mistake to think that this luxury market is nothing but white people. There are plenty of extremely wealthy African Americans, Hispanics, and particularly Asians. And there is also diversity in what they buy. But what is not diverse is their attachment to value. Maybe they can afford $1,000 for a watch, but if they see that same watch for $300, they'll go for that value."

In the 2010 Census, a predominant 80 percent of the affluent top 20 percent, and 82 percent of the top 5 percent of households, are headed by someone classified as white, non-Hispanic. Blacks, Asians, and Hispanics comprise the remaining 20 percent.

⮑ **Figure 4.2 Number of Affluent Households and Share of Market (SOM) by Ethnicity, 2009**

in thousands

	Top 20 percent	SOM	Top 5 percent	SOM
White, non-Hispanic	18,866	80%	4,809	82%
Black*	1,395	6	247	4
Asian*	1,560	7	492	8
Hispanic (any race)*	1,542	7	292	5

* Alone or in combination

Source: U.S. Census Bureau, Current Population Survey, 2010 Annual Social and Economic Supplement

The reason ethnic minorities, with the exception of Asians, are not more largely represented among the top 20 percent of affluents is the income gap found between the dominant white, non-Hispanic population segment and Blacks and Hispanics. A Black household needs an income of only $70,006 to be classified in the top 20 percent of all Black households, nearly a third less than the threshold for all households. Hispanics' top 20 percent income threshold ($76,040) also lags behind the income of the national average. Asians enjoy a higher level of affluence; $130,540, the income level that distinguishes the top 20 percent of Asian households, is considerably higher than that of white, non-Hispanics ($106,130).

Complicating matters for marketers in gaining greater insight into the affluent ethnic minority households is their innate reticence to talk about their wealth. Francese explains, "Minority affluents may be wealthy, but they wouldn't dream of telling you how much money they carry or what they are buying. Asians in particular are extremely closed-mouth about what they buy and how much money they make."

⮑ **Figure 4.3 Affluence Income Gap by Ethnicity**

	Average income Top 20 percent	Difference	Average income Top 5 percent	Difference
All	$100,000		$180,001	
White, non-Hispanic	106,130	6%	189,300	5%
Black	70,006	-30%	126,300	-30%
Asian	130,540	31%	233,300	30%
Hispanic	76,040	-24%	136,757	-24%

Source: U.S. Census Bureau, Current Population Survey, 2010 Annual Social and Economic Supplement

At the same time minorities are under-represented in the affluent market, they still make up an important 20 percent of the total. As the country overall becomes more diverse, diversity will also rise in the affluent market. This will be especially true for minorities following the other demographic markers that lead to affluence, namely high levels of education and being married.

Demographic shifts are reliable predictors of trends in the consumer market

One of the pleasures of studying population demographics is that many trends are largely predictable. All people age at the same rate; this allows the demographic make-up of the population to be reliably projected five, ten, or twenty years out. On the other hand, demographic study also uncovers unknowns. Peter points out one of the big unknowns in the demographics of affluence—how income will change. In the past, high-income professionals might have progressed through their careers in a fairly predictable pattern. Today, all bets are off when it comes to income trend lines. Technically called "social mobility," Peter foresees the composition of the top 20 percent will be especially fluid in the future.

"I think that it is entirely possible we will see coming out of this recession the distinct movement of many people down and out of affluence. People who once had a job that paid six figures are not only jobless now, but they also may be close to homeless," he explains. He points, for example, to the precipitous drop in per capita income in New York County (i.e., Manhattan) in 2008. The financial collapse of AIG, Lehman Brothers, and Bear Stearns is a compelling case study of downward social mobility. In 2005, Manhattan ranked number one nationally in per capita income (average income of each adult resident) at $147,000. By 2009 its per capita income had dropped by nearly one-fourth to $120,790.

But what the affluence gods take away from one person, they can give to another, as Peter points out. "You will see entrepreneurs who start a business of one kind or another working nights, days, and weekends to make that little business go. Ultimately they will pop up into that top 20 percent of income. The thing that will slow down mobility is the diminishment of immigration. Immigrants create social mobility. An awful lot of people who become very affluent are, in fact, immigrants or the children of immigrants. And so the first- or second-generation immigrants powered the movement up into that top 20 percent. And remember, it's always the top 20 percent. And so when somebody comes into the 20 percent, somebody else is going out."

Age defines window of affluence

For luxury marketers the most important demographic distinction that separates affluents from everybody else is age. Households reach their highest level of income and earnings between ages 35 and 54—the age window of affluence.

⊃ Figure 4.4 Income by Age of Householder

	Average income head of household	Average income individual	
15-to-24	$40,367	$13,620	
24-to-34	$62,064	$35,612	
35-to-44	$79,355	$47,265	Window of Affluence
45-to-54	$83,770	$49,301	
55-to-64	$77,512	$46,193	
65 and over	$46,363	$29,718	
Total	$73,895	$38,213	

Source: U.S. Census Bureau, Current Population Survey, 2010 Annual Social and Economic Supplement

The 35-to-54 age range also corresponds to the highest level of participation in the luxury market. This conforms to the age distribution of Unity Marketing's Luxury Tracking Survey. In that survey, which we conduct every three months, about 60 percent of the luxury consumers are aged 35 to 54. As a result, the age range from 35-to-54 is the window of affluence defining the prime target market for marketers looking for their best high-potential affluent customers.

As people age, they move in and out of the window of affluence in a predictable way. We can chart the course of the target affluent market over time by studying the number of people who fall between ages 35 and 54 from year to year. (*Note:* the Census doesn't provide household projections by age.)

But households within that twenty-year age span corresponding to the window of affluence don't participate to an equal extent in the luxury market. Households in the 35-to-44 age range, called young affluents, spend roughly 30 to 40 percent more on luxury goods and services than those aged 45 to 54, mature affluents. For luxury marketers, the young affluent consumers are of far higher value than the slightly older 45-to-54-year-olds. We will explore this difference in luxury consumer spending later in the chapter devoted to purchase behavior.

This difference in spending between young and mature affluents is attributed to younger people being in a more acquisitive lifestage: They are setting up new homes, having children, and generally acquiring the material trappings of a luxury lifestyle. Older affluents, aged 45-to-54, have already bought the basics and have less need to spend on luxury. Further, as people mature they start to look toward their senior years and funnel money they once would have spent on discretionary purchases into savings and investments. Given these trends in spending, luxury marketers are ultimately more dependent upon their younger affluent customers for revenues and growth.

That difference between the higher luxury spending behavior of young affluents as compared with more mature affluents, combined with the huge Baby Boom generation's rapid overall aging out of the window of affluence, is ushering in a drought in the luxury consumer market that will last until 2019 or 2020.

As Peter Francese says, Generation X is merely a "hiccup" between two baby booms. In the luxury drought we entered just about the time that the recession hit, Generation X affluents filled the 35-to-44 age bracket, the ages when people spend the most on luxury. GenX is much smaller in total numbers than the Baby Boom. It will never make up for the shortfall in luxury spending as Baby Boomers move through the second half of the window of affluence.

⊖ **Figure 4.5 U.S. Population Projections, 2001-2020**

in thousands

	2001	2005	2010	2015	2020	
25-to-34	37,063	36,933	38,851	41,248	42,794	
35-to-44	44,693	42,716	39,442	38,787	40,711	**Window of Affluence**
45-to-54	38,641	41,890	44,161	41,986	38,837	
55-to-64	24,549	29,690	35,429	39,919	42,108	

Source: Population Projections Program, Population Division, U.S. Census Bureau

Baby Boomers largely gave rise to the luxury boom that marketers enjoyed through the 1990s and first years of the 21st century. Consumers aged 35-to-44 years outnumbered the more mature 45-to-54-year-olds until 2006, when there were virtually equal numbers of Americans in both age ranges. Then the distribution started to shift, as the less indulgent and more mature population took dominance in the age window of affluence. Not until 2019 will consumers aged 35 to 44 once again outnumber the more mature segments as the next population boom, the Millennial generation, matures. For luxury marketers, that means that the good times of easy growth and prosperity are over. Competition will become especially fierce in the luxury industry as a smaller consumer market becomes the primary target.

Age projections also show powerful opportunities emerging for luxury marketers that can tap the potential of the 25-to-34-year-olds. These consumers have less income to spend on luxury, but being younger, they have a powerful appetite to acquire more material possessions. Furthermore, after 2020 today's young adults will move into the window of affluence that corresponds with high levels of spending on luxury. Thus after 2020, there is a potential for a new luxury boom as large in size and scope as the one just past.

Figure 4.6 Population Projections by Age for Consumers in Window of Affluence, 2001–2020

in thousands

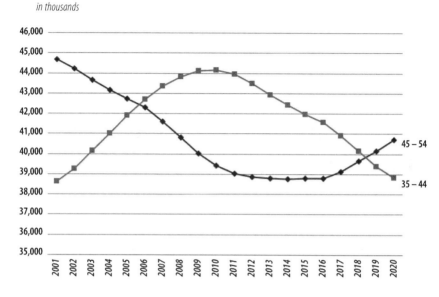

Source: Population Projections Program, Population Division, U.S. Census Bureau

In the next chapter we will explore in more depth the challenges and opportunities marketers will face as the generations shift in the luxury market and the luxury drought gains momentum.

chapter 5

The Next Generation of Affluents and the Changes They Bring to the Luxury Market

The next generation of the affluent are the kids of baby boomers. They are the future of luxury.

—Burton Tansky, president and CEO, Neiman Marcus

The recession and the global economic reordering that resulted from it lasted only about two years, a mere blip in time. But depending upon your point of reference, those two years can be an eternity. Just think of the internet and how many things that weren't available two years ago are widely available now—social media, flash sales, Kindle and other book-reading devices, iPads, iPhones, and the growing number of apps for both.

Today, 80 percent of all Americans, 248 million people, use the internet. From the consumer's perspective, two years is quite a long time too. It represents roughly 5 percent of an adult's 40-year consumer life span (ages 24 to 64), and 10 percent of the prime window of affluence period (ages 34 to 54). Luxury consumers who went into the recession in 2008 have come out in 2010 two years older, two years wiser, and equipped with new attitudes about their money and new ways of shopping. Steven Dennis says simply, "With a few exceptions, today's consumer is not the same person you served two years ago."

As luxury marketers look forward to the next decade, they will face the challenge of juggling the differing wants, needs, and desires of three distinct generational cohorts as they enter and move through the age window of affluence, that period from age 35 to 54 when households achieve their highest lifetime income and people have their greatest propensity to indulge in luxury.

Baby Boomers, the "Me-Generation," gave rise to the explosive growth in the luxury market throughout the 1990s and through the first half of the first decade of the 21st century. Boomers, aged 47 to 65 in 2011, will remain an important target market for luxury through 2019, when the entire generation ages out of the window of affluence. From 2020 and beyond, this generation will be a secondary target market for luxury, as Millennials take the helm as the primary high-value target consumers for luxury marketers.

Generation X is the cohort of consumers born from 1965 to 1979, who in 2011 are aged 31 to 45. Ultimately they will be of less importance to luxury marketers than Baby Boomers because this is a much smaller generation. However, right now GenXers are in the window of affluence, the most acquisitive lifestage. The leading edge of GenXers will reach age 55 in 2020 and mature beyond the window of affluence at that time, while the trailing edge of this generation will reach age 45 in 2023.

Millennials, also called Generation Y, born from 1980 through 1995, are the babies of Baby Boomers and the next great baby-boom generation. In 2015, leading-edge Millennials will mature into the window of affluence age range corresponding to their peak income period of life.

To the dismay of many marketers, the marketing and branding strategies that have worked so well with Baby Boomers are going to fall short when targeting the younger affluent generations. Peter Francese explains the challenges facing any marketer as the generation they target turns over to a new one, "Here is the generational challenge in a nutshell: If your aging Baby Boomer mother or father has been buying Louis Vuitton or whatever luxury brand, the chances are pretty slim that the next generation is going to buy into it. The way it has always worked is that whatever one generation embraces, the next generation avoids. It would behoove anybody who has been making money selling luxury to Baby Boomers to consider how they can reposition themselves to alter their products and perceptions for the next generation."

Francese points to the Greyhound Lines as a company that has tackled the challenge of marketing to a new generation and won.

· · · · ·

How Greyhound Created a New Bus Brand for a New Generation

The story of Greyhound Lines' BoltBus brand, while not a case study of a luxury brand transformation, clearly demonstrates what brands must do to change their marketing to address the next generation.

Peter explained, "Greyhound realized it had a real image problem as it looked to target the younger generation. Think about it, would you want your kids to go to a Greyhound bus station?"

My answer was an unequivocal "No!" since I associate bus stations with the sleazier side of most cities.

He continued, "Greyhound had an image that was not only downscale, but downright nasty. Recognizing this image problem, the company also wanted to capture the Millennial generation. This is a generation that travels a lot, and has lots of places to go. Greyhound wanted to capture this market, but rather than redoing its brand, it invented an entirely new bus company with a joint venture partner, Peter Pan, called BoltBus. Parents have no problem with their kids getting on a Bolt."

Not only did Greyhound create a new brand, they put new features on their Bolt buses that would appeal to young travelers. Peter explains, "The company realized if it invested and positioned Bolt as both safe and affordable with amenities that young people today want, it would make a fortune and that is exactly what it is doing."

Proof of the brand's success is its ridership topped 2 million within the first two years of service even though it was limited to travel among Washington, D.C., New York City, and Boston, with a few stops along the way in Philadelphia, Greenbelt, Maryland, and Cherry Hill, New Jersey.

Maybe bus travel isn't luxurious, but the orange BoltBus offerings take bus travel up a notch with leather seats and generous legroom, plus those extras today's technologically savvy travelers require, free wi-fi and seatback power outlets. "Even better," says Francese, "you don't go to the bus station to catch a Bolt. It picks you up at street corners or shopping centers where everybody's comfortable."

This curbside pickup strategy is good for both rider and company. It keeps overhead costs low and lets the company change routes and bus stops depending on demand. And most importantly, by investing in the features that matter most to its younger customers—luxurious, spacious seats equipped with technology and convenient, safe pickup locations—the company has tremendous flexibility with price, offering its now famous Bolt for a Buck promotion.

The pricing model is based strictly on supply and demand and offers riders high value for very reasonable costs. At least one $1 seat is available on any daily scheduled route, with other seats priced at different levels, but none over $25. If the seats sell fast, prices go up, but if sales drag, the company makes more $1 seats available. The company's loyalty program is also simple and customer friendly. Regardless of your miles traveled or ticket prices, if you travel eight times, the next ride is free.

Besides creating a new brand and a new market for a new generation, the company's launch strategy was also perfectly positioned to go viral. Heavy on social media and word-of-mouth, and based on the "rides for a buck" hook, it was what Seth Godin would call "remarkable." While the company has a Facebook page, Twitter is its riders' preferred means of communication. The company asks its riders to tag their tweets with #bolting so that they can stay in communication with their travelers.

Luxury marketers must be ready to transform their product and brands for each new generation, keeping what is best and forgetting the rest, as Greyhound has done with BoltBus. The first step is to realize that heritage and authenticity are vital to the success of a luxury brand and will help carry it to the next generation, but young people will demand their own unique take on a brand's heritage and authenticity. As Greyhound did, luxury brands need to recognize that change is required to connect with the younger generation, despite the fact that the change may threaten the very foundation on which the brand prospered through the later part of the 20th century.

• • • • •

Consider the recent announcement of Francois-Henri Pinault, PPR chairman and CEO, that Gucci Group is moving away from prominent display of its logos, "adjusting to this new perception of luxury, which is more subtle, more sophisticated." *Gucci products without the dominant GG!* Now that is a groundbreaking change, but right in line with the new sensibility of luxury consumers who want their luxury on the inside, not on the outside. Or, as I have heard numerous times in focus groups, "I don't want to wear any initials on my clothes but mine."

Peter Francese gives this practical advice to all luxury brands as they face the challenge of marketing their heritage brands to a new generation of consumers who definitely don't want to buy their mother's or grandmother's luxury brand. "Luxury brand providers will have to pull off a transformation like that of Bolt, making their brand, their product, their services, their prices, and their marketing relevant to a new generation."

That is what putting the luxe back in luxury means. Marketers must learn a whole new set of skills and a new way of communicating with the next generation of young affluents to inspire their passion. This will be crucial to the success of luxury brands through 2020, as GenX and Millennial affluents assume dominance in the luxury market.

A luxury drought sets in due to the aging of Baby Boomers

Until about 2020, luxury marketers will face a luxury drought, brought about by the dearth of high-spending affluent consumers aged 35-to-44 years, as the more mature downsizing Baby Boomer and maturing GenXer generation consumers dominate the market for luxury. Not until about 2019–2020 do the generations shift and young consumers aged 35-to-44 years start to dominate the luxury market once again. This shift may well signal a second luxury boom like the one from which we have just emerged, but the jury is still out on that.

During the luxury drought that started in 2007–2008, coincident with the recession but not caused by it, through about 2020, luxury marketers are going to confront a shortage of affluent shoppers who are willing to give up their hard-earned cash for what they perceive as over-priced luxury indulgences. Only two years earlier, these same consumers were more than willing to pay extravagantly for the same brands and products. What a difference those two years make when it comes to their willingness to indulge in luxury, as people aged from 44 to 46 years old! Until about 2020, highly indulgent young affluents will be thin on the ground as luxury marketers face an increasingly gray market of older and less indulgent affluent consumers.

For luxury marketers Baby Boomers still matter—a lot

It is a coincidence that the severity of the economic recession and the shift toward dominance of the 45-to-54-year-olds in the consumer economy took place at about the same time. The decline in the luxury market took shape totally independent of the recession due to the simple shift in the target market's age. However, the recession was the tipping point. It pushed the luxury drought along, increasing its intensity as luxury marketers experienced a decline in revenues brought about both by the demographic shift and the recession.

But for luxury marketers there is a silver lining to the recession's pain. It put them on notice that the world had changed and they must change in response. Without the loud wake-up call of the recession, many more luxury companies might have folded.

Luxury marketers were stunned by how quickly affluents closed up their wallets as the recession took hold. Affluents weren't supposed to feel the pain of recessions; at least they never had in the past. But this time was different. Not because of this recession's effects, but different because as the giant population of affluent Boomers aged the fundamental motivators for luxury consumer spending were beginning to shift. In effect, luxury marketers took a double hit—a one-two punch—breaking their previous high growth rates, and humbling many as they confronted sales declining as they never had before.

That is when the luxe went out of the luxury market, especially for Baby

Boomers. Many affluents simply stopped falling for luxury's temptations. They were no longer buying the old promises of luxury indulgence. For maturing affluent Baby Boomers, the luxury lifestyle just wasn't worth the price of admission anymore.

However, for luxury marketers through 2020, Baby Boomers still matter a lot. Putting the luxe back into *their* products and services and selling proposition is critical to seeing the way through until the Millennial generation reaches the window of affluence. Commenting on the importance of Boomers, Peter Francese puts it succinctly, "I am tired of hearing about how all Baby Boomers are going to retire tomorrow morning and bankrupt the country. Most Baby Boomers in 2011 are between the ages of 47 and 55 and in their peak money years. The substantial majority of Boomers are under age 60 and they aren't going to retire for a long time."

A new study from MainStay Investments focused on affluent and currently employed consumers aged 45 to 65. It highlights the vital economic role Boomers will continue to play for the next decade. Forty percent of the 1,049 Boomers surveyed said they will delay retirement to afford the lifestyle they want to live. Besides working later in life, Boomers also say they will save more to afford the luxuries that have evolved into necessities in their personal lifestyles.

Saving rather than spending is a favorite strategy affluent Boomers will practice. The MainStay survey found that 76 percent will spend less today to invest in a more comfortable lifestyle for the future. Where they are willing to make sacrifices in spending is largely in the area of luxury goods, more specifically those that fall into the personal luxury space, like clothing, fashion accessories, jewelry, and watches.

But Boomers are not willing to compromise on luxury experiences. The MainStay survey found that a large share of those surveyed looked at these experiences as necessities rather than as luxuries:

- weekend getaways – 46 percent;
- professional hair color/cut – 43 percent;
- children, grandchildren's education – 42 percent;
- dining out – 38 percent;
- domestic travel – 35 percent;

- ordering takeout – 34 percent; and
- movies – 30 percent.

As people mature and begin to prepare for their senior years, they look for something beyond acquiring another new designer handbag, another new necklace, or another thing that they really don't need. They start to demand more return from the hard-earned money they previously would have spent on material trappings of the luxury life. They come to realize that more things aren't going to make them happy. Their world changes and they want more of what really matters—quality of life, not quantity of possessions.

At the same time, few luxury brands or luxury retailers can afford to write off their Baby Boomer customers too soon. They need to keep them in the loop, active and involved. Marketers need Boomers engaged, and to do that they have to offer these mature, more discerning customers more value than bling, more substance over style. That is the new luxe these shoppers are looking for. Without keeping these mature customers engaged, many luxury marketers will face a very rough road ahead.

And it is worth noting that these changes in consumer priorities and values are organic and come along with the natural course of aging. Today's young affluents under age 45 will eventually exhibit the very same changes in their priorities as they grow older.

Keep your eyes on the prize—young affluents

Luxury marketers will gain much by developing strategies to keep maturing Baby Boomer affluents engaged through the next decade. But the ultimate prize is to capture the passion and loyalty of young affluents, those high-income consumers from Generation X, born from 1965 to 1979 and the emerging Millennial generation, born from 1980 to 1995. The reason why luxury brands must court the passion of young affluents is very simple: Young affluents have a hearty appetite for luxury and as a result spend more on luxury than their more mature counterparts.

Throughout the last decade young affluents, GenXers mostly, have consistently and significantly out-spent more mature Baby Boomer affluents in Unity Marketing's studies. Young affluents have been tracked spending roughly one-third more than Boomers on luxury through 2008. With the easing of the recession, the difference between young affluent and mature affluent spending more than doubled, with the mature affluent segment holding back on its spending while young affluents released pent-up demand for luxuries denied them during the depths of the recession.

⊃ **Figure 5.1 Difference in Luxury Spending, Young Affluents vs. Mature Affluents**

in percent

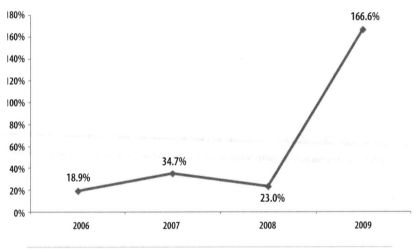

Source: Unity Marketing

Only time will tell whether young affluents will continue to outpace mature affluents in their spending. But one thing is sure, young affluents have a stronger appetite for luxury, and marketers need to think young to cultivate these consumers and build loyalty to their brands.

• • • • •

Mary J. Blige Is a Luxury Brand Designed for a New Generation

I think the beauty business needs some different thinking in it. We're going to keep looking for different ways to speak to the consumer where and how she wants to be spoken to.
                                        —Steve Stoute, Carol's Daughter

Born in 1971, Mary Jane Blige is a GenX musician. Among her peers, her fame and accomplishments are legendary, including nine Grammy awards. As a Baby Boomer who came of age with the Beatles and the Doors, I know Mary J. Blige only as a brand, but an extraordinary brand that followed a new era playbook in marketing.

With social media flash and celebrity sizzle, Mary J. Blige launched her signature fragrance, My Life, on July 31, 2010. Mary J. Blige My Life brand, a 1.7 ounce bottle retailing for $55, is remarkable for being a perfume that broke all kinds of records for sales of a scent with very limited sampling or traditional media involved. Sold exclusively through Home Shopping Network (HSN), Mary talked her scent into the virtual shopping bags of thousands of television shoppers, setting an HSN record. More than 72,000 bottles of fragrance and ancillary lotion products sold in the first 24 hours, generating over $3 million in sales. Not bad for a day's work.

The perfume was sold almost exclusively by telling Mary's life story, including her ups and downs, and how she worked to create the brand. It was marketing magic aimed at the psychology of a new generation of women consumers who expect more immediacy and connection with brands than traditional marketing allows.

As the HSN team headed by CEO Mindy Grossman looked at the opportunity, they felt the brand demanded a fresh approach in keeping with Mary J. Blige's personal story. According to Steve Stoute, founder and lead investor in Carol's Daughter, the company that manufactures the fragrance, "I'm a guy who has built my career by creating footsteps where they never existed and I entered the beauty business only a few years ago. The success of the launch changes the existing business model for a prestige fragrance launch. I think the beauty business needs some different thinking in it. We're going to keep looking for different ways to speak to the consumer where and how she wants to be spoken to."

How the HSN team spoke to their consumer, 20 percent of whom were new to HSN, encompassed what they described as a "360-degree marketing campaign." Prior to release, new customers were tempted with video clips, called "Chapters," featured on HSN and the HSN.com website, as well as Facebook and Twitter postings. HSN also distributed 100,000 direct mail brochures and 300,000 inserts to its existing customer base. Ads were run in *Allure, Glamour,* and *Essence* magazines and 50,000 snap bracelets embedded with My Life scent were distributed at the Essence Music Festival over the July 4, 2010 weekend.

Mary came on for her premier HSN show at midnight July 31. Oprah Winfrey later joined her by phone to give her some "you go girl' encouragement. Super-model Naomi Campbell also dialed in, as did many of Mary's fans to chat it up with the celeb. Customers can feel good about their purchases because a dollar from each unit sold is donated to the Foundation for the Advancement of Women Now (FFAWN). This is a non-profit created by Blige and Steve Stoute to assist women in need with education and training.

The playbook that Mary J. Blige and her partners HSN and Carol's Daughter created with the success of My Life perfume represents a marketing model that luxury brands wishing to attract younger consumers need to study.

For the new generation, master storytelling through compelling new mediums combined with an approachable and much-admired celebrity who embodies the brand takes precedence over product. But, celebrity isn't everything. The ultimate product must deliver. My Life does, as shown by its star rating of 4.8 out of 5 voted by HSN.com visitors. Impressario Steve Stoute offers advice for any brand looking to build loyalty among the next generation of affluent consumers. "This launch proves that consumers are looking for new ways to engage with a brand. Long gone are the days of traditional marketing that rely only on sampling and advertising. Consumers want to connect, believe, and immerse themselves in the experience. They want to see themselves fit into the story."

· · · · ·

Global Trend: Today's young affluents are the want-it-all generation

Meet young affluents, the "want-it-all, want-it-now" generation of luxury consumers. These consumers poised to assume control of the luxury market by the end of the next decade, taking domination away from the original "me-generation," Baby Boomers.

The ascent of the young affluents impacts not only the American luxury market, but is a global trend as well. Young affluents will be an increasingly important share of the target market for global luxury marketers over the next ten to twenty years beyond the United States (median age of 36.8*) and Europe (median age ranges around 40). In developing luxury markets like Brazil (median age 28.9), India (25.9), and China (35.2), the population as a whole is more youthful.

In the future, the global luxury market will be less culturally bound. Given the rise of the internet and other global media embraced by young people, trends in the luxury market will cross borders at alarming rates. The future of the international luxury market will be a "global village" made up of young affluent citizens of the world.

As the global luxury market trends younger, luxury marketers must learn to think young to survive and thrive. Global luxury marketers have gotten used to the passions and nuances of maturing Baby Boomers after so many years of targeting this generation. Now they have a new challenge to appeal to young affluents who have different ideas about luxury and different priorities in how they spend their wealth.

Key facts about the emerging generation of young affluents that luxury marketers need to understand:

The most highly educated generation ever

Compared with not quite 30 percent of 45-to-54-year-old Baby Boomers, 33 percent of 35-to-44-year-olds (GenXers) are college educated, and 11 percent have completed masters, professional, or doctorate degrees. Only 10 percent of Boomers have advanced education.

Reaching affluence at a younger age

Owing to their higher levels of education, young people can expect to reach higher levels of income at younger ages than their Boomer counterparts. Their rising income mobility will be helped out by relatively less competition for high-paying jobs than Boomers experienced when they entered the work force.

---

* All median ages according to the 2010 CIA World Fact Book

Grew up in more affluent circumstances

◔ Figure 5.2 Financial Status of Family of Origin by Generation

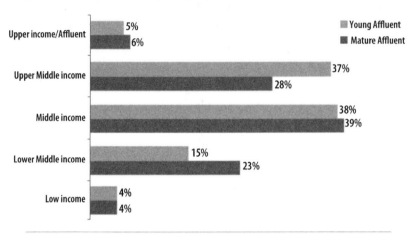

Source: Unity Marketing

A recent Unity Marketing survey of young affluents, most of whom were members of the GenX cohort, revealed they are far more likely than Boomers to have grown up in upper-middle income households. And Millennials, the babies of Baby Boomers, are going to arise from even more affluent circumstances. The lifestyle that people grow accustomed to in their youth sets them on a course to achieve a similar or an even more prosperous lifestyle.

Some of the differences in spending between the young and older affluents may well be explained by this. Younger consumers, having come from more affluent family backgrounds, may expect more luxury in their lives and so devote a greater share of their budgets to the pursuit of a luxury lifestyle. Older luxury consumers, on the other hand, are more likely to have "boot-strapped" their way to luxury and so view luxury more as a treat than something they expect to indulge in every day.

More consumer-savvy, more discerning, more brand aware

This is the generation that came of age with home computers, videogames, cable television, and the internet as a social and commercial tool. Gen Y has been in the vanguard of adopting email, texting, and instant messaging. They were first users of social media such as Myspace, YouTube, Facebook, and Twitter. They have had an exponentially larger world of media from which to draw knowledge, experience, and impressions than Boomers had growing up. This accounts for their greater sophistication as shoppers and far broader range of brand knowledge. "Gen Y Prestige Brand Ranking," a recent survey conducted by L2 among Millennial consumers worldwide, found that 65 percent of young women and 61 percent of young men consider themselves brand conscious. Only 1 percent of women and 3 percent of men claim to be immune to brands. Despite their greater level of brand awareness, there is little evidence it translates into greater brand loyalty than that found among the Boomer generation. In fact, their more sophisticated shopping styles tend to discourage young affluents from settling in with specific brands; being more aware of all the world has to offer brand-wise, they'd rather play the field.

They want it all, but especially superior quality and price/value that favors the consumer

Young affluents put their formidable consumer knowledge and shopping experience to work to find bargains and get the price they want to pay. In my research I have been impressed with the passion of young affluents for stretching their dollar to get better quality for less. They don't take price tags at face value, and they are unlikely to equate high price with high quality, as this young man expressed in a recent discussion group, "I expect luxury brands to cost more, but I still look for luxury brands on sale or on close out or on eBay. I always try to get luxury for less."

Young affluents are masters of the new global communications media, both formal media, like internet shopping and company-sponsored websites, and informal communications—chat rooms, blogs, MySpace, YouTube, and the whole host of social networking media. They use their command of information to give them real power as consumers. It's not just leveraging the power that comes from having a lot of money, as Boomers did, but the even greater power that comes from knowledge. Young affluents are incredibly smart about their money.

They know how to use their cash to get what they really want. And they don't buy traditional advertising spin and hype. They are entirely too smart for that. They want substance, proven quality, and above all, value for the money they spend. They won't accept anything less.

They most highly value the experience of luxury

Young people have a ravenous appetite to achieve the "good life." Whether built up by media or marketing, young affluents want to enjoy a luxury lifestyle. They want the bragging rights that come from having the best-of-the-best brands. They want bigger and more well-appointed houses than they grew up in. They want it all and they want it now.

As we look to the future, we see a luxury market in transition. Over the course of the next decade, young affluents, made up primarily of GenXers born between 1965 and 1979, and leading-edge Millennials, born from 1980 on, will grow into wealth and consumer power to replace Boomers as the prime target market for luxury brands.

Luxury brands that have mastered the nuances of marketing to the distinctive tastes and desires of affluent Baby Boomers are suddenly going to discover their well-honed strategies and proven tactics are obsolete when selling to the next generation of affluents. They will have to learn it all over again for this new generation of affluents, who have different priorities, different desires, and fundamentally different motivations for indulging in luxury goods and services.

· · · · ·

Peter Max, Artist and Marketer, Spans the Generations

I consider myself extremely lucky to be an artist. I come here every day with the will to paint.

—Peter Max

He first came to prominence in the counterculture 60s as the "artist laureate" of the Baby Boomer generation. Since then, Peter Max and his art have evolved through the 70s, 80s, 90s and into the 21st century, staying relevant to each succeeding generation. He has captured the distinctive iconography of each decade to present a body of work that includes U.S. commemorative postage stamps; a Statue of Liberty series; gigantic murals for the World's Fair, Winter Olympics, Woodstock Music Festival, and the Rock & Roll Hall of Fame; and portraits of each president since Jimmy Carter. Of his latest, President Barack Obama, Peter Max says, "I was very excited when he was nominated. And following that thrill, I realized he is the 44th president, so I painted 44 portraits." The full installation of the 44 Obama paintings debuted on CBS's *The Early Show.*

His honors and awards are too numerous to mention, but his seamless transition from Sixties counterculture to celebrating the historic icons of American culture is a valuable lesson for marketers to learn. Most impressive, Peter Max has created and managed his own dynamic art brand through almost five decades.

In his Upper West Side studio in New York, sitting next to a Ringo Starr–autographed baby grand piano, Peter Max tells his story. "As an artist, I was very, very fortunate to study realism at The Art Students League. My teacher was Frank Reilly, and he was trained in the same classroom where he trained me, under the tutelage of George Bridgeman, considered one of the great anatomists of the 20th century. Frank's classmate was a young student by the name of Norman Rockwell.

"When I came out of art school I was intent on being a realist, but I also had a tremendous passion for astronomy. I wanted to give a face to astronomy that you can't really see through a telescope. After all, when you look through a telescope all you see is white dots. So I started drawing these into characters and suddenly I was winning awards and selling posters in the millions. Then all this licensing came my way with big manufacturers like J.P. Stevens and Wrangler jeans. But after about two to three years, I no longer wanted to be in the licensing business, as I was no longer painting as much. I gave it all up and went back to my studio for a creative retreat to paint. I moved into Expressionism and Fauvism, and developed a whole new way of painting spontaneously with multi-colored brushstrokes. It was a great departure from my poster style of the 60s."

Today those 60s posters that sold in the millions for $2 a pop are available to the collector's market for $2,000 to $3,000. The people collecting them include both Peter's original Sixties generation of followers who once put his posters up in dorm rooms and now frame them for corporate offices and million-dollar homes, but also the MTV generation who still connect with the vibrancy and vision of his early works.

Essentially, Peter Max's transition as a brand has been from mass to class, with a host of attendance-breaking one-man museum shows and top-notch art dealers, including the 31 Wentworth Galleries where he shows frequently. Peter thrives on meeting and greeting his fans, from young to old. "When I have a gallery show, there is standing room only. I'm very lucky to be so well known and to have this kind of popularity."

It's at his packed gallery shows where Peter Max, the ultimate brand manager and marketer, does his consumer research. Through his shows he learns what themes excite his collectors and what images make the connection. "I see collectors as just being great fans. Some collectors buy very large and important pieces for a lot of money. And some collectors are fans that may not have the means to buy something that is tens of thousands of dollars, but there are works of art available in galleries for them too, such as works on paper, lithographs. And sometimes I meet really amazing people, like the man who came up to me at a show with a book of photographs. He had photographs of his walls filled with Peter Maxes. He had 74 Peter Maxes. He said, 'I have been a collector and a fan of yours for 25 years. Every year I've acquired one or two pieces.' I really enjoy the collectors," Max says.

Peter Max's *tour de force* as a luxury brand is thinking of his art work as a series, or collections. In marketer's parlance, each series is a product line under the Peter Max brand with product line extensions that give the line relevancy and direction for further development. Like Fendi's baguette or Hermès' Birkin or Kelly lines of bags, Peter Max envisions his brand and products over the long term. He gave me a glimpse inside his vision of his brand in describing a new series concept he is working on now, the Art Masters series. "I have started painting portraits of the great masters—from Van Gogh's self-portrait to the Mona Lisa. I am a big fan of the classic masters and have studied them all. When I paint an artist like Van Gogh, I will use different color ways, and build upon his iconic brushstrokes. We are considering doing a show with galleries that have some masters' portraits and an 'Homage to Picasso' etching series. We'll call it The Masters Series."

I came away from my discussion with Peter with a tremendous respect for him as an artist and humanitarian, environmentalist, and defender of human rights, as he is actively involved in many causes from Earth Day to the Humane Society of America. He created a series of fund-raising posters for the September 11th Fund, plus creating a portrait of each of the 356 firefighters who died that day. He made two portraits of each, one as part of an installation at his one-man museum show at the Colorado Springs Fine Arts Center, and another to give to each of the surviving families.

Beyond his artistic philanthropy, he also is an intuitive marketer who knows how to manage his brand and product. He says, "I consider myself extremely lucky to be an artist and create beautiful images that many people love. It gives me tremendous satisfaction that I am able to make something from a blank white canvas with a bunch of brushes and colors."

Some may think it unseemly in an artist, but I find nothing inconsistent in a great artist also being a great marketer and being a caring and conscientious human being as well. "We may be in a human body and a little kitty cat could be in a kitty cat body, but inside lives a similar spirit that we all have. There are a lot of nice things we can have, like seeing a Broadway show or having a chauffeur, but quality of life is really how you conduct yourself in life relative to other living things. When you start opening yourself up and you take care of other living things, it gives you a sense of real belonging to the universe. I met a swami many years ago who profoundly changed my life and opened me to this consciousness. He taught 'Love all, serve all, always.'"

* * * * *

part 2

Marketing Strategy Hinges on Understanding Consumer Purchase Behavior

chapter 6

Purchase Behavior Reveals What Luxury Consumers Buy, Where They Buy, and How Much They Spend

To find out what satisfies buyers, marketers must examine the main influences on what, where, when and how consumers buy.

—William Pride and O.C. Ferrell, *Foundations of Marketing*

In marketing circles conventional wisdom is that past behavior predicts future behavior, in the sense that certain patterns of behavior become habitual and routine. The often-unmentioned caveat to the conventional wisdom is that the context of that behavior must be constant. That means if the world remains the same, people will most often behave in habituated, routine ways.

Unfortunately for luxury marketers, the context in which luxury consumers make their purchase decisions has changed dramatically over the past several years, resulting in equally dramatic changes in their purchase behavior. As a market researcher, I reject the notion that past consumer behavior predicts future behavior, but I don't reject the critical importance of understanding consumer behavior. While past consumer behavior isn't predictive, it factors in mightily to your overall marketing strategies. Marketers need to understand basics about the consumers' behavior past and present so as to meet potential customers in their worlds, and make products and services available to consumers at prices they are likely to pay.

In Part 1 we looked at luxury consumer demographics, the *who* in the luxury marketing equation. In Part 2 we will look at the *what, where,* and *how much* that defines affluents' purchase behavior. Let's start with examining how the recession and the economic turmoil of the last two years changed affluent consumer purchase behavior dramatically.

Vast majority of affluents are still making changes

⤳ **Figure 6.1 Lifestyle Changes due to Recession**

How has the current economic recession affected you and your household in terms of shopping? During the past 12 months, have you . . .

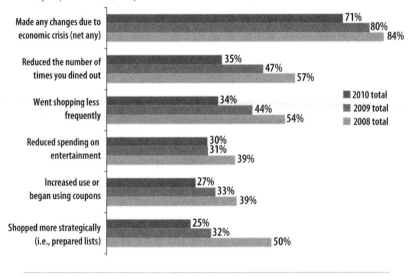

Source: Unity Marketing

Unity Marketing's quarterly Luxury Tracking Study is the best source of information about shifts in affluent consumers' luxury purchase behavior. Each quarter since 2008, as the recession gained force, the survey has included a question about what changes affluents are making in their lifestyles and their consumption patterns in response to the economy. Above are the ten most common changes affluent consumers have made and trends from 2008 to 2010. While this graph shows these changes in lifestyle are becoming less prominent, at the end of 2010 the vast majority of affluents (73 percent) report they still are modifying their lifestyles and spending habits in response to their current economic status. That things are getting better is without question, as 84 percent of luxury consumers surveyed at the end of 2008 said their lifestyles were in transition, but things are hardly back to normal.

Affluents are still making changes because most believe the country is still in recession and will remain so for the immediate future. In Unity's final 2010 survey (n = 1,364), 70 percent of affluent luxury consumers said they believed the recession is still in effect; only 21 percent believe the recession is over. The remaining 8 percent are undecided. For the majority who don't think the recession is over, we asked when they think it will end, and only 45 percent said 2011; the rest (65 percent) said 2012 or later.

This was an equal opportunity recession—people at all income levels felt the pain

⮕ Figure 6.2 Lifestyle Changes 2010, due to Recession by Income

How has the current economic crisis affected you and your household in terms of purchases and shopping? During the past 12 months, have you . . .

	HENRYs ($100k-$249k)	Ultra-affluents ($250k+)
Made any changes due to economic crisis (net any)	**77%**	**64%**
Reduced the number of times you dined out	41	25
Went shopping less frequently	40	24
Comparison shopped before making purchases	36	28
Reduced spending on entertainment	37	21
Increased or started to use coupons	33	19
Did more product research before shopping	29	24
Postponed or delayed purchases for the home	30	21
Shopped more strategically, such as prepared shopping lists	29	20
Postponed or delayed personal purchases, such as clothing and apparel, jewelry and watches, fashion accessories, etc.	29	20
Postponed or delayed plans to travel	29	17
Cut spending when making personal purchases, such as shopping for sales or at an outlet store, opting for less premium brands, etc.	28	16
Cut spending when dining out by choosing a less premium restaurant	28	14

	HENRYs ($100k-$249k)	Ultra-affluents ($250k+)
Reduced spending when dining out by choosing lower cost menu items or more budget-friendly wine or spirits, etc.	26	15
Cut spending when making purchases for the home, such as shopping for sales or at outlet stores, opting for less premium brands, etc.	24	15
Postponed or delayed routine personal services, such as spa visits, hair salon, manicures/pedicures	23	16
Limited shopping to stores that are having sales or special promotions that make my dollar go farther	23	15
Postponed or delayed routine household services, such as garden or landscape, housekeeping, pool	16	13
Changed the stores where you routinely shop in to find better prices	15	11
None of the above: I tend to do all these things regularly	7	6
None of the above: I have not had to change. The current economic crisis has not impacted my household	16	30

Source: Unity Marketing Luxury Tracking Study 2010

Significant lifestyle changes are taking place at all levels of affluence. More than three-fourths of the lower-income HENRY affluents are still making changes. Nearly two-thirds of the wealthiest ultra-affluents also continue to adjust their spending habits in light of the current economic reality. The number-one change ultra-affluents are making is comparison shopping before making purchases. In other words they are being smarter shoppers, taking time to do their research and find a better price or better deal if it is available. Another favorite strategy for ultra-affluents to save money is simply to shop less often, choosing to stay out of harm's way. HENRYs are doing these things and more to a much greater extent.

Despite more comparison shopping and more pre-purchase research, luxury consumers with the most money to spend are looking not necessarily for the lowest price, but the best value. As Warren Buffett says, "Price is what you pay, value is what you get." Affluent shoppers are looking for the purchase that makes the most sense and is the smartest purchase, when all factors are included.

I sat down with Ken Nisch, who is chairman of JGA, a brand strategy and environmental design group with a client roster that includes The North Face, Audi, British Airways, Estée Lauder, Lucy, Godiva Chocolatier,

Levenger, Origins, Saks Department Store Group, Jaguar, Hickey Freeman and Time Warner. We talked about the shift in luxury consumer values and how marketers must react at the brand level (i.e., making sure your brand is perceived as the best value in the consumer's comparison research) and at the retail level (i.e., giving people a compelling reason to come back into the store and run the retailers' gauntlet). He talks about changing the context in which people make their purchase decisions, so that they will ultimately buy and spend more.

• • • • •

Ken Nisch Shares Strategies to Change the Context of the Purchase

Luxury has become more democratic, so, for example, luxury is more inclusive, rather than exclusive, or just for the chosen few.

—Ken Nisch

According to Ken, the most profound change occurring in the luxury market today is that of the concept of luxury is fragmenting; Luxury means different things to different folks. There are no longer clear-cut boundaries that define value in the diverging luxury space.

Ken explains, "It all goes back to the definition of luxury. To some it is scarcity, to others it's price, or aspiration. Luxury has become more democratic, so, for example, luxury is more inclusive, rather than exclusive or just for the chosen few. But if we look at the luxury market today, as reflected in brands like Hermès, their audience may have widened because people have more income, but it hasn't widened because the company has lowered its price or broadened the availability of product. You don't see many shopping centers with an Hermès boutique, but you are apt to find a Louis Vuitton shop. A brand like Louis Vuitton is different than Hermès, because you can basically buy it in many places, at many price points, and it's not exclusive or hard to get. We are creating this new idea of super luxury, like Hermès, and mass luxury, like Vuitton."

What differentiates super luxury brands like Hermès, Bulgari, or Van Cleef, according to Ken, is "they haven't changed radically over the last ten years. They've certainly increased the number of people who can participate in the world they have created due to rising affluence, but they haven't changed their world to participate with more people." By contrast, he points to Louis Vuitton, David Yurman, or Swarovski, brands that are more mass luxury, having broadened their business in the past decade.

Ken asks, "This is the million dollar question: How big can you be as a luxury brand before you basically outgrow the definition of luxury?" The difference between mass luxury as represented by Louis Vuitton and super luxury like Hermès boils down to the natural limitation on production and the value of rarity and scarcity.

Ken says, "Mass luxury brands like Coach have fabulous products, but there is no real limit to the amount of product that can be in the marketplace besides the limitation the company imposes. They can set up production in Turkey or Brazil and make more product. Whereas with Hermès, you can only have so much of this product, based on the methods and materials that they use to make their products. It is becoming a gray area with customers wanting to know for sure that the product has all the key attributes and heritage. I expect the more discerning customers will ultimately abandon a brand that has gone too mass, if they are not getting the inherent values that they expect to pay a premium for. They won't pay a premium for a European brand if it is made in China, for example. A real danger for positioning luxury brands is that the ads are more about perception than reality."

Ken points to two recent ads from Louis Vuitton that brought down the wrath of the Advertising Standards Authority. The ads showed women hand stitching leather goods with text that implied LV products were handcrafted throughout most or all of the production process. Vuitton couldn't argue with the ASA's finding that the ads were misleading and therefore pulled them from the company's rotation.

The challenge for luxury brands is to clearly define what they are selling —whether heritage, hand-craftsmanship, exclusive material, cutting-edge design, or in the case of a brand like Apple, cutting-edge technology—and deliver that value to a customer who is willing to pay a premium for it. Brands that aren't living up to that standard need to assess exactly what their value is and who their value is for.

Ken goes on to say that the value is not about price. "True luxury marketers have to find a way to add value to the customer's perception of the products. This isn't lower price, but more service, more exclusivity, less availability. But price/value enters the picture at the lower levels of mass luxury or even down to premium brands. Procter & Gamble people talk about Rembrandt teeth whitening products or Pantene as being luxury in their segments, because they get a significant premium over the alternatives. Luxury in these spaces might be to have your hair colored in the salon for $300 or use this Pantene treatment for $75. Or have your teeth whitened at the dentist for $600 or use this Rembrandt kit for $300. In these cases you can get the same results, but spend less money. What you trade off is the service. Customers trade the experience, and get the same result if they can't afford the whole thing."

Ken then warns luxury marketers, both in the service sector like restaurants and hotels and also consumer goods manufacturers, that they need to pay keen attention to the idea of value and how it affects the customer's perception relative to the transaction.

"Marketers need to think about the value perception of their luxury but also address their customer's need for a deal. If you are a hotel, you might give away a spa treatment or a free night in a package for your customer. For example, a good friend of mine has a restaurant where they cellar a bottle of wine at $150, using the regular restaurant markup, pretty luxurious. But if you are a frequent diner, you can order that wine for only $50. Now even $50 is a lot for a bottle of wine, but my friend is selling an amazing number of those $150 bottles at $50, far more than she could sell of regular $50 bottles before. Her customers feel like they are getting this great value and this great experience. Marketers in the service sector have to rethink what the new normal means."

Ken talks about the lasting value of quality and how that will become even more important to customers in the future. "There is a dichotomy between the luxury of fashion and the luxury of quality. In fashion, luxury is ultimately disposable, because if it is fashionable today, it will be obsolete tomorrow. That is different from quality. Take a company like Ramblers Way Farm, founded by Tom Chappell who also founded Tom's of Maine. They make casual clothing and undergarments from this very special wool that is as soft as cashmere. The idea is you are buying Ramblers Way Farm clothing for a lifetime; it's a classic. You are not going to throw it out. You pay a significant premium but you are going to love every day that you have it on. That's a lot different than buying some piece of fashion that is going to be out of style by next fall. In the future people will think of luxury more as this lasting quality. People are going to still spend to get quality, but what is quality is evolving from what is purely fashionable to what is well made."

Ken concludes with the sage advice that a one-size-fits-all luxury marketing strategy is not going to work in the future as customer segments splinter and the distinction between luxury and premium, mass and class, continues to erode.

"There will be a new reality for luxury marketers in mature markets like the U.S. or Europe and in emerging markets, like China and India. This idea of putting luxury in a nice box and tying a ribbon around it with a simple, predictive formula will not exist. It will take a much more complex and thoughtful solution. Just because a luxury brand has been around for the last hundred years means relatively little for the next hundred years. Soon, I think, we will see new luxury brands emerge from places like Brazil and India, places where people increasingly want to define their own culture's role in the world and their own definition of luxury. Those cultures will reject many of the luxury brands we think of today as the natural inheritors of affluence. If I were a CEO of a traditional luxury brand, I would be trying to find a partner in one of these places where a new luxury will emerge—China, India, Brazil—and harness the brightest, most creative skills and sources to bring a whole new energy to the luxury market. I would be doing this with a big dose of humility in that search," Ken concludes.

• • • • •

What Unity Marketing's luxury consumer surveys point to, and Ken is alluding to, is an emerging consumer cost-benefit equation. Affluent consumers no longer rely on an outside arbiter to define luxury for them, be it a noted brand like Louis Vuitton, or a designer like Karl Lagerfeld, or a magazine editor like Anna Wintour of *Vogue*, or their peer group at the country club, or friends on Facebook. They may use these sources as references in their due-diligence research before making a purchase decision, but they ultimately are the final arbiter and decision-maker in their own world.

Affluent consumers are asking hard questions of brands and products that purport to be luxury and are finding that many brands and their products do not measure up to the test of true luxury. Does it make sense to pay $295 for a Jean Paul Gaultier ivory tank top made of polyamide/spandex, when you can buy a natural-fiber, USA-made, natural-dyed wool tank for $100 from Ramblers Way Farm and feel good about your purchase and wear it for years instead of just for this season or next? Which is more luxurious? Ask the luxury "experts" above and you are likely to get a very different answer than from affluent consumers who are in search of lasting value, good investments, and wise spending. As author Thomas J. Stanley, who wrote *The Millionaire Mind,* reminds us, millionaires repair their shoes rather than buying new ones because they buy shoes that are worth repairing in the first place.

How Spending on Luxury Has Changed

Marketing success is selling more stuff to more people more often for more money more efficiently.

—Sergio Zyman

As Unity Marketing's quarterly luxury tracking study has confirmed, as well as studies of consumer spending by American Express Publishing and its partner Harris Group, MasterCard's SpendingPulse, and American Affluence Research Center all agree American consumers are spending more on luxury goods and services in 2010 compared with 2009 and 2008—the depths of the recession. Unfortunately the media makes the most of the encouraging sound bites and doesn't delve deeply into the underlying reality these studies show. Unity's research clearly documents dramatic increases in luxury consumer spending, but the spending numbers are driven by dramatic increases among a very small portion of the market. However, spending, as Sergio Zyman reminds us, is only one metric that measures marketing success. Getting more people to buy luxury more often is the challenge, and Unity Marketing's data doesn't show that happening yet.

Strong uptick in spending doesn't tell the whole story

Spending on luxury goods and services rose dramatically, from an average of $21,909 per luxury consumer household in the first quarter of 2009 to $28,060 in the fourth quarter of 2010, a 28 percent increase. However, in the last two quarters of 2010, the average amount spent by a luxury consumer declined from the previous quarter. The quarter-by-quarter trajectory of spending increases has been steadily slowing since the third quarter 2009, suggesting that affluent consumers have released pent up demand for luxuries built up during the depths of the recession.

⮑ **Figure 7.1 Percent Change in Luxury Consumer Spending**

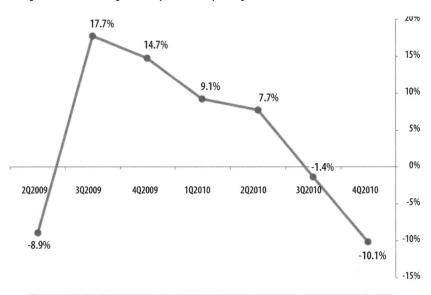

Source: Unity Marketing

However, the increases in luxury consumer spending were primarily driven by increased outlays among the very small segment of ultra-affluents who typically spend three to four times more on luxury than the HENRY households. These ultra-affluents, who represent only 2 percent of the total U.S. population and 10 percent of the top 20 percent of U.S. households by income, are major drivers of Unity's spending statistics, as this segment represents one-third of the survey sample. In statistical terms, the ultra-affluents are actually outliers, whose average or mean spending far exceeds the survey's norm, defined by the median value, when all values are ordered from highest to lowest.

For example, in the fourth quarter 2010 luxury tracking survey, the *average* (i.e., mean) amount spent by all affluents surveyed (n = 1,237) was

$28,060, four times higher than the survey's *median* or mid-point, a mere $6,817. Statistical averages or means are much more influenced by extremely high values in the survey. A small group of ultra-affluents who bought $100,000+ automobiles and expensive luxury vacations in one quarter can drive the overall survey *averages* to astronomical levels.

When we chart luxury spending by the two income segments, we find that the lower-income HENRYs increased the average amount they spent on luxury by only $3,000 from the first quarter 2009 to the fourth quarter in 2010. An overall 25 percent increase, but relatively modest when compared to the $13,50 increase in average amount spent by ultra-affluents in the same time period, a jump of 34 percent.

⤳ Figure 7.2 Luxury Spending by Income Segment

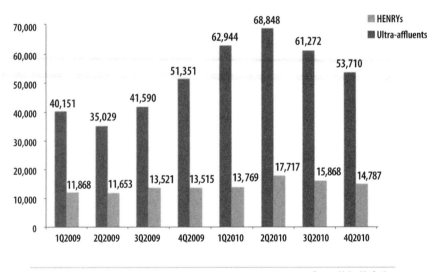

Source: Unity Marketing

Consumer spending doesn't measure the number of people actually buying luxury

The big problem with focusing on luxury spending is that it doesn't take into account *how many* people are actually buying luxury. This measure of the number of people buying is called *purchase incidence.* Since 2006 the actual percent making luxury purchases has been on a steady decline, from 55 percent of affluents in 2006 to 43 percent in both 2009 and 2010. In other words, we have experienced a dramatic loss of customers in the luxury market since before the recession with no signs yet of an uptick in participation. Even if those people who are currently buying are spending more money, there are now far fewer people in the luxury market than before the recession.

⤳ Figure 7.3 Share of Affluents Purchasing Luxury

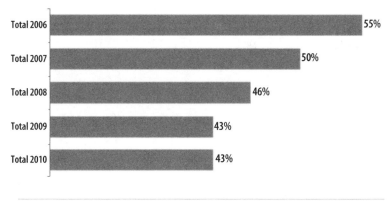

Source: Unity Marketing

Given the trend in fewer customers willing to indulge in luxury purchases, marketers can't rest on their laurels. The economic messages are mixed, with fewer people with means being enticed to indulge in luxury spending. Many affluents who have plenty of money have simply dropped out of the luxury market, gone back to buying mass, rather than class, because the value is just not there.

Premium mass brands like Banana Republic, Ann Taylor and Ann Taylor LOFT, for example, offer affluent shoppers a value proposition that is compelling in the current climate. They are being rewarded by the loyalty of ultra-affluent shoppers, who rank them as their most widely patronized fashion boutiques in 2010, ahead of such luxury brands as Chanel, Louis Vuitton, and Gucci.

⊃ **Figure 7.4 Ultra-Affluents' Favorite Fashion Boutiques, 2010**

in percent

Ann Taylor LOFT	17.8%
Banana Republic	16.4
Ann Taylor	15.1
Anthropologie	14.4
Chanel	13.0
J.Crew	12.8
Armani Exchange	12.8
Louis Vuitton	10.8
Coach	10.1
Calvin Klein	9.9
Talbots	8.4
Ralph Lauren	8.3
H&M	8.0
Kenneth Cole	7.7
Gucci	7.6
Chico's	7.3

Source: Unity Marketing Luxury Tracking Study 2010

• • • • •

Vera Wang Manages Her Luxe Brand Through Multiple Channels and Categories

Our objective is to continue to grow our lifestyle-product offering and keep pace with the evolving needs of the consumer.

—Vera Wang

Among fashion designers, Vera Wang is one of many who have broadened their reach to all price ranges, from bargain basement with Kohl's, mid-range through a new partnership with David's Bridal, and super high end with bridal fashions for her celebrity clientele, notably Chelsea Clinton, Alicia Keys, and Hilary Duff. What sets Vera Wang apart from other designers, most of whom have done limited low-end collections with single partners, is her determination to become a lifestyle brand, following in the footsteps of Ralph Lauren who moved out of the fashion sphere to play in a much bigger universe. Estimates of the size of her company vary from $700 million according to *Wall Street Journal* to $175 million from *Women's Wear Daily*. However big her enterprise is, it is only going to get larger in the years ahead as she continues to manage her brand to maximize sales across a growing range of products and retail channels.

Vera Wang launched her lifestyle brand from her platform as wedding designer to the stars. She started her fashion company in 1990 and got her first big bridal commission dressing the future daughter-in-law of Ethel Kennedy. Since then she has maintained a high profile as designer to socialites and celebrities for bridal and red carpet occasions as well as designer to the Olympic skating athletes such as Michelle Kwan and Nancy Kerrigan. (Vera's early training was in figure skating.)

From fashion bridal boutique to lifestyle brand was a leap, but one that Vera has managed strategically. She accomplished it through licensing, first into perfume with Unilever, a logical expansion strategy for many fashion designers, then fine jewelry with Rosy Fine Blue, a partnership that has since ended. The real innovation came when she created a two-pronged licensing strategy. One was keyed to her core competency, fashion. The other launched from the bridal platform to the bride's married lifestyle, what Vera describes as "creating a lifestyle that goes beyond core bridal."

For fashion the most noted license, and likely the one generating the most dollars, is Simply Vera Vera Wang. This license, with discount retailer Kohl's, reaches shoppers at 1,000 department stores and online at Kohls.com. The Simply Vera Vera Wang line is envisioned as real fashion women can mix with higher-end pieces, not another low-end cheap-chic line. She describes it on her website as, "For me, Simply Vera Vera Wang represents not just a fashion philosophy, but a vision about life and style. It's also a true expression of my own personal design vocabulary. This juxtaposition of ideas speaks to a modern sensibility that is fun, easy, and sophisticated."

Mario Graso, president of Vera Wang Inc. explains the business side of the Kohl's line, "It's very interesting and very similar to luxury. It's just quicker and the pieces are less expensive. It's a similar process. Kohl's has taught Vera that a lower price point is not a compromise."

Another high profile fashion license is a newly penned deal with David's

Bridal. The company will maintain a clear line of demarcation between the David's Bridal line of moderately priced bridal and bridesmaid's gowns in the $600 to $1,400 range featured in its 300 stores, and the high-end luxe Vera Wang gowns that start at $2,000 and range to as much as $20,000.

So far, there is no evidence that her entrée into the discount and middle markets has in any way hurt her high-end business; rather it provides capital to keep the high end growing. She plans to open a third boutique in Los Angeles in 2011 to attract more celebrity clientele. This helps make up for the significant loss of bridal shops in Saks and Neiman Marcus closed because of the recession.

Her expansion into more moderate price ranges for fashion are pretty much by the book these days, following in the footsteps of Isaac Mizrahi, Michael Kors, and others. What's really noteworthy and inspirational is how she extended her bridal brand into the bride's lifestyle. Wang says "Our authoritative position in bridal and bridal registry has allowed us to leverage this [consumer] trust into a lifestyle brand. The next logical step is to capitalize on our relationship with the client over the course of her life. Our objective is to continue to grow our lifestyle-product offering and keep pace with the evolving needs of the consumer."

The lifestyle branding includes a honeymoon suite at Honolulu's Halekulani Hotel, decked out with other Vera Wang products developed under licensing partnerships including Waterford Wedgwood Royal Doulton tabletop and dinnerware, flatware, and gifts; William Arthur stationery, including wedding announcements, invitations, note cards, and stationery; a new high-end home fragrance and candle line with Next Fragrances; and Serta mattresses that can be paired with bedding produced under partnership with Revman International. As Vera explains, "Seventy percent of the mattress business is when [people] get married."

Of course there are a number of dangers for any luxury brand to expand widely through licensing partnerships. Shoddy products or inferior designs can wreak havoc on a brand's reputation. At least for now, Vera Wang has successfully avoided the pitfalls through careful selection of partner companies that have a dedication to quality. The licensees highly value their partnership with Wang and are willing to work hard to keep it. Testifying to Kohl's commitment to Vera Wang, the company announced in its third quarter 2010 results that sales of its exclusive licensed products, the most important license being Wang's, accounted for 48 percent of total corporate sales. Kohl's also expanded the license to include Vera Wang cosmetics in 2011.

Vera Wang is diligently hands-on with all her licensing partners. She says, "I think my licensees have grown to depend on my participation, which is a challenge because I am one person. But I do control those businesses carefully. Each one of the businesses is different and I've had to come up to speed on all. I've had to understand what the market will bear and yet I try not to let go of my own aesthetic." That aesthetic or design philosophy ultimately underlies the Vera Wang brand's success, which Vera describes as "casualized couture." It's Vera Wang's casual luxury that resonates with consumers at the high-end or low, from functional housewares to fashion.

●　●　●　●　●

chapter 8

Shifts in the Luxuries People Buy and Where They Buy Them

> *They want something more special and they want more value for their money. We are facing the intelligence of the consumer; they expect more and we have to give more.*
>
> —Robert Coin, jewelry designer

The most profound contribution that Unity Marketing's Luxury Tracking Study makes in tracking the purchase behavior of affluent consumers is the Luxury Consumption Index (LCI). Each quarter, the LCI is calculated from how luxury consumers answer five key questions about trends in their spending on luxury during the past 12 months and expectations of spending in the coming 12 months. We also assess their feelings of personal financial well-being and financial prospects over the next 12 months, and the financial health of the country overall.

The LCI is very similar to various consumer confidence indexes, the most noted being those compiled by The Conference Board and the University of Michigan. What is distinctive about Unity Marketing's LCI is its focus on only the affluent sector of the consumer economy. It gives marketers, investment advisers, strategic planners, and business developers a view from the upper echelons of the consumer marketplace.

Luxury Consumer Index goes retrograde in 2010

○ Figure 8.1 LCI through 4Q2010

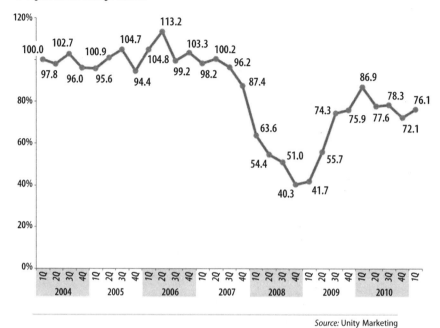

Source: Unity Marketing

This graph gives an historic view of the ups and downs of luxury consumer confidence and it tracks closely with the ups and downs in luxury consumer purchase behavior. Starting with a base of 100 in the first quarter of 2004, luxury consumer sentiment reached its highest point in the second quarter of 2006, corresponding to the boom in the luxury market. Sentiment remained high for about a year, but then started to go negative in the second and third quarters of 2007. Unity gave an early warning of this shift in luxury consumer sentiment a full two quarters before that decline in consumer sentiment began to play out in reduced spending at retail, which hit hard in the fourth quarter of 2007.

The LCI shows that luxury consumer sentiment reached its lowest point between fourth quarter 2008 and first quarter 2009; then it started to recover, along with the retail economy. By the first quarter of 2010 the LCI had recovered more than half of the points it lost during the downturn and recession. However, throughout 2010 the LCI has gone retrograde. Early in 2010 affluent consumers were optimistic about the year ahead, but reality came crashing down throughout the year and consumer confidence at the luxury level descended.

Let's look at some of the key ways changes in luxury consumer confidence have played out in consumption patterns.

All sectors of the luxury market lost volume

⊃ Figure 8.2 Luxury Purchases by Category: Home, Personal, Experiential

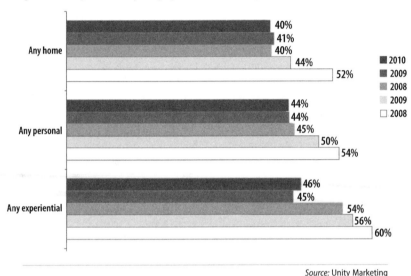

Source: Unity Marketing

In the last chapter we looked at total purchase incidence of any luxuries among all affluent households (see Figure 7.3). Here we delve deeper into the category of luxuries that affluents are buying to see how dramatically purchases are off in all sectors of the luxury market since 2006.

For example, among luxury consumers who bought any luxury goods or services in the study year, purchases of experiential luxuries, such as travel, dining, spa and beauty services, declined from 60 percent of all luxury purchasers in 2006 to 46 percent in 2010, a 14-point drop in consumer participation.

Purchases of home luxuries, the major category that includes art, furniture, linens, tabletop, and other luxuries for home, declined from 52 percent in 2006 to 40 percent in 2010, a 12-point drop.

Purchases of personal luxuries, which includes such traditional luxury goods as apparel, fashion accessories, jewelry, and watches dropped from 54 percent in 2006 to 44 percent in 2010, a 10-point decline.

These declines in purchases show that luxury goods and services are just not as relevant any more to a lot of people who bought luxury in the pre-recession period. So far there is little sign that the overall market for luxury goods and services is going to widen with an influx of new or returning affluent customers. Indeed, if purchases continue on their current trajectory into the future, luxury marketers are going to have to work harder to just keep their current customer bases, let alone attract new customers.

Shifts in the demographics of affluence examined in Part 1, specifically the rise in the number of less indulgent mature affluents and decline in the number of more luxury indulgent young affluents through 2020, present an unfavorable environment for natural growth in consumer demand for luxury goods and services. As a result, the luxury marketer's challenge for the future is to maintain relevance to those people who actually have the money to spend on their luxury goods and services. This is the new and painful reality for luxury marketers in the future.

However, all is not doom and gloom. There are some bright spots in consumer demand among the 22 different products and services that make up the three major categories of luxury mentioned above. Luxury goods and services categories that captured a greater share of affluent shoppers at the end of 2010 included luxury clothing and apparel, wine and spirits, fine dining, kitchen appliances, and travel. Prospects look particularly bright for the return of the luxury travelers in 2011, as more affluent consumers purchased luggage at the end of 2010 and attractive discounts still abound in this category.

Trends in purchasing luxuries for the home

Because a sharp drop in the housing market was one of the root causes of the recession, many luxury consumers turned to improving their "digs," when the market to sell their existing home was unfavorable. That led affluents to invest in home improvements that also boosted the value of their homes. Kitchen and bathroom upgrades including new luxury appliances were a priority.

Figure 8.3 Top Three Luxury Shopper Destinations for Home

Art

#1	Art galleries
#2	Internet/DTC
#3	Specialty home

Home electronics

#1	Electronics specialty
#2	Internet/DTC
#3	Discounter

Fabrics, wall & window coverings

#1	Specialty home
#2	Interior decorators
#3t	Internet/DTC	Department stores

Furniture, lamps, rugs & floor coverings

#1	Specialty home
#2	Home improvement
#3t	Department store

Garden/outdoor

#1	Home improvement
#2	Specialty home
#3	Internet/DTC

Kitchenware/Housewares

#1t	Specialty gourmet	Department stores
#2	Internet/DTC
#3t	Specialty home	Discount outlets

Kitchen appliances, bath, building products

#1	Home improvement
#2	Specialty appliance dealers
#3t	Department store	Internet/DTC

Linens & bedding

#1	Specialty home
#2	Internet/DTC
#3	Luxury branded shop

Tabletop

#1	Department store
#2	Specialty home
#3	Internet/DTC

Source: Unity Marketing Luxury Tracking Study 2010

With an eye toward upping the luxe experience of living in their homes, many higher-income affluents turned to home decorators or designers as a source for purchasing home decorating fabrics, and wall and window coverings. For the rest, the big-box home improvement stores, Lowe's and Home Depot, became a favorite destination for the new do-it-yourselfers and those interested in saving money. Home improvement stores were among the top destinations for affluents in the lamps and lighting, garden and outdoor, kitchen appliances, bath, and building products categories.

Luxury consumers also turned frequently to retailers that specialize in the product area they are interested in buying, making the assumption that specialty retailers offer better after-sale service and more highly trained sales personnel to guide in brand selection. Various specialty retailers lead in such categories as furniture, home electronics, kitchenware, specialty gourmet, and linens and bedding.

With affluent shoppers turning more often to specialty retailers, department stores declined in their share of affluent purchases, notably in linens and bedding and kitchen wares. Tabletop was the only home product category where department stores held onto first place as a shopping destination for affluents.

The internet and other direct-to-consumer channels are also notable in terms of affluent shopping destinations. While the internet and other direct-to-consumer channels account for roughly 10 percent of all retail, these channels rated among the top three destinations for affluent shoppers purchasing in all nine luxury home product categories, and as the second most popular destination in four home luxury products, specifically: art and antiques, home electronics, kitchenwares and housewares, and linens and bedding.

• • • • •

TAKE ACTION

Luxury Marketers Must Meet Affluent Customers Where They Gather, and They Like to Gather in Cyberspace

Why so many luxury brands have been so slow to adopt the internet as a marketing partner is totally inexplicable to me. Surely part of it is the illusion that maintaining exclusivity of the brand also requires inaccessibility. As a result, many luxury brands force affluents to be "window shoppers" online by not providing the means to make purchases through internet channels. Slowly luxury brands' internet anxiety is changing, but still such notable brands like Patek Philippe and Chanel, except for their beauty products, force website visitors to go to stores to make purchases.

An attitude that the customer experience delivered online is somehow inferior to that in the store is prevalent in luxury circles and it is just plain ridiculous. As we saw in our study of the demographics of affluent consumers, these are people with demanding jobs and very demanding personal lives who simply don't have a lot of extra time to shop. They want what they want when they want it, and online shopping certainly delivers on that. Internet shopping is most respectful of shoppers' time and that is an important area of customer service to this luxury shopper.

Let's look at the numbers on use of the internet and internet shopping from a study Unity Marketing conducted in early January 2010 for its luxury tracking clients (n=1,614 luxury consumers):

Everybody uses the internet

Virtually all affluent luxury consumers use the internet for personal, as opposed to professional, reasons, including shopping. Further, nearly 80 percent of affluents are social media users. Four out of five (78 percent) affluent consumers have profiles on one or more social networking sites. Facebook is the hands-down favorite among affluents.

Social networking isn't just for the young

Seventy percent of mature affluents (45 years or older) also have one or more social-media profiles.

Affluents use social media to look at brands, rather than commit to a relationship with them

About half of affluents have used social media to connect with a brand, by taking such actions as viewing news, products, or a video. But only one out of four affluents have "friended" a luxury brand. In other words, affluents are more likely to use social media to look at brands, rather than to commit to a relationship with them.

Affluents spend one-third of their time online shopping

The typical luxury consumer spends 13.5 hours weekly online, about 4.2 hours of it devoted to shopping. The most active internet shoppers spent 9.5 hours on shopping-related activities. These heavy users are more likely to be young and ultra-affluent ($250,000 and above). They spent three times more than the average on their online purchases. Heavy users make up about one-third of the affluent consumers.

Affluents that shop a lot online like it a lot more than shopping in stores

While the number of affluents who enjoy the shopping experience more online or in the store is evenly split, a majority (55 percent) of heavy users (i.e., those affluents who typically spend 4 or more hours shopping online each week) say they enjoy shopping online more than in the store. Affluent men, in particular, prefer the convenience and time-efficiency of internet shopping.

The research clearly shows that the internet attracts the kind of high-value luxury-indulgent customers that luxury brands need, especially affluent men who want to shop, but who don't want to go to the store. Internet shopping is just another way for luxury consumers to interact with their favorite brands and get the luxuries they desire. The simple fact is affluent customers want access to their favorite luxury brands in different ways at different times. For luxury brands there is nothing to fear from the internet. Rather, there is a whole lot to fear if luxury brands don't make themselves accessible online.

Today's luxury consumers are an internet shoppers who are drawn to the websites of stores where they have shopped before. Bricks-and-click retailers like Nordstrom.com, Neimanmarcus.com, and Saks.com have a distinct advantage in the online space, although the most used websites among affluents were exclusively internet retailers: Amazon, eBay, Overstock, Buy.com, and Zappos. Luxury shoppers value the time-saving convenience of internet shopping, along with its greater access to sales and discount offers and its ability to help them find the best deal.

· · · · ·

What's hot in home luxuries

At the home luxury product level, Unity Marketing's study has these found sectors of opportunity:

- In **art and antiques**, the big story is original art. Affluents want, and are willing to pay more for, that one-of-a-kind piece. It doesn't have to be an "old master." Affluents with a passion for art are buying up pieces they like from local art galleries, exhibitions, and shows.

- In **home electronics**, high-tech televisions are in great demand. Affluent shoppers are taking advantage of sales and discounts in this highly competitive category.

- Affluent home owners are investing in new **lamps and lighting accents**. They also are turning more to interior designers to help them decorate their spaces and give them access to higher-quality furniture, rugs and floor coverings, and lamps and lighting than are available in local furniture stores.

- In **outdoor living,** all things luxury are growing in popularity. From outdoor furniture, power equipment, lighting, and water features to barbecue grills, luxury consumers are investing more in their outdoor living spaces.

- Perhaps in response to less dining out, affluents are taking their home cooking up a notch. They are investing more in **gourmet cooks' tools** such as small kitchen appliances, cookware, cutlery, and bakeware.

- Affluents are sleeping better now, at least as measured by higher levels of purchase of luxe **mattresses and box springs** and bed linens.

Trends in purchasing personal luxuries

In shopping for personal luxuries, affluent shoppers continue to rely on department stores as their destination of choice, especially for clothing and apparel, fashion accessories, and cosmetics and beauty products. For affluents who want to make jewelry and watch purchases, specialty retailers, including luxury branded boutiques such as Louis Vuitton, Gucci, and Chanel are the destinations of choice.

⊃ **Figure 8.4 Top Three Luxury Shopper Destinations for Personal Luxuries**

Clothing & apparel	
#1	Department store
#2	Specialty fashion
#3t	Internet/DTC | Luxury branded shop

Fashion accessories	
#1	Department store
#2	Luxury branded shop
#3t	Discounter | Specialty fashion | Internet/DTC

Cosmetics/beauty products	
#1	Department store
#2	Personal care/beauty specialty
#3	Internet/DTC

Jewelry	
#1	Jewelry store
#2	Department store
#3t	Luxury branded shop | Internet/DTC | Specialty fashion

Watches	
#1	Jewelry store
#2	Internet/DTC
#3	Luxury branded shop

Personal electronics	
#1	Electronics specialty
#2	Internet/DTC
#3	Discounter

Source: Unity Marketing Luxury Tracking Study 2010

As in the home luxury space, affluent shoppers are also increasingly drawn to online and other direct-to-consumer channels. Internet ranks among the top three destinations in all six personal luxury product categories.

What's hot in personal luxury

At the product level in personal luxuries, these trends are worth noting:

- In the **luxury automobile sector**, more American affluents are turning to American-made luxe brands for their next car purchase. While European luxury car brands continue to take the lead in luxury car purchases, American brands increased their share of buyers to be a strong contender for second place ahead of Asian brands.

- In **luxury clothing and apparel,** men's clothing, including casual, business and outerwear, is shining bright, suggesting that men are returning to more business or professional attire. Ralph Lauren, Ann Taylor, and Calvin Klein ranked as affluents' favored apparel brands.

- In **fashion accessories,** budget-conscious affluents are more likely to trade down to mass brands in women's shoes than in handbags where luxe still rules, though they are finding more bargains in accessories purchases at discounters and outlet stores. As in clothing, men's accessories are also a bright spot. Coach, Gucci, and Ralph Lauren were their top brands in accessories.

- In **beauty** the fastest growing products in prestige are color cosmetics and makeup, displacing face care in the No. 1 slot it held in previous years. Perhaps the most important trend in prestige beauty is loss of share by department stores in favor of specialty personal care and cosmetics stores. While department stores are still the top destination for luxe beauty shoppers, specialty stores are rapidly closing the gap as measured by share of affluent shoppers' spending. In the latest surveys, Clinique, Lancôme, and Bare Escentuals were the leading prestige cosmetics brands, while Olay, Maybelline, and Cover Girl were the affluent shopper's favorite mass brands.

- In **luxury jewelry,** men's jewelry was a bright spot, again pointing to men picking up their professional appearance. Tiffany continues to hold the top spot in jewelry brands among affluent consumers.

- **Luxury watches** enjoyed increased spending by affluents in recent studies. Rolex, Movado, and TAG Heuer were the top brands overall in the latest surveys.

- In **personal electronics,** laptop computers, including iPads, were tops, followed by cellular and smart phones and MP3 players. Apple was the favored brand among the luxe shopper segment.

Luxury brands are increasingly dependent on the appetites of ultra-affluents

Of the recent shifts in consumer purchase behavior in the luxury space the most prominent and the one with the longest-term implications is the growing reliance of leading luxury name brands on the higher income ultra-affluent consumers. In key luxury goods categories, ultra-affluents are far more likely to make purchases of leading luxury brands than are the lower-income HENRY affluents.

☞ Figure 8.5 Luxury Brands Index by Income Segment

Product category	Overall purchase	Ultra-affluents	HENRYs
Sunglasses	100	257	67
Fashion accessories	100	196	77
Luxe department stores	100	174	81
Fashion boutiques	100	156	85
Clothing & apparel	100	147	86
Beauty products – prestige brands	100	142	88
Jewelry	100	140	83
Beauty products – mass brands	100	123	93
Internet websites	100	121	94
Watches	100	110	95

Source: Unity Marketing Luxury Tracking Study 2010

This table shows an index of the relative importance of ultra-affluents as compared with HENRYs for purchases of any luxe brand in these luxury goods categories. For example, in luxury sunglasses, which include such brands as Chanel, Oakley, and Gucci, ultra-affluents are 157 times more likely to purchase one or more of the brands as compared with the average customer. HENRYs by contrast have an index value of 67, meaning they are 33 percent less likely to purchase any of these brands.

Among the other categories that skew strongly toward the ultra-affluent sector are fashion accessories, where ultra-affluents are 96 percent more likely than average (index of 196) to buy one or more of the luxe brands, including such names as Coach, Gucci, Hermès; and luxury department stores where ultra-affluents are 74 percent more likely than average (index

174) to shop in Neiman Marcus, Saks Fifth Avenue, and Bloomingdale's, among others.

By contrast watches are a category where the difference between ultra-affluent and HENRY purchases of luxury brand names is smaller, though even here ultra-affluents are 10 percent more likely than average to buy a brand-name watch.

• • • • •

TAKE ACTION   Focus on Better Understanding All of Your Potential Customers, One-size-fits-all Marketing Doesn't Work

On the surface, the brand-purchase data above suggests luxury brands should focus more exclusively on the most affluent segment of consumers —the top 2 percent of the nation's households.

While brands certainly can't ignore their ultra-affluent customers, their challenge for the coming years is to entice the lower-income HENRYs back into the fold and encourage them to invest in their luxury brands again.

The key for luxury brands to generate growth in the present and coming economic climate is to learn about their customers: what they want, what they will pay for, and where and how they are buying. That means segmenting the target market by more than just demographics like income or gender, but by their psychological underpinnings as well.

With the luxury consumer market splintering into discreet segments, marketing at the luxury level demands different strategies for different types of customers. All ultra-affluents are not alike, nor are all HENRYs.

A recent study conducted by Boston Consulting Group gave a world-wide perspective to the growing diversity of interests and consumption among the world's highest income consumers. This report, "The New World of Luxury: Caught between Growing Momentum and Lasting Change," identified five different segments of affluent consumers residing in both developed (i.e., Europe, Japan, United States) and developing markets (i.e., Brazil, China, Russia). Their findings are not unexpected. Market segments that are the least "established" in their affluence make up the largest number of households worldwide, and account for the largest levels of spending in total. These include households with lower levels of income and wealth, and those "new moneyed" households who boot-strapped themselves from lower- or middle-class households to riches.

The BCG report's authors see increasing fragmentation of the luxury consumer market occurring between the developed and developing markets. Affluent consumers in developed markets, such as Europe and the U.S., are "less interested in acquiring status symbols and more interested in the actual worth of products," whereas those in emerging markets are eager for the status that luxury brands convey. That makes luxury marketing fundamentally easier in developing versus developed markets. Consumers in developing markets continue to respond to the image-based marketing that has dominated the industry for so long. Marketing luxury to affluent consumers in developed markets is harder because the old tricks don't work. They report, "In this new world of luxury, being iconic and exclusive is not enough to make a brand grow, and fewer consumers are willing to blithely accept high prices as the market of luxury. They need better reasons to buy."

But if it is easier for luxury brands to be marketed in developing countries, then there is a real danger that those brands will lose out or ignore opportunities in developed markets like the U.S., where they might have to work harder or more diligently. The BCG report warns, "Companies that devote too much time and effort penetrating emerging markets could end up de-emphasizing their presence in the traditional centers of demand, thus missing out on surprising opportunities for growth." Further they caution, "Companies that are enamored with emerging markets risk sacrificing some of the core traits of luxury—namely selectiveness, refinement, and service—in the rush to establish a foothold."

For marketing luxury brands, the report says, "There has been a shift from a push strategy, with companies and media outlets calling the tune, to a pull strategy with consumers more willing and able to decide what's desirable and what's not. In addition, it has become more critical for companies to differentiate their brands and retail offerings."

Push marketing strategies may still work in developing markets, but for brands to continue to gain traction in the new American luxury market, the key will be learning how to attract clients with compelling information about the brand, the product, its quality and value. They need to put the right bait out there to pull in their targets and that requires a deep understanding of the different consumer segments who are drawn to luxury offerings in their product space in general, and in their own brands in particular.

The BCG report concludes with important advice to luxury marketers: "Consumers remain hesitant to purchase goods on the basis of something as superficial as brand image or the urge to show off. Demand will need to be triggered by something more meaningful. Most luxury companies stand to benefit from a more rigorous approach to market research. BCG's studies have shown that consumer-facing companies, in general, are not doing enough to learn about their customers."

· · · · ·

Luxury branded companies are keenly interested in the shifts and changes in affluent consumer behavior. Moreover, investors watch what shifts and changes luxury branded companies make in response to shifts in the consumer market. That's why I spent time talking with Melanie Fouquet, managing director at J.P. Morgan with responsibility for advising investors in the luxury goods sector, specifically following companies such as LVMH, PPR, Richemont, Swatch, Bulgari, Burberry, and Hermès, to learn their perspective on luxury consumers that these companies serve.

· · · · ·

J.P. Morgan's Melanie Fouquet Views International Luxury Brands

Historically, it has taken two to three years for the luxury industry to recover from past dips. The fact that it's come back even half way from the bottom in some of the traditional markets is a good sign, but we could be facing another crisis right behind this one.

—Melanie Fouquet

After a full decade of following the luxury goods sector, including the last several years, Melanie remains bullish about luxury, "The luxury sector has been and continues to be a growth sector due to the strong appeal on the part of the consumer for branded goods that have a high level of craftsmanship. Much of the force of these luxury brands is the aura of quality they bring to the consumer."

That said, Melanie doesn't overlook the dramatic changes that have come to the luxury market recently. Indeed she says that luxury has traditionally been a cyclical business, though its cycles have historically not been as extreme as the recent past.

"A big element of the luxury industry is its cyclical nature. That has been most evident in profitability, especially considering that these are big businesses with very high costs—expensive stores, expensive advertising, and a highly skilled workforce. In the crisis of '08 and '09 we saw the biggest impact on sales, rather than profits, which historically we have not seen to such a degree. If you look back to '02–'03, the last previous crisis, it had more impact on operating profits rather than revenues. This time it was much more visible in sales, with declines around 8 to 12 percent. Several quarters of double digit declines in revenues are very unusual in this industry. At the same time we have been surprised by how quickly revenues have returned, most notably with growth coming from Asia and Japan."

Melanie puts the global luxury industry in perspective by explaining some major shifts she has observed in the operation of the companies she has followed over the last ten years. "The number one big shift has got to be geographic, first from old Europe to Japan, then toward the U.S. five years ago, and now more towards Asia. Second, we have seen a big shift in increased control of the companies' whole spectrum of operations, from owning the company's own design, its production, and its distribution. Ten years ago you had companies much more dependent upon licenses even in their core businesses. Because of this we see the third major shift in luxury goods companies and that is increased professionalization. The quality of management is much higher and we financial analysts see this very clearly with the focus on cash flow. This new professionalism is all part of the maturing of the industry and it is changing the landscape in which the companies operate, especially with more competitors coming into the space."

A critical part of Melanie's job is not just to analyze the past, but also to predict the future for her investment clients. While she has been surprised by the speed at which companies she follows recovered from the decline, a double-dip isn't out of the question. "Historically it has taken two to three years for the luxury industry to recover from past dips. The fact that it's come back even half way from the bottom in some of the traditional markets is a good sign, but we could be facing another crisis right behind this one. We could have a double-dip owing to the volatility of the stock market," she explained.

That led me to ask Melanie how the U.S. plays into her assessment of the luxury market in the future. Would the United States be as important a market for luxury brands going forward?

"It all depends," Melanie said. "Ten years ago the U.S. was not very important for luxury goods. It was a very small market up to six or seven years ago, then there was an undeniably big boom for European luxury brands in the U.S. market. You were talking about 25 to 30 percent growth per annum for the leading players. That growth completely stalled with the crisis of '08–'09. Not only did it stall, it completely collapsed, becoming a drag rather than a driver. Today the U.S. stands at roughly 18 to 20 percent of the sales for the industry. It could remain there in the future with recovery; there is a market for luxury goods in the U.S. When you look at the companies I cover, it's striking to see that even in the downturn some product categories, like leather goods and some very high-end brands, like Hermès, were still growing. But whether the U.S. can rise toward the 30 percent of global sales that Europe represents, is a big question mark. Luxury is more ingrained in Europe than it is in the U.S., which is why we have seen less of a downturn in Europe. Quite a lot of companies are no longer investing heavily in store expansion in the U.S., and real growth in this industry comes from adding stores. If you aren't opening new stores, you aren't going to deliver faster growth. But they are adding stores in Asia and Japan—your fastest growth is going to come from those markets."

As our discussion turned to companies opening their own captive retail outlets, we turned to the internet and its role in the future operations of these global luxury goods players. "The industry has been surprisingly slow in adapting to the internet. But times are changing. Richemont has just acquired Net-A-Porter (the U.K.–based internet-only luxury fashion retailer) which saw an opportunity for high-end, ready-to-wear with some sort of concierge advice on the back end. But we don't know yet whether that business can be scaled. We know there are places where it can do some business, but there isn't evidence yet that it's a big business in handbags or watches for example."

As we closed our discussion, I asked Melanie to weigh in on the changing perception of value and how it impacts sales of luxury goods. Her answer was simple: luxury goods are all about value. "The companies I cover are leading players in the industry and have very strong brands in their portfolios. You don't see trading down. Rather there is a chase for the best brands, ones with the highest perceived value, carrying very high price tags. For instance, Hermès bags retail on average at €3,000 (nearly $4,000) yet sales were up 16 percent in 2009, the year of the crisis. Obviously, the question is more about which brands are established and bring the truest and highest perceived brand value, like Hermès or Louis Vuitton, which even during the downturn did no promotional activity. This crisis brought out the value of leading brands and their enduring, lasting value. In the downturn we actually saw an upturn back to the world's iconic brands, the product and category leaders that offer enduring value."

But Melanie warns these companies can't rest on their laurels or become stale and old, they need to keep innovating. "As we think about the upturn, the big word is innovation. It's not good enough to just have an iconic product, you have to bring innovation with the product. For instance, if Burberry merely offered the old fashioned mac, I'm sure they would not be as successful as they are today. Burberry has had lots of new launches around the mac. Another good example would be Cartier watches or Chanel quilted bags. You have to rework your product culture, keeping the classic, but innovating with reference to the classics. You have to think of your customer. When things are buoyant, she might buy a few of your bags, but when things get tougher, she might only buy one or two. If you are the leader, you have to reference the classics but give her something new to buy, too."

Melanie's advice for other luxury companies that want to break through and achieve iconic status is pointed. "Customers are looking more for real craftsmanship. There has to be a greater focus on product quality, supported by a strong heritage and strong craftsmanship behind the product. An important part is educating the consumer and having a real message around your brand and your product. The customer is more sophisticated than ever before, and you need to plan for it. For example, lots of brands go in for super models and celebrities. But supermodels and celebrities didn't make the Louis Vuitton brand great or iconic. Louis Vuitton stands for travel and a brand has to stand for more than just the aspiration to look like a super model. Celebrities can give you all the publicity you could want, but it doesn't necessarily translate into people buying your brand."

• • • • •

Trends in purchasing experiential luxuries

Experiential luxuries are the class of luxury that includes services, such as travel, dining, spa, and beauty services spanning massage, manicures/pedicures, and physician services, home services, and entertainment. As a category of luxury, more affluents purchase experiential luxuries than either home or personal luxuries. This has remained consistent throughout the years I have studied luxury consumer purchase behavior (see Figure 8.2). But experiential luxuries lost the most since 2006, dropping from a participation rate of 60 percent in 2006 to 46 percent in 2010, a decline of 14 points in purchase incidence.

Luxury experiences has been one of the more popular areas where affluents made budgetary adjustments. These range from dining out less frequently to choosing less expensive restaurants and less expensive menu items, to postponing vacations, taking vacations of shorter duration, or making different destination choices. Yet experiences give the greatest return on investment in the lives of affluent consumers, a subject that we will explore more deeply in the next part. It may be that affluents cut back most on experiences during the worst of the recession because people really don't have to spend a lot of money to get the same happiness kick from experiences. How much does an afternoon walk in the park with your honey cost, compared to its return in happiness?

Using my family as an example, we have allocated spending on dining out and travel experiences differently, but with no noticeable effect on our overall enjoyment. We have become more creative in our choices, choosing boutique hotels over high-end chains, and becoming more adventurous in our destinations, touring within a 3 or 4 hour drive from home without the airport hassles. It seems there are a lot of people like us who really don't miss air travel, stays at the Ritz-Carlton or Four Seasons, and white tablecloth dining all that much.

If we look at the course of the recession, the experiential sector was the last to feel the effects of consumer cutbacks, and consequently, is the one most delayed in recovery. Further, we have consistently tracked a reverse correlation between spending on home luxuries and experiential. When spending on home luxuries goes up, spending on experiential goes down, and vice versa. This intuitively makes sense: when you in the midst of major home improvements, you are unlikely to go off on long and expensive vacations. Likewise when you take a two-week vacation to Hawaii in February, you are not likely to come back to renovate your kitchen in March.

Looking to the future, we continue to see experiences as a major focus of affluent consumers, but whether or not they trade back up to more luxe experiences or continue to find their pleasures in less costly options is a question. For marketers of luxury experiences, the same lessons apply: You have to offer the kind of value that affluents want most, at a price they are willing to pay. They are too smart to pay more for an experience when they can get the same or comparable experiences for less. Customers know how to find value, and service providers must continue to be creative in cutting costs while adding services that matter to the customer.

One good example we have seen throughout the recession is a big uptick in purchases of luxury cruises, originating in both foreign and domestic ports. In the luxe space, Royal Caribbean, Norwegian, Holland America, and Princess Cruise Lines have been the major beneficiaries of increased purchases, but smaller lines, notably Crystal, Regent Seven Seas, Silverseas, and Celebrity, have also benefited. The recession forced many cruise lines to sharply reduce fees and develop creative packages to appeal to affluents who wanted the cruise experience but were willing to sacrifice some of the extras. More of the same is the prescription for the future for experiential service providers looking to fill rooms and keep their tables occupied. They need to be vigilant in controlling costs, while also figuring out creative ways to generously deliver the experiences that their luxury customers value most. Not every dining couple wants a waiter hovering over their table to pour more wine. Affluents will pour it themselves, and favor establishments that offer a nice selection of under-$50 bottles or better yet, half-price wine specials on Tuesdays.

part 3

Psychographics Tell Us Why People Buy

Luxury Is Not Bought Out of Need, but from Desire

The single holistic principle that binds together the multiplicity of human motives is the tendency for a new and higher need to emerge as the lower need fulfills itself by being sufficiently gratified.

—Abraham Maslow, "hierarchy of needs" psychologist

Now that we have examined the demographics of the affluent market and their purchase behavior, the final piece of the puzzle needed to fully understand the luxury market is to study their psychographics. Wikipedia defines psychographics as "attributes relating to personality, values, attitudes, interests, or lifestyles." But I call it "why people buy."

Simply put, the more money a person has to spend in support of his or her lifestyle, the more important that person's underlying psychology is to the whole buying equation. Lower income consumers are much more tightly bound by their pocketbooks. They must allocate more to need-based purchases and less toward discretionary or desire-based purchases. Affluent consumers, on the other hand, with a surfeit of cash in hand can spend on luxury indulgences. When it comes to luxury goods and services, nobody needs any of it. All luxury is desire-based, making the psychological component that drives the consumer to buy so much more important to the marketer.

When I started to learn my trade of consumer research, the conventional wisdom was that studying why people buy was really not all that important.

I was taught that consumer research should focus on past buying behavior and demographics as the most reliable predictors of future behavior. Like the good student I am, I believed them and started my work at Unity Marketing with this quantitative perspective. However, it wasn't long before I discovered that past consumer behavior is no predictor of future behavior and that demographics, while valuable, don't explain why families that live next door to one another with similar incomes and nearly identical homes, choose different decorating styles, drive different brands of cars, shop in different stores, and belong to different political parties.

An understanding of psychographics or "why people buy" cuts to the chase and responds to these weaknesses in traditional market research. In terms of predicting future consumer behavior, past behavior is only suggestive, not predictive. While people do develop habits of consumer behavior, for example they regularly shop at Wegman's and always reach for the same brand of mayonnaise or ketchup, they can quickly change their behavior based on external factors, like loss of a job or other economic shift. They stop going to Wegman's and start shopping at Walmart, and instead of Heinz they choose the house brand of ketchup. While consumer behavior is fickle and can change quickly, the underlying psychology is far less changeable and much more stable over time. When consumer psychology changes, it is often due to more predictable factors like lifestage transitions from young single to young married, or the transition to empty nester associated with aging.

That is why I emphasize the psychology of the consumer as the single most important factor to direct and guide marketing and branding efforts. Understand why your customer buys and you will be able to use that insight to reach out to other consumers who have the same basic values and motivations and attract them to your store or your brand. Since one of the key challenges facing luxury marketers today is a values shift in the mindset of the consumers, Part 3 of this book explores consumer psychology, motivations, personalities, and values to offer luxury marketers the greatest insight into how to put the luxe back into their luxury brands.

chapter 10

When Good Enough Is Better than Best

The perfect is the enemy of the good. —Voltaire

All affluent consumers are not created equal! Some buy only the best of the best. Some choose to buy primarily the better option. Some buy good items, with an occasional foray into better or best. Some occasionally buy luxury but generally don't see luxury as part of their lives. All are affluent, but each consumer behaves in very different ways and should be targeted very differently.

⤳ **Figure 10.1 Lifestyle Approach to Luxury: The Good, the Better, the Best**

Which of the following statements best describes your lifestyle and approach to shopping?

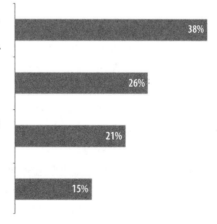

Better–The majority of the purchases I make, including travel and dining experiences, are better than average. I save "top of the line" for some things and/or experiences that really matter to me. — 38%

Good–In terms of good, better, and best, I mostly have good. I scale back a bit on some purchases in order that I can have the "good life" in areas that really matter to me. — 26%

Best of best–I tend to buy highest quality and aim for the best of the best. In terms of the good, better, and best . . . I always aim for the best. — 21%

I've been lucky to enjoy certain luxuries in my life, but luxury is not a part of my lifestyle. — 15%

Source: Unity Marketing

In the current market for luxury goods and services the largest percentage of customers are more likely to opt first for the better option when given a choice between the good, the better, and the best. The number that are predisposed to choose the good most often (26 percent) is nearly the same as the number that say they most often turn to the best of the best option (21 percent). And, in a worrisome trend, a fairly high number simply don't care that much about luxury at all.

This chart represents the tally of a survey of over 1,300 luxury consumers with an average income in excess of $300,000 (Note: 71 percent had incomes $100,000–$249,999 and 29 percent were ultra-affluents with incomes starting at $250,000 and above). Perspective on the "good-better-best," or "I just don't care," changes with rising income. Consumers at the ultra-affluent levels of income are able to afford the best of the best more often (49 percent) and far fewer of them choose the good option (12 percent). But interestingly the share of consumers that most often opt for the better with occasional best is nearly the same whether they have a HENRY level of income (40 percent) or are in the ultra-affluent segment (32 percent).

While the overall picture changes for marketers focused primarily on those at the top 2 percent of U.S. households, it is prudent for all luxury marketers to keep a level head and be realistic about the indulgence level of their consumer marketplace. It would be a big mistake to assume that all people who can afford their high-priced luxuries are actually willing to buy them.

Many people with high incomes, who value luxuries and are willing to spend on the best, view luxuries as an occasional indulgence, not an every-day occurrence. As marketers, it is easy to get caught up in the excitement of creating wonderful products and services and presenting superb, over-the-top brands to the marketplace. But the majority of affluent consumers simply don't share that level of excitement. Many of them can take it or leave it. They may appreciate superior quality, workmanship, and materials in luxury goods, or outstanding personalized service in the luxury services they participate in. They may *not* appreciate the added value enough to pay for the next level in the luxury hierarchy from good to better to best.

Where does luxury fit into a "new austerity" economy?

Time magazine dedicated its April 27, 2009 cover to the "new frugality," with a feature story chronicling how 17 people from vastly different walks of life and levels of income were adjusting their lifestyles in light of the new economy. By December 15 of that year, *Time*'s columnist Brad Tuttle was asking, "Is the New Frugality Here to Stay?"

I'll answer that in the affirmative. Unity Marketing has tracked affluent consumers releasing pent-up demand for luxury throughout 2010. But this hardly translates into a wholesale return to conspicuous consumption, or indicate "frugal fatigue" has taken hold and people are returning to their old ways. Luxury marketers need to err on the side of prudence and take seriously the shift in values marking a new post-materialism approach to spending. Pay heed to the fact that Merriam-Webster's editors named "austerity" the word of the year for 2010, based on the dramatic increase in the number of searches logged in the dictionary's free online website.

When marketers look at their luxury consumers, it is a big mistake to underestimate them. They are very smart about their money; they are experts at investing their money in value. They have learned that saving, rather than spending, is smart and prudent. Nobody gets rich by spending all they've got. They get rich by carefully evaluating their options and choosing to make smart purchases for the long term. That smart investment may well be to spend more on the highest quality product (best-of-the-best) that will deliver a lifetime's use. But they will be increasingly hesitant to splurge on something like fashion, a shirt just for this season, or an item that costs a lot but delivers mostly bragging rights.

As we look to the future, more marketers need to find inspiration beyond the simple product qualities and attributes which have traditionally defined high quality. They need to make a connection with the customer on a deeper, more meaningful level. That calls for luxury marketers to be vigilant in aligning the attributes, values, and qualities of their goods and services with what their target consumers truly value. They must continue to work harder and harder at elevating the luxury values of their products over and above the *good* and *better*, to help affluent consumers readily distinguish the added value of the *best*.

Only a handful of luxury consumers are truly invested in their luxury lifestyles and hanker after the best-of-the-best in the products they buy and the services they patronize. The rest are truly skeptical that the higher-priced offering is really worth it to them. They will often trade down to the better, premium offering, or to the brand that is simply as good as all the rest, rather than spend their hard-earned money on a luxury that just doesn't mean all that much to them or doesn't make a compelling argument why they should buy. In the new luxury market, the indulgent luxury consumer who aims for the best-of-the-best is a rare exception, rather than the rule.

• • • • •

The More Luxurious Your Product, the Harder You Must Work to Find the Right Customer

Very few people *can* afford to pay over $10,000 for a Patek Philippe wristwatch; even fewer *will* pay so much. The more luxurious the product, the harder a marketer must work to reach out and interest the right target customers in a dialogue they find compelling and engaging. That dialogue must begin by understanding the messages that the customer is receptive to and delivering those messages in a way that the customer will hear. There is so much marketing noise today. An oft-quoted statistic puts the average number of commercial messages an American receives at 3,000 per day. With the overnight explosion of mobile media, I suspect the number is even higher today. Marketers who want to be heard need to be sure that they are communicating in words, phrases, pictures, and impressions that mean something to the target consumer. Rather than using sheer volume to rise above the noise, they need to find the right frequency that resonates with their target. They need to talk a language of value to their customers.

Marketing isn't sitting back and waiting for the customer to come to you. Luxury marketers must take the right message to the right customer in the right media to make a connection. For example, Swans Island knows that $500 is a lot to pay for a woolen blanket. There are perfectly good blankets to keep you warm and look nice on your bed that cost one-fifth as much. Swan Island, founded in the early 1990s, hits all the right notes for a particular type of customer who is drawn to its artisanal, hand-loomed blankets crafted of the wool of rare black and brown sheep, dyed by hand using natural materials. Everything about Swans Island is special in a down-home, sustainable, back-to-basics, back-to-the-land sort of way. The company's products aren't for everyone, but they appeal—and appeal strongly—to a limited few.

While located out-of the-way in its Northport, Maine headquarters, the company maintains an extremely active public relations program targeting "influentials" who reach an affluent audience. Martha Stewart has written about their blankets on her blog and the *New York Times* has featured the company in its Home and Garden section. The company gained stature on the national scene by winning the prestigious Smithsonian Blue Ribbon for Craft. It is the brand of blankets the cognoscenti know about and covet. The company smartly sells its wares through carefully vetted retailers who can effectively communicate the values inherent in a $500 blanket, and through the company website, which tells the full back story of where the brand comes from and how each of its products is made.

● ● ● ● ●

Constellation Brands Uses Psychographics to Focus in on Customers for Premium Wines

Social media becomes important because taste is highly personal, you need to find somebody else with a similar taste profile to connect with.

—Leslie Joseph

Just back from a presentation to the Direct-to-Consumer Wine Symposium in Sonoma County, California, I discovered how sobering the luxury wine business is for scores of wineries that share the same artisanal values as Swans Island. U.S. consumers purchased $25.4 billion in wine off-premise (for consumption at home) in 2009, according to the Bureau of Economic Analysis, up a miniscule 1.2 percent from the $25.1 billion spent in 2008.

Out of the nation's roughly 225 million adults, fewer than half drink any wine at all and most of that is sold at price points far below $25 per bottle. The premium wine industry has been hammered by the same economic forces that have hit many luxury market segments, and with many wineries being vertically integrated businesses, they have had few resources to fall back on when confronted with falling sales and scarce customers. The result is that many high-quality, artisanally produced premium wines that in the boom time commanded a significant premium, have had to respond to the old laws of supply and demand.

Rob McMillian an industry analyst for Silicon Valley Bank who authors its annual State of the Wine Industry report, said, "We expect continued downward price pressure in all but those wineries selling on allocation [i.e., presold shipments to members of a winery's vintage club], large scale producers, or established brands in wide distribution."

Leslie Joseph, vice president of Consumer Research & Consumer Affairs at Constellation Wines, explains, "Only 30 percent of U.S. adults drink wine at least once a week or more often. Of that group, only 16 percent of wine consumers drink 91 percent of all wine."

When it comes to the premium wine sector, the price point that defines premium from mass market wine is surprisingly low, only $5 and above. The wine consumer market is razor thin and those who are willing to pay $25 or more per bottle even thinner. For Constellation Wines, a marketer heavily invested in the premium space with brands like Kim Crawford, Robert Mondavi, Clois du Bois, and Ravenswood, understanding the motivations and attitudes of their customers is critically important.

Leslie explains that this is the reason behind Constellation's Project Genome, a psychographic segmentation study of the different personalities of regular wine drinkers. "Through Project Genome we identified six different segments or personalities of wine drinkers. As a large company with many wine brands, we target all six of the segments, but in the premium space we are more focused on just a few. For example, there is the group we call **Image Seekers**. These are status-conscious people who like to flaunt wine brands and their knowledge. They are early adopters, people who are interested in what's new and leading edge, so they respond to stickers on the grocery shelves that say 'new.'"

The Image Seeker values newness above all, highlighting one of the special marketing challenges that makes the luxury wine market different than many others—much of the enjoyment of wine is exploration and discovery. It is hard to build brand loyalty and repeat purchase when much of the fun is trying out new brands, new vintages, new varietals, and new places of origin. But Image Seekers, at least when confronted with a challenge of which new wine to buy, are more likely to turn to price as a guide to the good, better, best. "Image Seekers go for the trendy and being on the cutting edge. They also think that if you pay more, you can be more confident in your wine choice. They believe that spending more money will get them a better bottle of wine," Leslie says.

Another important personality that purchases premium wines is the **Enthusiast.** Leslie explains, "There are people who buy wine priced over $15. They are more likely to go for small vineyard wines released in quantities of 500 cases or so. They are the people on vineyards' lists to be called about new releases and who say, 'Ship it and charge it to my American Express.'" Marketing to this Enthusiast customer who values single-vineyard wines is a special challenge in today's patchwork of state liquor laws, Leslie says. "We can legally ship to only about half of the U.S. states. In some states, I can't even post an online application to tell you where to buy a brand."

With laws and regulations like these, the online wine experience in many states focuses exclusively on education and branding rather than sales or distribution. Social media then becomes a key component for marketing and branding in the premium wine sector. "We are starting to do a lot of work in social media with the Wine Market Council, our industry trade group, where I am on their research committee. Social media becomes important because taste is highly personal, you need to find somebody else with a similar taste profile to connect with. That's the challenge of the *Wine Spectator* and *Wine Enthusiast* ratings. If your profile doesn't match the profile of people doing the ratings, then you are not going to like the wine you buy. It is interesting that one of our most active social media sites around one of our wine brands is Arbor Mist, which is not in our premium group, but it has a huge Facebook following."

"Lots of different people talk about things other than wine on the Arbor Mist Facebook site. It's all about life," Leslie says. She also notes that some of the company's higher-end wine brands are starting to venture into social media, including Ravenswood which now has 13,000 fans on Facebook. Kim Crawford, a brand out of New Zealand, is testing the waters of Facebook on a global scale.

Leslie reminds us that the business of luxury wines ultimately is very different from so many other categories in the luxury market. "Exclusivity and rarity are real when you talk about single-vineyard wines that produce only 250 or 350 cases. You can't get more. It's not like purses or dinner plates where you can just make more in the factory.

As a leading producer of premium wines all over the world, Leslie explains the critical importance of getting up close and personal with the inner psychology, drives, and motivations of all their different target customers. "Even though the total number of wine consumers in the U.S. is small, there is no one kind of wine consumer, and in the luxury end there are different people looking for different things. The **Enthusiast** is looking for more wine knowledge; the Image Seeker is looking for newness or the latest trend. Then there is the **Traditionalist,** another personality we found, who wants a wine from a well-known and respected brand. It is not one-size-fits-all. We need to target all of the different segments of consumers who drink our wines. Kim Crawford appeals to one type of customer and Robert Mondavi to another, or to the same customer who wants a really good wine to drink during the week and picks up a magnum of Woodbridge, but on the weekend trades up to a Robert Mondavi Private Selection."

· · · · ·

As Leslie Joseph explains, one-size-fits-all marketing strategies don't work, nor does one-size-fits-all all-the-time, as in her later example where someone chooses the better option on a day-to-day basis but a best-of-the-best option on weekends. The learning for all those in the luxury space is to view their lines more fluidly with recognition that there is room for luxe at each step in the good-better-best pricing and product levels.

· · · · ·

Work Good-Better-Best Pricing for You and Your Customers

With the largest percentage of affluents most often gravitating to the better option (38 percent) with the occasional best, and about an equal but lower percentage choosing the good (26 percent) or the best-of-the-best (21 percent) most often, luxury marketers need to design their product lines to give their customers a choice from good, to better, to best. For now and in the future luxury sector, a high-quality better product or service offered at a fair price is a real winner.

Because luxury consumers are more likely to go for the better with the occasional best, you need to make sure that you have offerings that cover all the bases, like designer Ralph Lauren. Polo Ralph Lauren provides the best case study of a luxury brand that gets it right. At the high end, appealing to that segment who regularly shops for the best-of-the-best, or for better customers who trade up for that occasional indulgence, the company offers women Ralph Lauren Black Label, and offers men Purple Collection. Their better offerings include Polo by Ralph Lauren for men, Blue Label for women, and some of the various sportswear (RLX Polo). Licensed brands, such as Chaps, Polo Jeans, and women's Ralph by Ralph Lauren, round out the good selections. This gives opportunities for customers to build a relationship with the Ralph Lauren brand at many different levels in the pricing continuum that can mirror the customer's rise up the income ladder. As Ashley writes on her Eurbanista blog, "PRL is creating something for everyone in most price ranges to ensure that anyone who WANTS to own a piece of this imagined American lifestyle can."

But while you are looking at your product lines to be sure your bases are covered, it may well be a time to take your best-of-the-best and move it up a notch, going up in price at the very high end, as opposed to down. Adding a more expensive product at the top of a brand's price range can help to reposition the brand's better offerings, helping to bolster the better's price and giving people justification to spend more for better, even if they aren't going to venture all the way up to the best. Fashion designers have used this strategy for years. They make very little money, and probably even less profit, on their extremely high-end couture lines. But the buzz and excitement built around their couture offerings supports their brand where the real money is, in their better ready-to-wear or good bridge lines.

Take, for example, Burberry. As the Burberry brand exploded into mass market popularity and its signature Burberry check got over-exposed, the company decided that the best way to put the luxe back in the Burberry brand was to offer a new, more exclusive, high-end line called Burberry Prorsum. This line gives the company a new platform to attract a fashion-forward customer desiring a luxury look that isn't so common or ubiquitous as the now better Burberry offering. Coach, too, is following a similar repositioning strategy, shifting its higher end and extending its brand further across the good-better-best range. While it launched the new lower-priced Poppy line to open up a lower-priced good spot in its range, the company also moved up the price spectrum with a new Reed Krakoff line named for the company's president and executive creative director.

• • • • •

Personalities Who Make Up
the Luxury Market

Brands, like people, have personalities.

> —Dr. Michael R. Solomon, professor, St. Joseph's University

There are several commercially available syndicated studies that look at the psychographic dimension of the broad consumer marketplace. Perhaps the most well known is the VALS study developed by Strategic Business Insights (formerly SRI). The VALS segmentation strategy is based on three basic consumer motivations that are active in all people to a greater or lesser extent:

- Ideals where consumers are motivated by knowledge and principles;
- Achievement where consumers are primarily focused on purchases that demonstrate success to their peers; and
- Self-expression, where consumers who purchase as a means to connect socially or express themselves physically.

Based on how high or low one rates on these three motivations, the VALS study segments consumers into eight different personality types, such as **Innovators**, described as "successful, sophisticated, take-charge people with high self-esteem. They are change leaders and are the most receptive to new ideas and technologies. Innovators are very active consumers, and their purchases reflect cultivated tastes for upscale, niche products and services. Image is important to Innovators, not as evidence of status or power but as an expression of their taste, independence, and personality," or

Experiencers, which VALS defines as consumers "motivated by self-expression. Young, enthusiastic, and impulsive consumers, Experiencers quickly become enthusiastic about new possibilities but are equally quick to cool. They seek variety and excitement, savoring the new, the offbeat, and the risky. Their energy finds an outlet in exercise, sports, outdoor recreation, and social activities."

• • • • •

Why People Buy Luxury: A View from SRI

In an article published in the November 2002 issue of *American Demographics* magazine, researcher Kristen Thomas, with Menlo Park, California–based SRI Consulting Business Intelligence (now known as Strategic Business Insights), shared three key motivations behind consumers' purchase of luxury goods and services. These reasons why people buy luxury have not changed noticeably since then, so it is useful to return to understanding the key underlying motivations for luxury, besides the simple fact that luxury feels good.

Luxury as Function

Kristen explains that consumers primarily motivated by function buy luxury products because they perform better and because of their overall higher quality. Consumers with function as their primary motivation tend to be older and wealthier, and are willing to spend more money to buy things that will last and have enduring value. She says, "These consumers buy a wide array of luxury goods, from luxury automobiles to artwork to vacations. They conduct extensive pre-purchase research and make logical decisions rather than emotional or impulsive decisions. Messages that highlight product quality and are information-intensive are powerful with this group."

Luxury as Reward

Reward-oriented consumers, who SRI research indicates are younger than the functional group but older than the indulgence group, often use luxury goods as status symbols or to say, "I've made it." Kristen explains,

"The desire to be successful and to demonstrate their success to others motivates these consumers to purchase conspicuous luxury items, such as luxury automobiles and homes in exclusive communities. Luxury brands that have widespread recognition are popular with this segment. And yet, this segment is also concerned that owning luxury goods might make them appear lavish or hedonistic, especially in these economic times. They want to purchase 'smart' luxury that demonstrates their importance, while not leaving them open to criticism. Marketing messages that communicate acceptable exclusivity resonate with this group."

Luxury as Indulgence

The indulgence-focused group is the smallest of the three, Kristin says, and tends to include younger consumers and slightly more males than the other two groups. She says, "To these consumers, the purpose of owning luxury is to be extremely lavish and self-indulgent. This group is willing to pay a premium for goods that express their individuality and make others take notice. These consumers are not overly concerned with product quality or longevity, or with the possibility that others might criticize their purchases. Rather, they enjoy luxury for the way it makes them feel. If a product makes them feel good, they will likely make the purchase. These consumers have a more emotional approach to luxury spending, and are more likely than the other two groups to make impulse purchases. They respond well to messages that highlight the unique and emotional qualities of a product."

* * * * *

Unity Marketing presents an exclusive psychographic segmentation of the luxury consumer market

For years, Unity Marketing has maintained a close look at the psychology that guides and directs affluent consumers in the pursuit of a luxury lifestyle. In 2005 when my book, *Let Them Eat Cake: Marketing Luxury to the Masses—as well as the Classes,* was published I profiled four distinct personalities in the luxury market. At that time they were:

Butterflies (30 percent): highly evolved, experiential luxury consumers;

Aspirers (26 percent): those who have not yet reached the level of luxury to which they aspire;

Cocooners (24 percent): luxury consumers who express luxury through their homes, what they have, and what they own;

X-Fluents (20 percent): eXtreme Affluents who live luxury large.

Since the publication of *Cake* and coincident with, though not a result of, the global recession, a new personality emerged in the luxury market—the **Temperate Pragmatist**. The distinguishing characteristic of this personality type is a lack of desire for the trappings of a luxury lifestyle. They can take or leave luxury; it just doesn't matter all that much to them.

These three simultaneous events—the worldwide recession, the generational shift of the affluent market toward an older, less indulgent consumer, and the emergence of the Temperate Pragmatist personality—set up a perfect storm that will challenge luxury marketers for many years to come. But before we examine the five personalities that make up the luxury market today, let's briefly review how the makeup of the luxury market has shifted in the last decade.

From 2002, when Unity Marketing did its first major study of the luxury consumer marketer, until 2007, four personalities—Butterflies, Cocooners, Aspirers, and X-Fluents—dominated the luxury market. Then in the 2007 study, the new Temperate Pragmatist personality reached critical mass and emerged as a separate segment. By 2009 this new personality—which evolved mainly from Butterflies and Aspirers personalities—accounted for 20 percent of the total luxury market.

⊃ Figure 11.1 Luxury Personalities, 2003 and 2009

Personality type	2003	2009	Direction of change
Butterflies	30%	20%	-10
Aspirers	26%	18%	-8
Cocooners	24%	19%	-5
X-Fluents	20%	23%	+3
Temperate Pragmatists		20%	

Source: Unity Marketing

When a new consumer personality emerges, it is big news in a market researcher's world. People's underlying motivations and consumer psychology on which psychographic segmentation is based remains fairly stable over time. For researchers, the emergence of a personality, like the Temperate Pragmatist, represents a significant shift in the luxury market.

In laymen's terms, one out of every five affluent consumers is a Temperate Pragmatist. This customer is every luxury marketer's worst nightmare—a person with means who doesn't respond to the traditional marketing cues and clues of luxury that attract people to indulge in their brands. Temperate Pragmatists are affluent consumers who marches to their own drummers, who need no status symbols or brand badges to bestow stature, who disdain conspicuous consumption, ostentation, or pretense, yet who have a significant level of wealth and income. Temperate Pragmatists are the prototypical "millionaires next door," borrowing a term coined by author Thomas Stanley to describe people who live in modest middle-class houses, drive modest middle-class cars, wear modest middle-class clothes, yet have millions in the bank.

Luxury marketers: meet your customers

Let's take a closer look at the five distinctive personalities that make up the luxury consumer market in order of their luxury spending, starting with the least indulgent to the highest spender:

⮑ Figure 11.2 Personalities of Luxury Consumers

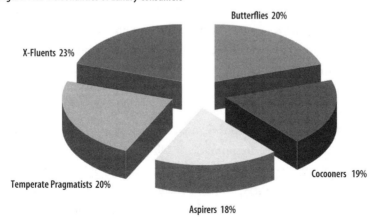

Source: Unity Marketing

Temperate Pragmatists

Temperate Pragmatists have a take-it-or-leave-it attitude about luxury. For consumers with this personality, luxury and the pursuit of a luxurious lifestyle is simply not that important to them. They mostly agree with this lifestyle statement: "I've been lucky to enjoy certain luxuries in my life, but luxury is not a part of my lifestyle." When it comes to luxury, they represent the personality the least likely to indulge and the personality that spends the least amount of money buying luxuries as well. The hugely rich, but modest-living Warren Buffett, the oracle of Omaha and reputed to be the second wealthiest American after Bill Gates, is the prototype of the Temperate Pragmatist, as is the quirky Ed Begley Jr., who expresses his environmental consciousness through recycling and thoughtful consumption.

Butterflies

Representing 20 percent of the luxury consumers surveyed in 2009, Butterflies are luxury consumers who have emerged from their "cocoon" of materialistic luxury comfort in which they previously enveloped themselves. They have turned away from their self-indulgent ways to become more connected and concerned with their spending and its impact on the world. Their luxury spending reflects egalitarian attitudes toward luxury; they take a strong anti-status point of view when it comes to luxury. Nearly 85 percent of Butterflies, the highest percentage overall, agreed with the statement, "At my stage in life, I am less interested in buying more luxury 'things,' and more interested in spending my money on special experiences." Butterflies are highly experiential and view their luxury lifestyles as a form of self-expression. At the same time they enjoy the pleasures they experience through their possessions. Butterflies are looking for new meaning in their lives and recognize that conspicuous consumption will not help them achieve a more meaningful lifestyle. Butterflies are primarily made up of Baby Boomer–generation consumers. Along with Cocooners, they are the oldest personality segment. Oprah Winfrey, Bill and Melinda Gates, and Michelle Obama are prototypical Butterflies who, while enjoying a luxurious lifestyle, believe in giving back.

Luxury Aspirers

The smallest of the personality segments, Aspiring Luxury consumers are best defined as those who have not yet achieved the level of luxury to which they aspire. They view luxury as an expression of what they have and what they own. Highly materialistic, they are more likely to link luxury with specific brands and to shop for brands with luxury "badge" value. These consumers do not embrace luxury so much as a feeling or an experience. Rather, for them luxury is expressed through their consumption, what they buy and what they own. This segment tends to be younger than Butterflies or Cocooners. Prototypical Aspirers are young celebrities like Jennifer Lopez, Sean P. Diddy Combs, and Britney Spears—all of whom came from less than upper-class backgrounds.

Luxury Cocooners

Luxury Cocooners wrap themselves up in a luxurious home "cocoon" for safety and shelter. When it comes to buying luxuries like fashion or jewelry for themselves, they are cautious and careful in their spending. On the other hand, they are indulgent regarding purchases for their homes. Their priority in luxury spending is home. They tend to view luxury materialistically, as objects one has or owns, rather than luxury as an experience. Characteristic of the Luxury Cocooners' personality is agreement with this statement: "While luxury experiences like travel are nice, they are fleeting, so I prefer to buy luxury items that I can keep." The prototypical Cocooner is Martha Stewart, or at least the carefully crafted public image she projects through her television show and magazine.

X-Fluents (eXtreme Affluents)

This segment lives luxury large. They are the über-spenders in the luxury market and they can afford it. They deny themselves nothing and freely indulge in all kinds of luxuries, including experiences as well as luxury goods for their homes and themselves. While they share many of the experiential values of Butterflies, they are different in that they are significantly more materialistic and brand-oriented than Butterflies. They are highly invested in maintaining their luxury lifestyles, and they are the personality segment with the highest percentage of people who describe their lifestyle as a persistent search for the "best-of-the-best." X-Fluents have the highest average income; after all, they need high incomes to achieve their desired lifestyle, and are more likely than any of the other personalities to live in the downtown area of a major city. Paris Hilton, Ivana, and daughter Ivanka, Trump are prototypical X-Fluents.

• • • • •

John Gerzema Shares How Consumers' Values Are in Motion

John Gerzema, chief insights officer for Young & Rubicam, and co-author Michael D'Antonio, examine how a shift in values is taking root in the American consumer psyche in their new book, *Spend Shift: How the Post-Crisis Values Revolution is Changing the Way We Buy, Sell, and Live.* Focusing on the dramatic loss of consumer confidence resulting from the recession, the authors document changes in purchasing behavior caused by the overall loss of $13 trillion of consumer wealth and nearly 45 percent in American equities and housing values.

In his book, Gerzema says people are "disentangling themselves from the risk, tension, and liability created by excess in everyday life." Consumers are deleveraging debt and refusing to continue on with their spendthrift ways. "After decades of unfettered indulgence, Americans are spent," and making profound changes in their consumption habits by redefining wants and needs.

In a recent interview with *Inc.* magazine, Gerzema speaks to how Americans are finally getting back to basics after going on an extended spending spree. They are returning to values like self-reliance and self-sufficiency that have been a part of the culture's character since its founding, "People are finding happiness in old-fashioned virtues—thrift, do-it-yourself projects, self-improvement, faith, and community—and in activities and relationships outside the consumer realm. Our data show large numbers saying money is no longer as important to them. Seventy-six percent say the number of possessions they own doesn't affect how happy they are."

In answer to the question, does this mean consumerism is dead? He says, "No. But we are moving from mindless to mindful consumption." This trend toward living within one's means shifts the focus in consuming from materialism, based on old status symbols, toward a new values-based purchase decision. In the new paradigm, consumers are more adaptable as they weigh the long-term implications of a purchase against short-term gains.

For example, he points to Blu Homes, a maker of pre-fabricated, modular homes. Blu Home customers can grow their home by adding rooms as their needs and income increase, rather than buying more house than they can afford. This is the ultimate anti-McMansion concept, and one perfectly attuned to the new value of living within one's means.

Part of the new consideration set that will inform people's consuming behavior, Gerzema argues, will be the values reflected by companies and brands with which people choose to do business. He explains the results of attitude research, "Seventy-one percent of people said, 'I make it a point to buy brands from companies whose values are similar to my own.' Nearly the same number rejected companies whose values don't match." He identifies the corporate values resonant today with American consumers as transparency, honesty, kindness, good stewardship, ethics, and humor. For example Whole Foods, a brand recognized as very expensive, presents values that its target customers value highly. Whole Foods remains a company people want to do business with because they believe in what the company stands for.

To luxury marketers, Gerzema warns, "It is a challenging world for anyone selling a $1,000 item that is the latest version of something already in the American home. You have to convince people that your product gives a better experience and that advances in energy efficiency and quality will yield some kind of savings."

Luxury market consumers, who are endowed with the highest levels of education and informational resources and who hold high-paying jobs in business and government, tend to be the consumers most likely to pay the most attention to what a company, its leaders, and its brands really stand for. Commenting on the importance of a company's core values, Gerzema says that in his research Microsoft outranks Apple in values including reputation, leadership, and being the "best brand." He explains, "Much of that has to do with the philanthropy of Bill Gates, who represents a wise and generous kind of capitalism. If you allow your founder, your executives, and your workers to be personally identified with making the world a better place, they will burnish the image of the company."

Burnishing the tarnished image of self-centered, self-congratulatory, self-consumed luxury brands is called for in the new economy. That will go a long way toward putting the luxe back in the luxury purchase equation. People with means will pay more for high quality brands that deliver values in line with their personal value system and beliefs.

• • • • •

Different strokes for different folks: positioning and selling luxury to the five different luxury personalities

Given their different attitudes and motivations in pursuit of a luxury lifestyle, here are some key ideas for marketers and retailers can put to work to maximize their connection with each unique personality.

Butterflies go for the experience

Butterflies are highly experiential luxury consumers. They are far more likely to be motivated by purchases of luxury services, such as a luxury cruise or resort, a celebrity chef restaurant, and the most upscale spa, rather than buying more "stuff." When they are inclined to purchase material goods, their primary motivation is the feelings or experiences that come from having, owning, wearing, or using the item. For this luxury consumer, experiences, rather than things, are key.

How to identify a Butterfly

Unlike X-Fluents or Aspirers who can be identified by the clothes they wear and the cars they drive, Butterflies are not prone to luxury-branded status displays. They are likely to dress in a more subdued manner without showy logos, but in classic styles, think Talbots not Burberry; Brooks Brothers not Dolce & Gabbana; Levi's not Diesel; Coach not Louis Vuitton; Estée Lauder not MAC; Cole Hahn not Louboutin. As a rule, Butterflies are older than X-Fluents or Aspirers, so if you see someone with a little gray in her hair, noticeable lines around her eyes, and dressed in more mature-skewing premium brands as above, then you are likely dealing with a Butterfly.

Where Butterflies are likely to be found

Butterflies might occasionally be found in luxury department stores, but most likely only when those stores offer a sale or a special promotion. On the other hand, they are very unlikely to ever open the door to a luxury branded boutique, since they are not given to conspicuous consumption. They are more likely to shop at the local mall, which offers access to premium, as opposed to luxury brands. Their premium mall destinations are likely to be Ann Taylor and Ann Taylor LOFT, Chico's, Jos. A. Banks, Men's Wearhouse, White House|Black Market, Talbots, Eileen Fisher, and Brooks Brothers. When it comes to luxury, they are more likely to frequent Nordstrom rather than Neiman Marcus or Saks. For this shopper value and quality are important, but so is a fair and reasonable price. Butterflies feel they get good value from premium brands without having to venture into the high-end luxury branded world.

How to sell to Butterflies

Unlike X-Fluents and Aspirers who shop for fun, Butterflies tend to shop mostly when they need something. That makes selling them fairly easy: Find out why they are in your store, probe into the values that are most important to them in their purchase, then give them one or two options to chose from. Butterflies tend to put high priority on getting in and out of the store fast and efficiently, so they will reward establishments that make shopping as quick, easy, and painless as possible. They like a bargain as much as the next person, but Butterflies are willing to trade off price for convenience and service. So the key word when selling to a Butterfly is service.

Aspirers go for flash and bling and want luxury brands that convey status

Aspirers yearn for the good life and are eager to get more of it. Unlike X-Fluents, Aspirers feel uncertain about their status and achievement, so they seek confidence by wearing and displaying the most prominent and well-known luxury brand name logos. They are highly materialistic and eager to follow the next hot fashion trend or celebrity fashion icon.

How to identify an Aspirer

On the surface Aspirers may look very much like X-Fluents, but they are more likely to be found carrying an even trendier handbag with an even bigger brand-name logo. These shoppers, in particular, want the flash and status that luxury brands give them, so they are more likely to sport the latest hot brands and logos that people will know immediately. When X-Fluents wear similar high-end luxury brands, the labels and logos will be more subtle, worn on the "inside" rather than on the outside for everyone to see. An Aspirer will be sure her Burberry raincoat is worn with the brand's logo check accenting the collar and with a matching, highly visible and immediately identifiable Burberry check scarf. The X-Fluent will likely have an even more exclusive brand of Burberry raincoat, say the Prorsum, paired with an even more expensive scarf of impeccable design, say one from Hermès, made from the finest, softest, most luminous cashmere. Sales professionals need to be attentive to the cues and clues that distinguish between the trendy, status-conscious Aspirers and X-Fluents with classic tastes who have really made it.

Where Aspirers are likely to be found

Aspirers are likely to be found in many of the same shopping venues as X-Fluents, especially where luxury branded boutiques and high-end department stores are found. In fact, they are drawn to these official luxury-branded destinations even more than X-Fluents, who are just as likely to be attracted by out-of-the-way boutiques or clandestine destinations that wouldn't appeal to the see-and-be-seen Aspirer. In general, Aspirers are less adventurous when it comes to shopping and are likely to go with leading luxury brand names for their shopping fix. They want the vibe and status that comes from shopping in the branded stores, where everybody recognizes the names and the bags, and where they will be noticed.

How to sell to Aspirers

Aspirers go first and foremost for the most showy brands and most prominent logos. With their focus on the externals, they will notice which brands celebrities are wearing, which brands magazines are covering, which brands are hot and trendy now. Sales associates can gloss over quality details with this customer and go straight for the jugular—the gossip and trend news that will hook them and encourage the Aspirer to buy. But be careful. If you make the mistake of using Aspirer messaging with X-Fluent customers, you are more likely to turn them off rather than on. X-Fluents want the brand that is more exclusive, more subtle, quieter, and not so showy. Aspirers need the reassurance of choosing brands to which an external arbiter of style, such as a fashion magazine editor or celebrity endorser, has given a seal of approval.

Cocooners seek out luxury for their homes, not for themselves

Cocooners get their luxury thrills from their homes, rather than from fashion or experiences they might indulge in. Their ultimate pleasure is centered around feathering their nests, which has profound implications in how marketers identify them and where they are likely to find them shopping. An avid HGTV viewer, the Cocooner will also be a heavy consumer of home decorating magazines and books.

How to identify a Cocooner

Cocooners are likely to be unremarkable, even dowdy, in their dress or appearance. Not prone to luxury indulgences in fashion. The Cocooner is more fashion victim than fashionista, so comfort (think mommy jeans or sweat pants and big, baggy t-shirts) will rule. This personality is also among the oldest in the luxury market, so their age can also be an identifying characteristic. Her car of choice, for the majority of Cocooners are female, is most likely to be a mini-van, station wagon, or SUV cross-over model, big enough to cart home her furniture and home-furnishing finds.

Where Cocooners are likely to be found

Cocooners are most likely to be found in home furnishings or furniture stores, home improvement centers, and the home departments of a department store. Cocooners are not likely to turn up in luxury branded or fashion boutiques—it's just not their style—though they might be drawn to more upscale home or gift boutiques and luxury-leaning garden centers where they can find interesting decorative items.

How to sell to Cocooners

For this shopper you should stress the decorating possibilities of the home items you are trying to encourage her to buy. She will eat up decorating and styling advice and can become a regular, high-spending customer at shops that teach her new and different ideas for home decorating. While she is decidedly "what not to wear" in her personal style, she is very interested in home decorating, so give her creative ideas, then fit your store's items into that design and watch her buy.

X-Fluents are eager for what you are selling

For many traditional or heritage luxury brands, the X-Fluent personality makes up the lions' share of their customer base. These consumers are high spending, highly indulgent, and eager to buy what luxury marketers are selling. While they are the best prospects for anything luxury, they aren't about to waste money on brands that don't measure up to their high standards.

How to identify an X-Fluent

X-Fluents often can be identified by the clothes they wear, the brands they select, and the bags they carry, jewelry and watches with which they adorn themselves, the cars they drive, and the hotels where they stay. They go first-class all the way and are likely to dress the part when they shop. They have learned that they get better service and access to more exclusive items when they turn up at the store dressed to the nines, so this personality is fairly easy to identify by their plumage.

Where are X-Fluents likely to be found

These consumers are likely to be found shopping in neighborhoods where the major luxury brands congregate: L.A.'s Rodeo Drive, Chicago's Miracle Mile, and New York's Fifth and Madison Avenues. But they are also recreational shoppers who pursue shopping as a sport, so they are always in search of shops that offer them something special. They are drawn to shopping destinations of all kinds that offer a different or unique experience or product assortment—specialty boutiques, downtown shopping areas filled with interesting shops, and luxury outlet malls. For them, members-only sample or flash sale websites are particularly appealing. They want to uncover the hidden gems when shopping. Places that only a select few know about give them bragging rights for their great shopping finds.

By contrast, this shopper is not likely to be attracted to big mass-retail chains or shopping centers and malls that cater to the masses. X-Fluent shoppers want shopping experiences that are out-of-the-ordinary and special in one way or another. Retailers draw the X-Fluent shopper through 1) exclusive brands; 2) advertising that evokes curiosity rather than emphasizes discount prices; and 3) special events that give the shopper new exposure to brands or designs, and ideas about how to put those brands to work in their lives. They are highly experiential shoppers in search of special shopping experiences, in addition to more stuff. Extra-attentive services and special events in the store are very attractive indeed to this shopper.

How to sell more to X-Fluents

X-Fluent shoppers expect first-class service, attention to their needs, and sales professionals who care. They want to know more about the products, brands, items in the store than the label tells them. Sales clerks who can fill in these missing links will be appreciated. This shopper responds to messages about superior quality, how items are made, and distinctive materials used in manufacture. They seek exceptional design and distinctive style. When an X-Fluent zeros in on one item, the savvy sales professional will offer up complementary pieces that work with it to boost sales. When selling to X-Fluents, sales professionals need to give them a reason to buy; if the seller goes that extra mile, X-Fluents will often reward them with an extra purchase. For this shopper, the sales professional needs to find ways to give something extra special, not just the ordinary or same old thing. Sales professionals should go to the trouble to pull a single display item out of the window or undress a mannequin to let them try on that one-of-a-kind piece. Your extra effort will often pay off in a larger sale.

Temperate Pragmatists make careful shopping decisions with a view to the long term

The quintessential Temperate Pragmatist is Ed Begley Jr., star of his reality cable television series *Living with Ed.* His latest book is *Ed Begley Jr.'s Guide to Sustainable Living,* which says it all. He is a movie and television star who lives in Studio City, California, but rejects the conspicuous consumption lifestyle and all that it stands for. In the vanguard of renewable energy and sustainable living, Begley augments the power of his home's solar energy system by pedaling his stationary bike. Rather than a car, he gets around town on his bicycle. He saves gray water to use in his garden, has solar collectors on his roof, and resists buying new, in favor of repurposing old cast-offs or making it from scratch. Many Temperate Pragmatists may not take their lifestyle as far as Ed does, but they definitely lean toward a green lifestyle where conserving and preserving are key.

How to identify a Temperate Pragmatist

One thing for sure: you won't find a Temperate Pragmatist carrying a logo-ridden Louis Vuitton handbag, but after that, all bets are off. This personality won't necessarily be decked out in organic cotton t-shirts and Birkenstocks, but they also don't appear as much of a fashion victim as the typical Cocooner, either. What is distinguishing about Temperate Pragmatists is their casual lifestyle and casual, non-trendy approach to fashion. Further, they are likely to be concerned with health and fitness and are unlikely to have the typical couch-potato body shape associated with the Cocooners.

Where Temperate Pragmatists are likely to be found

Like Butterflies, Temperate Pragmatists are not recreational shoppers, so they are not likely to turn up in your store unless there is something they really need. But when they shop, they are less likely than Butterflies to venture into luxury-leaning establishments, with the exception of food and health stores like Whole Foods or Trader Joe's. They are willing to pay a premium for organic produce and grass-feed beef, and desire access to a wide selection of healthy living products. For most other shopping they will patronize down-scale, mass-market stores where they can find good prices and good value, or they turn to outlet stores, discount shops, and especially their favorite destination store: members-only club warehouse stores like Costco or Sam's Club.

How to sell to Temperate Pragmatists

These shoppers are cautious and careful and not about to spend a penny more than absolutely necessary. They will respond to discounts and sales, coupons, and other promotional offers. They will pay full price, but only when the value is there. For this shopper positioning a product's price in terms of lifetime use or price per wear is a good strategy. They also will respond to information about a manufacturer's or retailer's green marketing practices. Stores and brands that are environmentally conscious will win their loyalty and repeat business.

chapter 12

Values Shift: How Consumer's Values Are Shifting and How Marketers Must Respond

We've been talking about two things: One is, value is in, and the second is, high-end spending is tough.

—Scott Tuhy, Moody's Investors Service

Through the course of the economic recession, luxury marketers have seemed to discover the concept of value, as if value were some new idea their customers just embraced. Luxury consumers have always been and always will be the ultimate value customer. It is a luxury to be able to vote with your dollars on value and values alone. Unfortunately, the word *value* has gotten corrupted in marketing circles. Today it is often used to signify cheap or discount, as in Walmart's adoption of "Great Value" as its store brand.

But value doesn't mean cheap; it means worth the price. When you are a Gucci or Louis Vuitton and trying to sell handbags for $995 and up or shoes for $695 or more, you better be sure that you justify the price to your affluent customers. Value is far less important when you are selling something that isn't priced so dearly.

Luxury marketers' sudden discovery of value as part of their brand proposition is symptomatic of a fundamental change in how their customers view value. Back in the boom times for luxury, brands didn't have to do too much work to encourage people to buy. Having a prominent logo seemed to be the key. But with the economic downturn, luxury brands got the values "religion" and started to think long and hard about what value and values really mean to their customers. They discovered that values were the platform on which they could build lasting relationships with their customers; before, they were mainly focused on simply having a transaction.

Steven Lussier, executive director of DeBeers Group, expressed the new values proposition in the luxury market: "Luxury has long been associated with superior quality, design, and craftsmanship. But the time is turning with a new breed of consumers who are seeking style with substance. These new consumers desire something more meaningful than just an expensive piece; they want brands to live and breathe their *values* through the way they do business. Our future is entwined with our ability to ride these new waves of change."

Values are the platform for creating customer relationships

Today's consumers will be loyal to brands that speak to their unique lifestyles. What do they hold dear? What is truly important to them? Marketers must discover the way their customers define value, and how they balance that inner scale that measures perceived value against actual cost. *Value* is more than product features; it goes much deeper than quality, workmanship, and materials. It's what the company stands for, how the company's values align with the customer's personal value system, and how the company talks to me, with me, about me. What does it say about me and my personal value system when I choose to buy this brand, stay in that hotel, wear that designer? It's why someone might refuse to carry a Louis Vuitton handbag; favor boutique hotels over Ritz-Carlton or Four Seasons; won't buy jewelry that might get her killed in a dark alley; and drive an American car, not an import. Consumer choices say a lot about the individual making them. That is why your customers' values are so critically important for you to understand. High income consumers can choose widely across a whole range of brand choices at all different price points, unlike lower-income consumers who have far fewer options.

The customer becomes the focus of the brand's value proposition. As senior lecturer Paurav Shukla, at Brighton Business School, University of Brighton, puts it, "Managers will have to change their core message and value proposition to reflect the market conditions and consumer motivations. The question which managers need to ask is what is the value proposition in the present circumstances most of my customers are looking for, and how can I develop and convey a message which reflects consumers' reality, rather than the brand's own reality?"

Unity Marketing focuses much of its research efforts on affluent consumer values in different product and service categories. Insights from this perspective can prove extremely fruitful for marketers' within a particular market segment. But since consumers operate across a wide range of product and service categories, we recently took a different approach to our values research. We looked across the luxury consumers' lifestyles to measure their personal values sets, to examine individual's "reality," not just shopping and buying behaviors. Let's look more closely at what the values research uncovered about the luxury consumer and get inspired in ways to use these insights to power your luxury marketing and branding.

Examining the Key Facets of Luxury Consumers' Lives

People have many areas of responsibilities and concerns in their lives and their personal values help them prioritize those different responsibilities. To understand the different dimensions or facets of their lifestyles and their responsibilities, we asked affluents to tell us what was important to them. A total of 21 issues were examined, which fell into four key facets of the luxury consumers' lives.

In a nutshell: Family comes first for the affluent customer. Affluents' number one priority is supporting and caring for their families. That includes providing for their families financially, as well as emotionally. These individuals know that they have to take care of themselves in order to take care of their spouses and their children. So they make finding time to emotionally recharge a priority, including pursing a satisfying sexual relationships. They work at careers that not only provide financial rewards, but personal rewards as well, recognizing that having an emotionally rewarding career is important for personal health. In the midst of a very busy schedule they make time to exercise, plan for and eat a healthy diet, and spend time with their friends, since these are also critically important in their family-first value system.

⮑ **Figure 12.1 Key Facets of Affluents' Lives**

importance index: 100 = average

Family and emotional health	116
Career and finances	106
Society and politics	91
Health and wellness	89

Source: Unity Marketing

Affluent consumers rate their family and emotional health as the most important priority in their lives, as measured by an index value of 115 where 100 equals average, meaning this facet is 15 percent more important to affluent consumers than the average for all consumers. With nearly 90 percent of affluents married and most of those with children, it is not surprising that family and emotional health are the utmost personal priority.

Luxury watch marketer Patek Philippe taps affluents' family-first orientation in its *Generations* campaign which, since being launched in 1996, has stood the test of time. In a recent ad a little boy sits deep in concentration, working through a thorny homework problem. His father sits with him, mirroring his position of deep thought, a Patek Philippe timepiece evident on his wrist. The tag line accompanying this installment by photographer Peter Lindberg of the *Generations* advertising campaign reads, "You never actually own a Patek Philippe. You merely look after it for the next generation." The success of this ad campaign is how it conveys the brand's quality and value, as well as how it forges connections within the family across generations.

Through its *Generations* campaign, Patek Philippe has reinforced its position as a lifestyle brand—a brand that aligns itself with the values and aspirations of its consumers. With its lifestyle marketing approach, Patek Philippe emphasizes the inherent values its customers cherish, making its products a seamless part of that lifestyle. The company could easily market its products on exceptional quality; or its heritage, dating back to 1839; or on innovation, as it holds 70 patents. But that isn't enough for the company whose mission states, "Lasting value is both material and emotional." The brand's marketing makes its connection, both emotionally and rationally, through the values its ideal customer holds most dear.

Figure 12.2 Family Comes First for Affluents

	Index	Extremely/Very Important
Caring and supporting the needs of my family	127	90%
Setting priorities and boundaries in my life to keep family needs first	118	83%
Finding time to emotionally recharge and refresh	118	83%
Enjoying a satisfying sexual relationship with my partner	112	79%
Spending time with friends and keeping an active social life	103	72%
Overall	116	

Source: Unity Marketing

For the affluent luxury consumer, family and emotional health is the number one priority, whether male or female, young (under 45 years) or mature (45 years and above); HENRY income ($100,000–$249,999) or ultra-affluent ($250,000+); high-net-worth ($1 million or more) or low-net-worth (less than $1 million).

• • • • •

Find Ways to Help Your Luxury Customers Do More in Less Time

- Time is the ultimate luxury.
- Time is what people need to attend to their families' needs and their personal emotional health.

It has become a cliché that time is the ultimate luxury. However, when we examine the facets of affluent consumers' lives we see that time is indeed their first priority, time is their issue, time is their personal challenge. They need time to care and support their families. They have to set priorities and boundaries to find time to fulfill their families' needs. They need alone-time when they can escape from the stresses and demands of their lives to recharge and refresh. They need to spend quality time with their spouse or partner to generate sexual excitement and build a satisfying relationship. They must have time to share with friends and their social circle.

Multi-tasking is how affluent consumers manage to do more with less time. It's how they keep all the balls in the air and meet the many demands of their busy lives.

As a luxury marketer, you can respond by giving your luxury consumers solutions that help them save time or do more with the time available. Needless to say, being respectful of affluent customers' time is a critical priority. You must make sure that you deliver the utmost luxury in the most time-efficient way. That could be offering online shopping, home delivery, express check out, or mobile phone apps that allow a shopper to order an item displayed in your store window and have it sent same-day, so it arrives home almost before she does.

Marketers can learn from retailers like Apple, who lets customers schedule appointments with its support "geniuses" before leaving their home or office. Retailers Coach and Nordstrom offer in-store pickup. A customer can order a handbag or dress online in the morning, then pick it up at the store in the afternoon for a party that evening, rather than having to wait the standard 5 to 7 business days for delivery.

Saving time doesn't extend only into the retail store or service sector. Just look at Rachel Ray's business empire built on teaching people to prepare a "healthful and delicious meal" in only 30 minutes, or personal trainer Tony Horton's exercise program guaranteed to give results in only 10 minutes a day. Opportunities abound for marketers who are clued into their customer's personal priority and chief personal challenge: finding ways to do more in less time.

• • • • •

Achieving financial goals is a priority for affluents—it makes their luxury lifestyles possible.

In the end, affluent consumers' lifestyles depend on their financial status, so it is no surprise that the facet of career and finances figures so prominently in their value systems. Next after emotional health, the affluent consumer is concerned with career and finances. These individuals are working hard to achieve their financial goals with a view toward the short term as well as the long term and eventual retirement. They gain emotional satisfaction from their work and rewards from pursuing their careers. Like most Americans, they want to achieve the "good life" which includes having wealth and financial stability.

⊃ **Figure 12.3 Career & Finances**

	Index	Extremely/ Very Important
Achieving financial goals and saving for retirement	121	85%
Doing work I enjoy and a job that provides personal fulfillment	114	80%
Pursuing a career that is rewarding and emotionally satisfying	109	76%
Achieving career success and my personal career goals	99	70%
Gaining wealth so that I can live the good life	89	63%
Overall	106	

Source: Unity Marketing

The values in the table above that pertain to career rewards and success are rated more important by men than women. On the other hand, women are more attuned to achieving financial goals and saving for retirement.

When it comes to using their wealth to live the "good life," men, young affluents (45 and under), ultra-affluents, and high-net-worth individuals are more motivated than are women, mature affluents, HENRYs, or lower-wealth affluents.

Affluents with diverse ethnic backgrounds are more likely to emphasize career achievement as the stepping-stone to a luxury lifestyle, than are the majority Caucasian affluents.

• • • • •

TAKE ACTION

Just Because They Have It, Doesn't Mean They Want to Spend It—Affluent Customers Know the Real Value of Money

- Affluent consumers are shrewd money managers.
- They believe that money is power and they know how to use that power to achieve their goals.

To understand affluent consumers, luxury marketers need to understand how shrewd at managing their money they are. They take full responsibility for their families' financial well-being. They know how to manage their finances for the short term, balancing their weekly or monthly budgets, and the long term, planning for retirement and saving for the future. Affluents know their money is the ticket to their luxury lifestyles, and they aren't about to jeopardize that by unwise spending or careless borrowing.

Affluent consumers are often leaders in business, having achieved senior levels of corporate management, entrepreneurial success, or accomplishment in their professional lives. They are highly paid and rewarded for their skills and talents. They read the *Wall Street Journal, Fortune,* and *Forbes*; they watch CNBC and listen to Bloomberg News for business developments. They know the score and how to play the game to win. They are business people who don't leave their business savvy at the office when they go home at night.

We must all remember: Affluent consumers didn't get "rich" by being wasteful and spendthrift. People gain affluence by paying careful attention to their money, keeping it, conserving it, and spending it wisely.

Affluent consumers know money is power and how to use that power. The challenge for you as a luxury marketer therefore, is to get these customers to spend some of their resources with you. You need to understand first that they are careful with money, but not afraid to spend. The key thing you have to do is add value in the pricing equation, as Warren Buffett reminds us, "Price is what you pay. Value is what you get."

You need to apply the "new math" at work in the luxury market for establishing prices. Affluent shoppers with a focus on high quality are also looking for that quality delivered at a more reasonable price. They are no longer willing to spend ten times more for a luxury item that is only three times better than a comparable product offered by a mass-market brand. With a focus on adding value, rather than reducing price, there are many ways that luxury marketers and retailers can give their affluent customers more for less, such as:

- Gift with purchase; multiple item discounts; online or email exclusives; special feature items; special limited time sales; gift certificates or rebates linked to next purchase.

- Internet retailers can offer free shipping and handling. Paying for shipping is a particular rub among affluents who value the convenience of internet shopping, but hate the extra charges.

Luxury leaders LVMH, Valentino, Gucci, Giorgio Armani, and Tod's are all taking steps to cut costs by shifting a portion of their production to countries where manufacturing costs are lower.

Luxury leading brands and designers continue to expand their brands into lower-price lines. Lanvin recently teamed with fast-fashion retailer H&M for a secondary line with dresses in the $300 range, high for H&M, but low compared with Lanvin's $3,000 price points. Karl Lagerfeld announced the introduction of a new affordable line with Macy's. Narciso Rodriguez, famous for dressing First Lady Michelle Obama, launched a lower-priced line early in 2010 through an exclusive arrangement with eBay. He is also reducing the prices of his ready-to-wear dresses that used to average $1,800 down to price points under $1,000.

Luxury retailers, notably Saks Fifth Avenue and Neiman Marcus, are demanding lower-price points from their luxury vendors and getting results. Saks now offers a Prada bag with an opening price point of $700, rather than $1,000, and Christian Dior features a bag at $950 instead of $1,500.

In a recent earnings call, Neiman Marcus described its new merchandising strategy at its full-priced stores of adding lower-priced goods while still maintaining its premium image. In a *Wall Street Journal* article titled "Neiman Marcus Opens Customer Door Wider," the company is reported to have increased its assortment of lower-priced merchandise over a period of 18 months and trained its sales staff to offer customers lower-priced items, rather than always upsell. Beyond the company's 30 or so Last Call outlet stores, which sell mostly clearance merchandise transferred out of full-price stores, Neiman Marcus wants still more traction in what it calls the "value" space. It has announced an even newer lower-priced offering, Last Call Studio, targeting shoppers who may find even Last Call outlet stores too expensive. Last Call Studio will sell new merchandise bought directly from manufacturers at more affordable price points, not clearance product. According to Karen Katz, NM's CEO, the goal behind the Last Call Studio is to bring fashionable young career women "into the fold and move them up as their incomes rise." Its strategy, then, would be correctly called aspirational. Wanda Gierhart, NM's chief marketing officer, says her Last Call Studio shopper, "may not have the reach level to buy the fine apparel that Neiman Marcus offers." Now that's a play that makes sense to me.

• • • • •

Society and political issues are important to affluents— education, schools, and local politics are a priority

⇒ Figure 12.4 Society & Politics

	Index	Extremely/ Very Important
Educational issues, including local schools	98	69%
Following local and state government actions and policies	96	68%
World affairs and U.S. policy in global setting	93	66%
Following political candidates, their platforms and positions	88	62%
Environmental issues, such as global warming, pollution, etc.	84	59%
Philanthropy and giving toward worthy social causes	84	59%
Overall	91	

Source: Unity Marketing

Another important aspect of affluent consumers' lives is how they relate in society and politics. When it comes to politics, affluents tend to think locally, rather than globally. They place educational issues, especially local schools, as one of their top priorities. They follow local and state governmental actions, as well as following political candidates, their platforms and positions. They know what is going on in the world at large and pay close attention to how the United States pursues its agenda on the world stage. Finally, affluent consumers are attuned to environmental issues and believe strongly in supporting philanthropic causes.

• • • • •

A Shift in the Culture from "Me" to "We" Perspective— Our Society Is Moving from Being a Consuming Culture to Being a Caring and Sharing Culture

There is a profound shift taking place throughout the culture. We can see it among companies as diverse as Gap, American Express, Hallmark, and Microsoft supporting the Product Red campaign, a global fund to fight AIDS; by the federal government focusing on health care for all citizens; among celebrities from Angelina Jolie to Bono who prominently support causes; among individual citizens who together gave over $220 million to charities and non-profits in 2009, according to statistics compiled by the Giving USA Foundation.

We are transitioning from a consuming culture, where more is better and "he who dies with the most toys wins," to a new caring, sharing, and saving culture where people think about leaving their children and grand-children a better world. People want to make a difference; buying another Mercedes-Benz, diamond ring, or mink coat just won't cut it any more.

Affluent customers are values-based consumers, looking to align them-selves with brands and companies that care about what they care about. These are customers who care and who give. They support brands and companies that care and give as well.

The ultimate challenge for each brand and each company is to align with customers' core values, to build a more meaningful relationship with them. Cause-related marketing is here to stay. Marketers have to relate to their customers' issues and values across all facets of their lives, and address the many issues that are important in their value systems. There are many different causes to choose from, but the key is to align your brand, your company with a cause that is authentic and meaningful to affluent consum-ers and their families.

Supporting the right causes and presenting the right core values to the affluent consumer can pay dividends to your company's bottom line. In our values investigation, Unity Marketing asked affluents how important it was for them to buy from companies whose values align with their own. The majority (50 percent) said it was important to them. Specifically 27 percent said shared values were very important and 23 percent said it was extremely important for the companies from which they buy to share their values.

Values are the ties that bind people with each other and to companies they choose to work for, and those with which they do business. Values are at the heart of people's connections, personally, professionally, and com-mercially. Values ultimately count more to affluent consumers. Given their high levels of income, these are customers who can be most picky about the companies and brands with which they choose to do business. Lower-income shoppers need to worry about pocketbook issues when it comes to the brands they buy and the retailers they patronize. The affluent have the means to let other values besides price determine their business partners.

Brands, companies, retailers, and service providers that want to attract these high-potential, high-spending customers need to be the most attentive to those lifestyle and personal values that are important to them.

• • • • •

Affluents take health and wellness for granted, or at least it doesn't play as strong a role in their lifestyle—being active and following a healthy diet are tops for affluents lifestyles

⇒ Figure 12.5 Health & Wellness

	Index	Extremely/ Very Important
Maintaining an active lifestyle, keeping fit and exercising regularly	107	75%
Following a healthy diet by watching calories and without a lot of fast foods, additives, excess fats	103	73%
Setting an example for healthy living for family, friends	94	66%
Following the latest news on health and wellness	80	56%
Buying organic and more natural foods	63	44%
Overall	89	

Source: Unity Marketing

It's surprising that the Health & Wellness facet ranks as the least important of the facets examined in this survey. However, note that the overall ranking for Health & Wellness was dragged down by the survey's lowest value, buying organic and more natural foods.

Eating organic just doesn't figure all that prominently as a means to health among affluent Americans, while following a healthy diet by watching calories and avoiding fast foods is much more of a priority. This consumer is dedicated to maintaining an active lifestyle, keeping fit, and exercising regularly. Given their values toward healthful living through exercise and good diet, it is not surprising that obesity generally doesn't characterize the affluent in this country. Study after study has shown obesity is linked to lower income. Perhaps it isn't only a function of access to healthy foods, but that affluent people value an active lifestyle supported by a healthy diet.

• • • • •

Affluents Focus on Health and Wellness Is Prime for Any Brand Marketing a Lifestyle

These findings about the importance of a healthy lifestyle among affluent consumers is valuable not just to brands like Whole Foods, FIJI, POM Wonderful, Nike, Gaiam, or Seasons 52—a new restaurant concept from Darden offering a menu where no item has more than 475 calories. It is relevant for any luxury marketer that is focusing on lifestyle marketing and branding. These insights can help marketers build a connection with their customers by taking the message of health and wellness to them.

For example, an affluent's health consciousness may connect to his growing environmental awareness. Product packaging based on recycled content or that can be recycled will resonate with this customer. How your products are made and manufactured (e.g., clothing manufactured from organic cotton), is another health component. There are many ways to creatively align your brand to the growing health consciousness and awareness of this customer, even if you are not selling health, per se, but fashion, home luxury, or services.

As we found, the affluent consumer wants to set a good example of health and wellness. Your brand and company should do the same by being a good example of health and wellness in the business community. Take the Roll International Corporation, which markets healthful products, notably FIJI Water and POM Wonderful. The company makes employee wellness programs an important part of its corporate mission. Its website states, "Consistent with its portfolio of healthy, good-for-you products, Roll International and its companies are committed to encouraging wellness, promoting a healthy lifestyle, and providing peace of mind for employees and their families."

In the beauty business today, health and wellness factors highly. Research confirms that health factors such as diet, exercise, and sleep are far more important to beauty than being born with symmetrical features. In a nod to healthful beauty, Saks Fifth Avenue launched a new concept, "The Beauty of Living Well," in five of its stores. It features exclusive nutraceutical beauty products, including a skin care line from Canyon Ranch, and Vinita, a line based on ancient Eastern beauty principles. With success, this concept of promoting wellness and an holistic approach to beauty may be a launching pad for more health-related products and supplements at Saks.

• • • • •

The Chief End of Business Is to Create Commercial Relationships with Customers

- **Specifically, we want them to buy what we are selling. But we need more than just a transaction—we need a personal connection. It is the difference between finding a customer who buys once and finding one who buys for life.**

Values are the platform on which marketers can build deeper, more lasting connections with their customers. While having a commercial relationship is important, brand loyalty is based on a true and meaningful connection.

As marketers we seek to build a customer relationship with affluent shoppers. Essentially, we want to attract them to our brands, our stores, our companies, to make a sale. But executing a transaction with the customer isn't building a relationship. The marketers' goal has to be more than just making a sale; it's about making a true and meaningful connection with the customer.

To make that connection, marketers and their brands must engage customers as individuals with lives beyond the store, and with values that guide them in the many facets of their lives. It extends far beyond their identities as customers. Therefore, we need to engage our customers and potential customers as complete people who are passionate about their lives, their families, their careers, their society, and also passionate about shopping.

To build a true connection with the customer, not just a transaction, you need to take a 360-degree lifestyle approach. You need to understand the many different dimensions, values, and priorities of your customers and use that understanding as a platform to build a long-term, lasting brand connection with them.

• • • • •

Values your company must exhibit to build connection with luxury consumers

In probing the values of utmost importance to affluent consumers when it comes to doing business with companies, customers are keen on these three values:

- the company offers high quality products and services;
- it behaves ethically, honestly, and lawfully (e.g., no sweatshops, no child labor, no shoddy business practices);
- it asks fair and reasonable prices for its products and services, with the emphasis on fair and reasonable.

⮑ **Figure 12.6 Corporate Values Affluents' Rate Extremely Important**

How important is it to buy from a company whose values are aligned with yours . . .

	Index 100 = Average	Extremely Important
Offers quality products and services	155	58%
Behaves ethically, honestly, lawfully	145	55%
Asks fair prices for products and services	135	51%
Treats employees well, equal opportunity employer, good pay/benefits	107	40%
Self-regulates, is accountable, is transparent	89	34%
Is environmentally responsible	79	30%
Cares about public, gives back, helps people	79	30%
Gives back to the community, locally concerned	73	27%
Offers energy-efficient products	72	27%
Donates to charities, sponsors, volunteers	65	25%

Source: Unity Marketing

Luxury consumers look first for high quality products and services from the companies with which they choose to do business. Using an index where 100 is average, luxury consumers rate product and service quality 55 percent more important than average in a scale of the ten key corporate values. Also of highest importance to luxury consumers is that the companies with which they do business behave ethically, honestly and lawfully, with an index value of 145, making this value 45 percent more important than average. The third most important value for a company that luxury consumers choose to do business with is that it asks fair prices for products and services, 35 percent more important than average.

In the realm of what is traditionally considered "corporate responsibility," luxury consumers give higher marks to a company that treats its employees well, than to the company's environmental policies, its donations to charities, or its community involvement. How a company treats its employees has an index of 107 on the importance scale, or 7 percent above average. This value ranks way above these other values considered synonymous with corporate responsibility, specifically environmental policy (index of 79); gives back to the community (index 73); donates to charities, sponsors, volunteers (index 65). *Note:* These corporate values are ranked lower when compared with others like quality products, ethical behavior and fair prices, but they still are extremely important to more than one-fourth of luxury consumers.

Women are luxury marketers' most values-oriented shoppers

Women are the most value-oriented shoppers, far more concerned with value compared with men. Women rate each of the following values higher than men to a statistically significant degree:

- offers quality products and services;
- asks fair prices for products and services;
- behaves ethically, honestly, lawfully;
- treats employees well, equal opportunity employer, good pay/ benefits;
- cares about public, gives back, helps people;
- offers energy-efficient products; and
- is environmentally responsible.

Of note for luxury brands' long-term planning, the youngest luxury consumers surveyed, aged 24-to-34 years, placed a higher priority on the social and environmental values included in the survey than those consumers aged 35 and older. So for the youngest affluents, environmental responsibility, community service, and charitable giving programs are much more important than they are for their older cohorts.

This suggests that as the younger generations of consumers move into the affluent market, luxury brands may well have to move their social and environmental policies up a notch in relative importance. At the same time, for the short term, today's luxury consumers are more apt to measure the values of a company or brand based on how well its employees are treated.

· · · · ·

The Key to Success in the Luxury Market Is Very Simple

- Offer quality products and services.
- Operate your company ethnically and responsibly in dealing with all business constituencies, including employees, business partners, and customers.
- Ask fair prices for the products and services that you deliver to luxury consumers.

A surprise from this survey is the emphasis luxury consumers place on the ethics and honesty of the companies with which they choose to do business. They expect, even *demand,* that companies behave in an upright manner, obey the laws that pertain to their business, and give frank and honest answers to questions and customer concerns. Some may argue this emphasis on business ethics is a direct result of the many recently publicized business and Wall Street scandals, but that likely is not the case. How responsibly and ethically a company deals with the public, its employees, its business partners, and its shareholders is a reflection of how ethically it deals with its customers. An ethical company dedicated to good business practices isn't going to short change its customers with materials, workmanship or service of lesser quality than what they promise. Ethical companies will stand behind their products and services and deliver the best to customers who are voting with their dollars. They will be honest in their corporate and marketing communications and not promise more than they deliver.

This survey shows that companies have to do their good works first close to home, within the company family, starting with their employees. Environmental policies and corporate contributions are important for luxury companies, but first they have to treat their employees fairly, justly, and right. Starting there, employees then are empowered and motivated to treat the businesses' customers fairly, justly, and right in each of the ways they touch the customer, whether in product design, manufacture, service, retail, operations, marketing, or public relations.

• • • • •

M&C Saatchi's Kate Bristow and Huw Griffith Share Secrets of Communicating and Connecting with Affluent Consumers

Advertising is the essential way brands communicate their lifestyle values to the target customer. Having never worked in the advertising field directly, only with advertising professionals tangentially, I defer to advertising experts like my colleagues at M&C Saatchi, a global advertising agency founded in 1995 by brothers Maurice and Charles Saatchi. We sat down with Kate Bristow, chief strategy officer, and Huw Griffith, CEO, North America in their Santa Monica, California, offices to talk about the challenges of communicating with the new luxury market.

"Demographics are key," said Kate when asked about the luxury clientele their clients target. "The essential challenge for us all is the numbers; there is a gap without a lot of new people coming into the market. It's very easy when the market is growing with lots of people coming in like we had in the luxury sector for a long time. But now you don't have the luxury of sheer volume any more. Now you have to be so much smarter because you've got less people."

She continues, "With that there also has been a shift in values. They started to ask, 'Do I need another car? Do I need another flat screen TV?' So their values shifted toward memories and creating experiences. I think that the luxury brands are going to have to think long and hard about their role in people's lives and what it could be in their lives."

Huw turns the discussion to the younger generation who will be so vitally important to the fortunes of luxury goods companies in the coming decades. "We also have to ask whether this younger group of consumers will adopt aspirations born out from the older generation or be completely different? Will it be spend, spend and be very materialistic, or will they be interested in such things like luxury products? Luxury brands are going to be tested to see how good they adapt; it will be survival of the fittest."

I share Huw's concerns about assuming the aspirations of the younger generations will be the same as the older generations. While time will tell, Huw cautions luxury brands to ask the hard questions about whether their core brand values really connect with the younger generation's mindset. "There are certain symbols of success to older generations that are linked to materialism that many young people see no relevance for. For previous generations Rolex and Mercedes were symbols of success, but for the young I think other, newer brands are evolving that will have just as much cache. Take Apple. It is a price-premium brand that keeps adding functions and features and has great appeal as it keeps people repeating the cycle of buying and upgrading."

Kate offers BMW and Audi as brands with cachet for a younger audience. "We worked several years ago on BMW and of course Mercedes was our big competitor. Mercedes is a brand that is headed for trouble because it is older, whereas BMW or Audi both offer the same German engineering, but they are symbols for the younger generation. They are cool brands that have actually overcome the generation gap. You have a 70-year-old CEO still driving a high-end BMW and younger kids desperate for a 3 Series. Mercedes and Rolex are brands that have a major issue. I can't even imagine what they are going to do with this younger generation."

What makes one brand cool for one generation and another cool to the next revolves around their media habits. Huw explains, "The younger generation has such different media consumption habits and how they come to understand about brands are very different. Back in the 70s and 80s people understood advertising; they liked watching advertising; people would pay attention to it during the breaks in TV. But now the younger generation is finding information elsewhere."

Kate adds, "Brands today are being built in the trenches. They are being built one-on-one, through conversations, social media. A brand can be built on Facebook and a brand can be built because it Tweets really well. That was unheard of before. Now brands are no longer being built on the big billboards or TV ads, they are built by people coming into contact with them one at a time and saying to their friends, 'This is a really cool brand. You need to be a part of this brand.'"

Kate points to British Airways as a brand that knows how to handle challenges and work social-media chatter to its advantage. "Take the Icelandic volcano that caused a crisis for the airlines in Europe where so many people were stranded and couldn't fly. British Airways came out better than any other airline because they decided rather than just do what they were legally supposed to do, they were going to go above and beyond. Every stranded BA passenger in North America was taken out of the airport, given a hotel room, given all their meals until they could get them back on a plane. The other airlines didn't do that. They put cots up if you were lucky. Here is a brand, which recognized its moral duty in this situation. And it will pay dividends in the future. People were tweeting about it. The *New York Times* wrote a whole story about it. British Airways will get such loyalty from people. Customers will say it is worth paying extra for a British Airways ticket, because they will really look after me."

Huw adds, "British Airways is expensive, but it will take share from American and United. They give real value."

Exclusivity is changing for the younger generation— exclusive accessibility

Kate and Huw both join in on how luxury brands have to start thinking about transforming the old idea of exclusivity toward a more all-inclusive accessibility and openness. Huw explains, "The younger people can't continue to stand for the loftiness of certain premium brands. If it's trendy, it has got to be accessible." Kate points to the Firmdale Hotels as an example of a new type of luxury hotel experience that is cool and hip. "This is a British group of hotels that just opened in New York's Soho district. It's an incredibly cool luxury chain; each hotel is individual and fits into its locale. The Soho hotel feels very Soho, and the Charlotte Street hotel in London feels very Charlotte Street. These hotels are in historic buildings and very quirky. They feel independent and individual and trendy. In Charlotte Street there is a bar and restaurant on the street, so you become part of the world that's going on outside the hotel, as well as inside the hotel. It's exclusive in that to stay there costs money, but there is an openness that is interesting and you can participate in it being cool. It's an incredibly cool brand that would appeal to a 25-year-old as much as a 60-year-old."

Huw adds, "The young generation demands access to the brands and won't listen to a brand that cuts itself off or turns down people because they aren't the right sort of person or dressed in the right sort of clothes."

Kate continues, "The Millennial generation is very democratic. Millennials care about the planet so all these other things come into play. You can be a luxury brand, but now you have to care about the planet. You have to be conscious of your impact on other people and their sustainability. All of these things matter to the younger generation, more than they ever did for Boomers."

All of which brings our discussion back to value and price. Huw says "It's been on the table for discussion for a long time since this recession hit: How do you say that this particular product is worth paying more for? Whether it is a hotel, or a destination or a cruise, this recession forced everybody to say, 'If this is what it costs, what is the value?' What does value mean."

Part of the value proposition is tangible—product features, or extra service. But increasingly, the value proposition is bigger than just what you are buying, it's what the company stands for. Kate says, "It's about passion and touching people's hearts. I am in the middle of a Pet Care Foundation project for Petco that is taking aim at abuse and stopping puppy mills. Petco is a brand that is socially involved and I think luxury brands have to do even more of it. Have a higher cause, that gets people to say, 'I like this brand because they are doing something, they are giving back. They exist for more than just making money.' Jim Collins wrote in his books *Good to Great* and *Built to Last* that great companies have a purpose. And that is even more so today, and more so even for luxury brands. The generation coming up passionately believes that. They are much more aware of the world they live in."

We close discussing how the new global awakening of young people is transforming the values of American young people forever. As a Brit,

Kate can look more objectively at Americans. "I think America's greatest success and its biggest weakness is its desire for stuff. It's driven Americans ever since this country was developed. It's driven by a desire to be more successful as an individual and that's what made it such a great country. But it's a big issue in the last ten years; people just got completely carried away with materialism. But now the kids can travel to Europe and debate European values versus American values. They travel to places like Sweden and Norway and come back transformed. They see people who are happier with a lower monetary standard of living but a much higher emotional standard of living. People in these countries don't have as much money as Americans do, but they are happier as a result."

Kate talks about Italians she knows. "They buy the most expensive shoes. The shoes aren't posh, but they are superb, Italian-made handcrafted shoes. They may not own as many as the average American, but every pair they own is superbly made. That's a cool way of spending your money. You've going to have one really expensive pair of shoes that you know is locally made and handcrafted of beautiful leather. They are going to last for a long time." Huw adds, "It's about quality of life. People may have simple things, fewer things, but very good quality. It is giving a new idea of luxury."

• • • • •

That, in a nutshell, is the new view of luxury where less is more, and we need less if it is the very best. It represents a positive attitude to life. And that brings us back to the fundamental value that the M&C Saatchi company stands for: "brutal simplicity of thought." Its website says, "It is easier to complicate than to simplify. Simple messages enter the brain quicker and stay longer. Brutal Simplicity of Thought is therefore a painful necessity." The brutal simplicity for luxury marketers is that they have to earn their place in the customer's closet, as in the case of a pair of shoes; or at their table, as in a bottle of wine; or as their travel partner, as their hotel or airline. They must align their values with those of their customers to earn their business.

Key lessons to embrace for the future: Values are the foundation for lifestyle branding and marketing

It is not good enough to be simply a luxury brand representing the ultimate in quality, workmanship, design, and exclusivity. Many luxury brands today have a new goal to become a lifestyle brand—one that aligns its values and aspirations with the group it targets in its marketing. It is no longer enough for luxury brands to present a lifestyle ideal to which they want their target customers to aspire. Rather, they need to understand the lifestyle that their customers already have, and use the values and priorities that guide and direct the customer in pursuit of that lifestyle to forge connections with them.

Lifestyle marketing is not about demographics or income; it's about values, priorities, and ideals. This investigation into the lifestyles of affluent luxury consumers, the facets of their lives, what they hold dear, what they value, can help marketers find a new way to connect with their target customers. Here are some final thoughts:

You need to engage the whole person

Affluent consumers are passionate about their lives, their families, their careers, their finances, their place in society. They are also passionate about shopping and luxury brands. Luxury brand marketers need to care about the many facets of their luxury consumers' lifestyle, what they care about, what they value.

The affluent are empowered consumers

The affluent consumers' power comes not just from having money, but from their knowledge and experience as shoppers. These consumers invest their valuable time—their most valuable currency—to learn more, to be smarter people and smarter shoppers. In marketing to these customers, you need to provide them with more than just a product or service. You need to provide insights and knowledge that will support them in their lifestyles and help them become better shoppers, better consumers. You have to become as smart about affluent consumers as customers are about their favorite luxury brands, retailers, companies, and ways of doing business.

These are business people, they apply their business acumen to their lives

First and foremost, affluent consumers are incredibly savvy about money. They know what they have and where it is all going. They are good money managers and have learned that they can actually live one or two rungs up on the income ladder simply by being better, smarter, more savvy consumers.

The affluent consumer is in a constant search for value. Being a value shopper doesn't mean buying the cheapest thing. This customer is willing to pay more—sometimes lots more—if the value is there. But they know how to assess value and put a price tag on what something is truly worth to them.

Luxury brand marketers must understand the many facets and dimensions of value in their product categories, among their competitors both up and down market. They must deliver more value to this customer, not necessarily the cheapest price, but always the best quality, and do business in an ethical, honest, and moral way.

part 4

Rainmaking in the Luxury Drought

chapter 13

A Perfect Storm Has Hit the Luxury Market: How to Transform Your Business and Your Marketing for the Future

The world is big now. If you continue to think in the same way, you'll restrict yourself to a small world

—Miuccia Prada

The consumer market in the United States has been hit by a rare combination of consumer-driven shifts that threaten to significantly downsize the luxury sector throughout the next decade. The demographic shifts toward an older customer base came just about the same time as the recession marked the beginning of the luxury drought. Then the brutal reality of the recession with its negative impact on the wealth of affluent consumers resulted in people asking questions about what they really needed as opposed to what they wanted to buy. They found it increasingly difficult to answer in the affirmative for luxury. Just as people started to ask hard questions about their luxury indulgences, a critical mass of aging affluent consumers simply decided enough was enough, and that a temperate pragmatic approach to their lifestyle was in order.

Affluents are questioning the true value of luxury. They wonder whether they need to spend so much money for expensive brands that really aren't all that much better than mass-market brands. Increasingly they are deciding there are better things to do with their money than to spend it indiscriminately. In recognition of that fundamental shift in values and priorities, editors at *Time* magazine dedicated their April 27, 2009 cover to "The New Frugality." They wrote, "The recession has changed more than just how we live. It's changed what we value and what we expect—even after the economy recovers." As mentioned earlier, Merriam-Webster named "austerity" the word of the year in 2010, based on the sharp spike in searches of its online dictionary.

As I have talked with industry insiders, my colleagues, and the people I interviewed for this book, many held the opinion that *Time*'s "new frugality" and Merriam-Webster's "austerity" are mere blips in the consumer culture. They believe that once unemployment returns to a more normal 5–6 percent and after the recession fades in memory, consumers will go back to their old ways, their old habits, the old retail playing field, and indulge once again. I don't buy it. I have talked with scores of affluent consumers and every three months I survey 1,200+ affluent luxury customers. They continue to be skeptical about the foundation on which the traditional luxury market is based.

They say, who needs more when we already have more stuff than we know what to do with? Who needs to buy the best of the best when the better will work just as well and cost one-tenth of what the best does? What really matters when you have to carefully budget your limited time to get more, get ahead, move up? Who pays the ultimate price for that luxury lifestyle? You do and your family does. The older people get, the more they realize time isn't on their side. They can no longer afford to trade off their precious time to make more money to get more things. They inevitably make new and different choices about their work, their lifestyles, the things they need vs. the things they want. Then the marketers of luxury goods and services lose as their customers the affluent, who are the only ones who can afford what they have to sell, as they focus on personal happiness and fulfillment, rather than on accumulating more material wealth.

Luxury marketers: Meet the customer in your future

Marketing starts and ends with consumers. If we keep our eyes on the prize, getting and keeping our customers, all the other issues about our businesses, products, brands, and strategies will resolve themselves. Throughout the first three parts of this book, we've delved deeply into the changing demographics, psychographics, and purchase behavior of the affluent consumer. In this section we put all those pieces of information together to help you transform your business, your marketing, your products, your brands, and your strategies to align with the customer of your future.

Step 1: Integrate consumer insights

Integrating insights about consumers, learning what they need, what they want, what they desire, and where they are going, is the first step in the process of putting the luxe back into luxury. You have to understand the demographics, psychographics, and purchase behavior of your current and future target customers and make those insights the platform on which to create a new vision of luxury. Before we get to the inspiring and innovating parts of the puzzle, let's review the key findings that we must integrate into our thinking.

- The most important consumer insight is that the luxury market is never going back to the vibrant boom period it experienced in the early years of the 21st century. Americans' appetite for luxury was fueled by their perception of growing wealth. Their homes were escalating in value. Their investments, 401(k) and other savings were rapidly growing in value. They felt wealthy and spent accordingly. However, with the recession, all that wealth disappeared and people had to adjust their spending to their real incomes instead of their perceived wealth. With an average income of about $170,000 among the top 20 percent of U.S. households, that doesn't leave a lot of money for indulgences after everyday expenses are paid.

- Fewer young affluents and more older affluents means that luxury marketers have a smaller number of potential high-income consumers they can target until about 2020. Even once the Millennial generation reaches the window of affluence marked by high levels of income, the jury is still out on whether they will crave the same brands, the same types of luxury goods and services that their parents and their older siblings did.

- Affluents are making different decisions when it comes to shopping, buying, and consuming. They are shopping in new ways, using the technology to empower them. They have learned that they can live one or two steps up the income ladder, simply by being careful with their spending. In the past, luxury consumers gained power by the amount of money in their wallets. Today affluent consumers gain power by how smart they are. They know where to shop and how to get the best deals.

- The new luxury-consumer mindset is to hold and not squander. Today's affluent consumers are in a persistent search for real value that frequently can be satisfied by purchases at many different price levels. They don't need to always buy the best of the best, when good or better purchases at half, one-third, or one-tenth the price will do. This is bringing real and meaningful competition to luxury brands and the mass market.

- One-size-fits-all marketing for the affluent consumer segment won't work. There are five different and distinct personalities, each characterized by different motivations, different priorities, and different attitudes related to their luxury lifestyles. We have to stop using "aspirational" as the catchall term to describe them.

Step 2: Inspire your customers, your employees, your self.
Stop thinking *aspirational* when it comes to the luxury consumer market —think *inspirational*.

The words we use to talk about our customers, to think about our businesses, to plan for the future powerfully influence the conclusions we come to in our thinking and planning. I'm convinced that the word "aspirational" is a term that has done and continues to do more harm to the future of the luxury market than any other. My research shows that about 20 percent of the overall affluent consumer base is aspirational. But aspiration and all that the term implies doesn't apply to 80 percent of the total luxury consumer market. By so freely and indiscriminately using that term to describe their customers, luxury marketers lose the impetus and motivation to do the hard work to build their brands. If aspiration is the key to getting people to buy their brands, marketers only need to create dreams to which people can aspire. We find page after page of *Vogue* magazine ads showing beautiful young, skinny "glamazons" modeling luxury brands with the brand logo displayed most prominently.

The overuse of the term "aspiration" and "aspirational" in this business of luxury is damaging to marketer's view of their customers. It assumes that the desire for their brand or product is already there. Merriam-Webster defines aspiration as "a strong desire to achieve something high or great *or* an object of such desire." Marketers need to start using and thinking of "inspiration" and "inspirational," defined as, "*b:* the action or power of moving the intellect or emotions *c:* the act of influencing or suggesting opinions."

The smart luxury customers of today and tomorrow aren't going to buy luxury brands because beautiful people have them. Smart customers need specific reasons to buy a luxury brand and to justify paying so much more for the brand than a competing premium or mass brand commands. It isn't about image or status; they buy because they believe that the luxury brand is better for them and their special needs than the mass-market alternative. Yes, it is about superior quality, but "quality" is also overused in marketing circles. Marketers need to probe with their customers to uncover the many dimensions that quality represents in their product category and brand. For some product categories and some consumers, quality is defined by rarity, workmanship, special services, and fit; for others quality is about color, complexity, lasting performance, and timelessness. The marketer's inspiration lies in delving deeply into the many dimensions that describe and define the brand and the product, then using those specifics to create a narrative that will inspire the customer to buy.

For each brand, each product, each consumer, quality means different things, but it is that special something that justifies a person paying $1,500 for a *best-of-the-best* bright yellow patent leather Dolce & Gabbana satchel handbag versus a look-alike *better* bag from Dooney & Bourke for $345 or a "look for less" *good enough* Nine West model on sale for $19.95. When all things are perceived as equal, affluents will not spend a penny more than what they perceive the item to be worth. To succeed, luxury marketers need to face the truth that aspiration isn't going to cut it anymore. They must focus on inspiring their customers to buy their brands by building their products' perceived value that justifies a customer's decision to pay more. They need to build a case why, for example, the Dolce & Gabbana handbag is $1,155 better than the Dooney & Bourke look-alike version, and it has to be more than simply the status value of the D&G brand logo. Or they need to figure out clever ways to price that $1,500 bag at a more reasonable $795, without changing the fabrication from leather to fabric.

Marketers need to recognize that for today's smart shoppers, there is a kind of status in finding a great deal and making a great purchase—what I call "anti-status." Bluefly.com is an exclusive online discounter of high-end designer fashion that has expertly tapped the mindset of the bargain-hunting shopper who takes pride in finding the best for less. The company's CEO, Melissa Payner, who reported a 17 percent year-over-year growth in profit for 2010, says, "Bluefly has always been the go-to destination for luxury goods because people are forever looking for designer brands at a good price. It's always been our focus and we excel at bringing our customers the designer products they crave at a significant value."

• • • • •

Marketers Need to Think More Like
Consumer Reports than *Vogue*

You need to put substance before image and prestige in the marketing mix. *Consumer Reports* lays outs the pros and cons of different products based on objective criteria. Unlike *Vogue, Consumer Reports* puts substance before image and that is the new way luxury brands need to start thinking about communicating with their customers. The brand messages in *Vogue* are almost exclusively aspirational and image-focused. Putting the luxe back in your luxury brand requires that you dial back on the image and status messages, and amp up the substance, or the facts and figures that give a person a real reason to spend more for the luxury label.

Today's resistant, over-exposed, highly educated, and super-savvy affluent consumers are not looking for image or status display when they buy a luxury brand. They want measurable, quantifiably superior quality and product experience when they trade up to a luxury brand. For years the mantra in advertising circles was "Sell the sizzle, not the steak." But today, when you are promoting luxury, you need to swing the pendulum back and focus on selling the steak along with the sizzle.

Fortunately today's luxury brands have many more ways of communicating with their target customers than print advertising vehicles like *Vogue*. They can take their message directly to consumers in ways that support the fact-based, substance-over-image marketing messaging that I advocate. We'll explore those new mediums a little later.

· · · · ·

How Leo Schachter Diamonds Listened to Consumers to Give Them a New Reason to Buy Diamonds

We started with the consumer to try and understand what the consumer cared about at that moment in time. We were digging for insights that could generate new product design.

—Anne Valentzas, Leo Schachter Diamonds

In the luxury market no category is more luxurious than jewelry, since nobody ever really *needs* to buy it. Also, no purchase is more emotionally charged and culturally driven than the purchase of a diamond engagement ring. It often represents the first real luxury purchase any young man, or couple, makes. Because consumers come to this purchase with a lot of trepidation, the industry has propped up the purchase of a diamond around four key objective measures of quality called the 4Cs: cut, color, clarity, and carat. Young men and their future wives study up on the 4Cs, learn how each factor impacts price, and try to figure out how to trade off a little bit of clarity for a little better color or lesser color for more carats. As much as the industry tries to make a diamond purchase more scientific, the process still awfully confusing.

That's why I valued sitting down with Anne Valentzas, former vice president of marketing at Leo Schachter Diamonds, to learn how Leo Schachter discovered a new way to look at and evaluate diamonds that puts a consumer-centric spin on this most daunting of purchases. While Leo Schachter still rates its diamonds according to the 4Cs, it introduced a new measure, *brilliance*, that customers can see and experience. Customers no longer have to look through a loupe and, as an untrained novice, try to read features that only a trained jeweler can see.

Anne explains, "We train sales people not to start the dialogue around the 4Cs, but rather about the customers' relationship with the diamond, and what they are trying to communicate with their loved one through the diamond they are going to purchase. A consumer may want to have the conversation about the 4Cs, but we ask her to take a step back and tell us about what she values, how she is going to wear it, what she wants to see. Inevitably, what she wants to see is a beautiful diamond and that is measured in brilliance—the fire and sparkle of the stone. Brilliance is actually a function of cut that produces a diamond that is visibly brighter than other diamonds of comparable carat weight, color, and clarity."

Rather than talking to customers about cut and the other Cs and trying to explain what each means to the untrained eye, Leo Schachter translated the concept of cut into what that really means to the consumer: how brightly the diamond shines. The customer has a reason to buy a Leo Diamond: the unique Leo cut means more brilliance and anyone can see that one stone sparkles more than another.

Starting with the consumer first and design second translates into success for Leo Schachter Diamonds in the midst of the recession

Leo Schachter Diamonds not only innovated by giving consumers a new and more meaningful way to measure quality in a diamond, but it also went against standard jewelry practice to focus on consumer needs and desires. Anne points to the Love's Embrace line as one that started with consumer insights that led to a distinctive design. "Rather than start with a design inspiration, it started with consumer inspiration and design followed. The truth is consumers love diamond jewelry, but what they need is a justifying narrative to help provide an excuse for purchase. We used consumer insights to find a justifying narrative that best meets consumers' needs. This is a process that is common to consumer-packaged goods, but doesn't operate in this industry. Luxury brands typically want to carve out their own unique space driven by their own creative vision. They seem to be terrified of doing consumer research. But that is where we started when I came to Schachter in the fall of 2008."

Anne warns that luxury brands need to learn lessons from their mass-market counterparts to remain competitive. She says the time when a creative director at a luxury brand could force his or her vision on the consumer is over. "I think the consumers still look up to the vision of the creative designer at a luxury brand where you expect them to have more vision than you do. But the marketplace is getting more complex and the brands will have to become more sophisticated in the way they operate. We will have to work harder to get consumers' attention. We are going to have to be more strategic. The marketing has to become more customer-driven. For luxury brands it isn't about leading the customer or following them anymore, but it's about partnering, having a dialogue with your customers. As a designer, you still have your vision and customers respect and want your vision, but they have a lot of important perspectives to share too."

Anne closes, "Whether you have a household income of $25,000 or $250,000, the consumer mindset is the same; diamond jewelry is primarily given as a gift of love. So as marketers we are looking at different ways to dimensionalize what loves means and how to express that love through diamond jewelry. And that's why we need to listen to our customers, because we are all going to have to work harder to convince them to part with their dollars. You have to give them more meaning. That's where the gift of diamond jewelry comes in. It isn't about adorning yourself; it's about something that is much more meaningful. It says, 'I care about the ones that I love.'"

• • • • •

Step 3: Innovate

Innovation distinguishes between a leader and a follower. —Steve Jobs

Companies often ask me to help them in ideation sessions by acting as the "luxury marketing expert." More and more I find mass-market companies want to leverage themselves into the luxury market space. Knowing these companies, their marketing savvy, and their willingness to invest whatever it takes to move up market, I counsel luxury brands to think about their businesses in new ways and move outside their comfort zone into other areas.

Innovation is a challenge for any company, but especially for market leaders who want to defend their turf. Frankly I think being a new entrant into an established market space is a far better place to be than to be the market leader, the "big dog." The new entrant can redefine the playing field, turn the leaders' defensive moves against them, or play a new way to attract a customer that is looking for a new, innovative solution, rather than the same-old, same-old. The dominant competitors have invested too much in playing the game the old way and are often extremely resistant to change. They don't want to take the risk.

As the new entrants take aim at the established luxury players, the "big dogs" in the market may well be done in by ingrained and old-fashioned attitudes best exemplified by the following statements I hear often in luxury marketing circles, "Well, after all, they aren't our competition," or "They really aren't true luxury." In other words, they feel safe in their "true luxury" domain, but I am putting everyone on notice: This attitude will doom your business in the new consumer-powered marketplace.

The secret for luxury brands to defend themselves is to stop thinking like the big dog and start behaving like a little one. The big dog always loses when he tries to run with the faster, smarter little one.

Luxury marketers need to be committed to innovation and true trans-formation. Too often ideation sessions turn from imagining new ideas into problem-solving exercises focused on figuring out ways to offer up the same solutions to the same customers in virtually the same way. Big dogs feel more comfortable tweaking old ideas, not imagining concepts that would make a real difference.

It's easier for companies to come up with new ideas than to let go of the old ones.
                                                    —Peter Drucker

The challenge for luxury brands is to innovate around ways to change the playing field, to explore ways of meeting a new luxury consumer in a marketplace that operates under a new set of rules. Essential to innovation is exploring the possibilities. Earlier we looked at BoltBus, a perfect example of a game-changing innovator transforming the market for inter-city bus travel. While bus travel is hardly luxurious, Bolt brought luxury to its customers and made inroads among the kind of highly educated consumers who will be luxury marketers' targets when their incomes catch up with their smarts. BoltBus is noteworthy because big dog Greyhound Lines created it by thinking and acting like a little dog.

Other examples of how big dogs lose when they ignore the little dogs until it's too late include—

- The big dog Blockbuster, now taking its last breath, beaten by Red Box on the one hand and Netflix on the other.

- Borders, the first to innovate with "big box" book stores, now entering bankruptcy as Barnes & Noble thrives by envisioning a new way to sell the same thing, and Amazon comes at them delivering the same product but in a totally different format.

- Or Bed Bath & Beyond, the big dog that now owns the home furnishings retail space, having done in its chief competitor Linens & Things. The retailing world is ready for an innovative and expansive type of home furnishings retailer that has never been thought of before. The market is there for the taking by someone who can imagine the possibilities, and not just try to beat Bed Bath & Beyond at its own game.

• • • • •

Derrick Palmer, InnovationPoint, Helps Companies Uncover New Value in Their Brands Through Innovation

There's no shortage of good ideas. What's lacking is the will to implement.
 —Derrick Palmer, InnovationPoint

As co-founder of InnovationPoint, a consulting firm focused on "strategic innovation," Derrick Palmer works with companies to bring the chaos that often results from innovation "to clarity," as he describes it. InnovationPoint offers its clients a process to guide and direct the erratic nature of innovation. At each step along the way, it offers checks and balances to bring the best and brightest innovation ideas to market on an established timetable. The danger in all innovation projects, as Derrick describes it, is "to have an innovation process that delivers more than just a binder full of bright ideas that sit on the shelf."

He explains, "When it comes to innovation, most companies have no trouble generating ideas. The tough part comes after that: prioritizing the most promising opportunities, getting people inside the company to embrace and support those ideas, and then committing to action in the face of internal resistance and uncertain outcomes. That support requires what I call 'strategic alignment.' If you don't take the time to align the organization's key stakeholders around new opportunities, at the end of the day the ideas will just sit in that binder and nothing will happen."

Another aspect of the innovation process that Derrick finds frequently overlooked is industry trend foresight. "Most companies work hard to understand the needs of their customers. But if you only take the customer's perspective and don't look at where the world overall is going, you only have half the picture. Henry Ford said, 'If I'd asked what my customers wanted, they would have said a faster horse.' Ford looked at the future and realized that emerging technology would open up entirely new avenues for the world of transportation. Certainly listening to customers is very important, but it is not enough. For luxury brands, this includes things like emerging payment processing technologies, mobile shopping, the evolving economic climate, changes in consumption patterns of luxury goods and demographic shifts. All these factors have to be incorporated into innovation mix."

I asked Derrick about any special challenges when it comes to innovating classic, heritage luxury brands, many of which have been around for a hundred years. He gave a very pointed answer. "There's good news and bad news. If you've got a name like Louis Vuitton or Chanel you really have something very powerful to take to market. But successful luxury brands may face significant internal resistance to change—sometimes there's an arrogance that comes from what I call 'the tyranny of success.' Long-term employees often say: 'We've been successful for over 100 years, and our formula works, so why do we need to change or take risks?' Combine this view with the 'don't rock the boat' mentality of senior execs and managers whose compensation is tied to delivering predictable quarterly results, and you can see why companies are reluctant to innovate."

Derrick stresses that while luxury companies may resist innovation, there is danger in not innovating, not evolving. "All brands have to stay relevant. They need to take look at where the world is going. Right now emerging markets like China and India obviously look very inviting to these brands. They know these nouveau riche consumers are eager to buy Western goods. But it's more complex than that, because at the same time, consumer tastes in the core (U.S.) market may be evolving. Big brands constantly face this question of balance: maintaining the core business, while concurrently moving into new high growth opportunities. On their journey of innovation, they must look critically at a wide array of emerging trends—both in their existing (core) markets and also in emerging ones. Managing the trade-offs and getting through the tough decision are very much part of the innovation process. And it can be pretty tricky."

Derrick suggests companies in the luxury space look outside their vertical market and beyond their competitive set to get fresh ideas and approaches for innovation. "An upscale company looking to innovate should try to find analogies in other industries and study what other companies have done. For example, we worked recently with a credit-card company. You'd imagine that they would bring in a bunch of accountants and think about ways to do credit cards better. We did that, but we *also* brought in *external* subject matter experts from a wide array of completely unrelated industries to inspire their thinking with very different perspectives. You need to broaden your point of view. If you are an upscale travel company, for example, there may be lessons to be learned from how an automotive company (like BMW) is tapping into the wisdom of its customer base; what a fashion brand (like Louis Vuitton) is doing to position itself for future growth; or how a logistics company (like FedEx) is transforming distribution models in the food & beverage industry. That kind of "out-of-industry" divergent thinking often brings fresh sparks of innovative thinking."

Derrick advises companies to scout out new ideas anywhere and everywhere that they happen, especially from sectors that aren't directly competitive or what he calls non-adjacent worlds. "People are enamored by Apple as being tops in innovation. But I look at a company like Procter & Gamble as being right up there too. Here is a company with an army of MBAs and a strong bench full of vibrant and young marketing and branding specialists, but they also have the wisdom and the humility to recognize that all the smart people in the world aren't on their payroll. So P&G has developed an innovation approach called "Connect & Develop" that looks outside the company and invites small companies, scientists, and inventors to present innovative ideas with which they can partner to create new products."

Derrick offers a final thought on how luxury companies can face new competition from unexpected quarters. He points out, "One of the common pitfalls in innovation is 'the rush to convergence.' In other words, companies are operating under all kinds of performance pressures, and often want 'the answer' by noon. My job is to slow the process down, to help impatient people look for breakthroughs by taking the time to think divergently. A head of a Fortune 200 company once told me, 'You know, we're really good at implementing bad ideas.' This is a common pitfall for a lot of companies anxious to race to a decision. This often means they end up with obvious ideas that are not exactly earth-shattering. Divergent thinking takes time, but if you're looking for the real breakthroughs you have to be willing to enter into an ambiguous world of uncertainty, and explore ideas that aren't immediately obvious. For sure, your competitors are looking at all the obvious stuff too, so you need to take it up a notch or three."

You can learn more about the Connect & Develop innovation program at www.pg.com.

• • • • •

Burberry is recognized by *Fast Company* for innovation

Burberry is one heritage luxury goods company being rewarded by its customers for its willingness to innovate. *Fast Company* magazine listed it as one of the 100 most innovative companies for 2011. Burberry gave a new twist to its iconic check, taking it undercover and making it less prominent in many of its designs. It also introduced the Burberry Prorsum line that raised the brand's credibility in fashionista circles. (*Prorsum* is the Latin word for "forward.") The company has drawn notice for how effectively it has embraced electronic communications, including social media through its highly regarded *Art of the Trench* website, where it invites ordinary people to post pictures of themselves in their Burberrys. The company was among the first to simulcast runway shows online and setup iPads in its stores so that customers could order runway looks immediately. With sales now reaching $2 billion, the 155-year-old brand is reinvigorated because the company fearlessly interpreted its heritage and tradition for its future customers.

Now let's turn to look at the innovative new opportunities available to inspire your customers of the future. It is through innovation that you will be able to make rain through the next decade of the luxury drought.

Rainmaking in the Luxury Drought
#1 Enhance the Quality of People's Lives

A man's life does not consist in the abundance of his possessions.

—Jesus, Luke 12:15

As marketers, our single biggest challenge is to look at our products, our services, our brands, what we are trying to sell, in a totally new way. If we are working on a brand or in a company we believe in what we are trying to sell. We like it, we think it is valuable, worthwhile, important, so therefore the customer must also. But that is rarely the case. We need to step outside our own world, our own prejudices, our own belief system, and take an unbiased view of our luxuries. We have to strip our marketing messages and our brands down to their core, and then build them back up in a totally fresh, transformative way. What you will find is that no matter how fine your products or services, or how much you believe they are important to people, they totally don't need it. Once you realize that nobody needs any of the luxuries you have to sell, then you are on your way to making money. You'll gain a new respect for your customer and that is where marketing must begin.

As a researcher I am fascinated by the study of happiness. Beyond subsistence consumption, food, clothing, and shelter, we buy products and services to increase our happiness in meaningful, measurable ways. Presumably the pursuit of a luxury lifestyle and all that it means will make us happier, more fulfilled individuals. We are happier driving a Mercedes-Benz than a

Ford Focus; we are happier with a Sub-Zero refrigerator, Wolfe range, and granite countertops than with a basic kitchen with Kenmore appliances and laminate countertops; we are happier drinking Moët & Chandon from a Riedel glass than we are drinking a no-name cava or prosecco from a paper cup. But not really, not always, not necessarily.

The entire consumer economy is built on a simple idea: Material things will make us happy and more things will make us happier. Cross-cultural happiness research has shown that after people succeed beyond a certain subsistence level, their happiness does not go up measurably with rising incomes. Recent research also suggests that people have a certain innate happiness "set point" that doesn't vary much as circumstances in their lives change. Part of this innate set point is a function of how they measure their happiness. Do they tend to define themselves and their values intrinsically based on their internal reference scale (more experiential) or extrinsically based on external measures, such as financial success, social standing, or material wealth (more materialistic)? Those who are more intrinsically-oriented tend to be happier than those who view themselves in comparison with others or outside factors.

How we experience happiness also has to do with how we experienced it in the past. People adjust or adapt to certain standards of living, experiences, and circumstances. This is called the hedonic adaptation. We initially gain pleasure from a new acquisition or a new experience, but then we adjust and the initial happiness wears off. Happiness then seems to relate to newness and disappears with continued consumption.

As happiness pertains to income, some research suggests that happier people tend to make more money so they can afford to live a more luxurious lifestyle. Other research finds that people gain happiness through achievement. The more they achieve, the more they want to achieve. They are never satisfied. Once they have achieved something, they want to achieve even more. This is called the theory of "rising aspirations" and it holds for material goods and services, but also for many immaterial things like career achievements. For example, a promotion tends to make us happier, but then it sets up an expectation and aspiration for further promotions. For those interested in learning more about happiness and how it relates to economic matters, see the paper by Bruno S. Frey and Alois Stutzer, "What

Can Economists Learn from Happiness Research?" published in *Journal of Economic Literature*, October 2001.

Whenever I talk about luxury in my research with consumers, what it is and how they feel about it, I get one set of answers. When I talk about happiness, I get another set, with very little correlation between the two. It is this dichotomy—that luxury isn't happiness and happiness isn't luxury—that led me to the research work of Thomas Gilovich of Cornell University and Leaf Van Boven of the University of Colorado. In 2003 their research found that "people tend to derive more enduring satisfaction from their experiential purchases than their material purchases."

In subsequent research, Gilovich, working with Travis Carter, found that people tend to be less satisfied with their material purchases and are more likely to "ruminate about the other options they might have chosen." Experiences on the other hand are more satisfying or more happiness-producing because "our experiences become our memories, they are more truly a part of the self than are possessions." Experiences "are less easily undone or mentally exchanged for something else. Mentally exchanging an experience involves deleting a part of the self, something that people are understandably reluctant to do. Experiences therefore tend to be experienced, remembered, and evaluated more on their own terms, and less in terms of how they compare to alternative experiences." (See Travis J. Carter and Thomas Gilovich, The Relative Relativity of Material and Experiential Purchases, *Journal of Personality and Social Psychology*, volume 98, issue 1, January 2010).

As luxury marketers we need to understand that experiences will inevitably trump material goods. Spending $1,500 for a quick three-day vacation with your honey will always be a better use of your money than spending it on a handbag, suit, television, or anything you can have and hold. Therefore, should all of us involved in marketing luxury goods just pack up our bags and go home? Not yet, because there is opportunity. Many purchases fall somewhere between material and experiential. By understanding and exploiting the intersection of the two, marketers will find opportunity in the luxury drought. They need to turn their luxury goods into experiences.

The specifics of how you can turn your luxury good product into an experience differ for each product category and each specific brand, but the springboard for any marketer is to be inspired to change the dialogue they have with their customers and prospects. Rather than presenting your brand as just a better thing, for example, a higher-quality watch, think of ways to translate your better thing into an experience, a Patek Philippe watch that is passed down through generations, connecting father to son, mother to daughter, a thing to be treasured as an heirloom from one generation to the next.

Make shopping an experience, too

Another source of inspiration is an essential understanding that customers experience shopping. Thinking of ways to transform your customers' shopping experience with your luxury brand can pay big dividends in surviving in the luxury drought.

A product brand that translates things into an experience is American Girl dolls. Now owned by Mattel, American Girl was founded by Pleasant Roland, a former teacher and publisher of educational books. A trip to Williamsburg, Virginia, gave her the inspiration to create a line of dolls combined with books that would "celebrate girls." The idea was to combine play with learning by creating doll characters who lived in challenging times in American history. The storybooks gave context for each doll character and were sold first in bookstores. In effect the books built the "buzz" for the 1986 launch of the luxuriously priced play doll line sold exclusively through a mail order catalog. The company exploded through viral marketing long before anyone thought of social media or the internet. The product line also included a line of doll accessories, which enhanced girls' play experience, and the company's coffers.

But what is outstanding about American Girl is its stores. The first appeared on Chicago's Miracle Mile, followed by another on New York's Fifth Avenue, right across from Saks. In all, the company has expanded to nine locations. The American Girl Place stores are the ultimate in experiential shopping. The stores, of course, sell dolls, doll accessories, and matching girl outfits, but each store also hosts a wide range of special events including crafts, doll hair styling, grandparent days, book signings, and sleepovers. They even take girl parties to local attractions, like ice-skating at

Rockefeller Center or a Shedd Aquarium trip in Chicago. A café offers tea parties, lunches, and dinners where girls can host parties that include their doll "friends" who also are given seats at the table. The stores also feature a doll hair salon and photography studio where girls can have portraits made with their dolls.

The American Girl Place is a true destination, not just a store selling doll stuff. It involves and engages customers, giving them many different ways to interact and become part of the experience. Shopping becomes secondary, or an adjunct, to the overall experience at American Girl Place.

Giving shoppers a reason to be there, besides shopping, can make such a difference. That's why Saks' flagship Fifth Avenue store has several dining alternatives, plus the excitement of an entire floor large enough to have its own zip code devoted to shoes. It's also behind the addition of an exclusive restaurant to the new Ralph Lauren Paris boutique. The opportunities to turn shopping into an experience are endless. It just takes imagination. Take a suggestion from Derrick Palmer's innovation playbook and study tangential businesses and brands to find creative sparks to transform your brand into an experience for the customer.

• • • • •

Larry Korman on Succeeding in Marketing Luxury Strictly on a "Need to Know" Basis

There is a new luxury and it has to be unpretentious. It has to fly under the radar.
—Larry Korman, president, AKA Hotel Residences

Larry Korman, co-president of AKA Communities along with his brother, is the scion of a real estate family that extends back four generations. Since 1909, the company founded by Larry's great-grandfather, Hyman Korman, and now headed by Steven Korman, Larry's father, has built more than 30,000 single-family homes, and 12,000 apartments and town houses, along with six million square feet of industrial and commercial space in Pennsylvania and New Jersey. Recognizing a lack of upscale extended-stay hotels in New York City, the Kormans saw an opportunity for an innovative concept that is called AKA Hotels Residences. "We were operating Korman Suites in Philadelphia during the 70s and 80s. Then our Fortune 500 companies asked us to bring our offering to New York City and AKA was born."

Larry explains the concept behind the AKA hotel experience, "We've taken a furnished apartment and evolved it, enhanced it, and honed it for a luxury audience. We found that when senior executives or celebrities visit New York City, they prefer a real home away from home with a spacious living room, full kitchen, and luxuriously-appointed king-sized bed. They do not want to be hassled with a crowded lobby or be out on display. They value the privacy of an intimate lobby as well as being able to reside in their own condo-quality suite. AKA provides the preferred locations, to be where the guests want or need to be. When it comes to people having to leave home and the comfort of their family for a new location, they want to be in a place that for a time can feel like home."

AKA Hotel Residences are located near such key New York locations as Central Park, the United Nations, and Times Square. The Kormans are working to open new AKA properties in lower Manhattan and in Los Angeles. "We offer luxury but without the overt opulence associated with names like The Four Seasons, The Ritz-Carlton, or The Plaza. Additionally, AKA doesn't have the daily check-ins and check-outs, small rooms, and crowded lobbies." The typical AKA guest stays for a couple of weeks to several months, with corporations or movie production companies often picking up the tab.

Larry explains that AKA's success is based as much on what their brand is not, as on what it is. "We are neither a boutique hotel, nor an extended-stay hotel. We aren't a condominium, or a furnished apartment. We are AKA. We serve guests looking for a place where they can feel at home when they aren't at home; they want an environment where they can be part of a community. But we're like a boutique hotel in that we appreciate contemporary style and design. We're like a furnished apartment in that we have spacious suites. We are like a condominium in that we have full-size kitchens with Sub-Zero refrigerators. We are like a hotel because we offer

Frette linens and robes. We have to explain all of these things, because we are unique. We have to let people know that AKA is a legitimate luxury option and help them understand the truly unique qualities that our brand has to offer."

To spread the special story of AKA, they rely on getting the word out to the people who need to know. He says, "Diane Keaton was booked to stay with us at AKA Sutton Place through her production company. She was so impressed with our concept that she told other people in the entertainment industry who trust her taste, so they came at AKA, too. When Florence Henderson came to New York for a week to sing at Feinstein's, she stayed at AKA. Ms. Henderson then recommended AKA to her friend Judith Sheindlin—better know as Judge Judy—who was coming to do a two-month engagement in New York, and she stayed at AKA. We find that the longer someone stays at AKA, the greater the 'wow' factor becomes and the more they spread the word about AKA as the new luxury alternative to the staid luxury hotel."

AKA satisfies its guests' needs for quiet, restrained, unpretentious luxury that delivers on the values their high-profile guests want: convenience, comfort, peace, and anonymity. Larry says, "We offer extremely high levels of luxury and service, but we don't shout it. Some of the top celebrities and business leaders stay with us because it meets their sense of refinement. They prefer not to stay in the presidential suite at The Plaza, for example. Their staying at AKA instead makes a statement about who they are and their connection to the community. They relish flying under the radar but still enjoy a special experience that meets their needs both personally and professionally."

• • • • •

chapter 15

Rainmaking in the Luxury Drought
#2 Sell to a Doubly Bifurcated Luxury Market

I think the idea of mixing luxury and mass-market fashion is very modern—wearing head-to-toe designer has become a bit passé. It's a new era in fashion—there are no rules. It's all about the individual and personal style, wearing high-end, low-end, classic labels, and up-and-coming designers all together.

—Alexander McQueen, fashion designer

As a researcher and marketer in the business of ideas, I know the value my clients place on simplicity. They want me to simplify the message, turn complexity and nuance into a PowerPoint slide with three key takeaways, or tell them the story in a 140-character tweet. Unfortunately when it comes to putting the luxe back in luxury, the future for marketers is full of complexity and nuance. In the past, people who bought luxury were more alike than different, making the job of marketing to them fairly straightforward. Today, the luxury consumer market has segmented, split into smaller and smaller micro-segments that share little in common with other micro-segments. While we may drive to find simpler solutions, you have to get ready to sell to a doubly bifurcated market, one that is split into a four-quadrant matrix defined by age and income. The simplicity-minded want to make only one of these factors the key; most marketers will opt for income as the critical factor, but income alone can't do it.

Marketers offering goods and services at the high-end space need to understand the four key segments of their target market defined by age and income. Then they need to figure out in which space or spaces they want to play. Different strategies and business models will apply depending on their answers.

➲ Figure 15.1 A Doubly Bifurcated Market

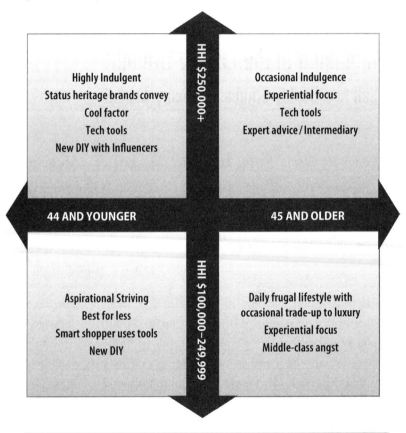

Source: Unity Marketing

High income/young age are most indulgent, but thin on the ground

This is the ideal customer profile for any true luxury goods brand: the young shopper with means. Easily influenced, drawn to the status that luxury brands give, these young shoppers crave what you are selling. They yearn for luxury brands and service providers that have a "cool" factor. They use technology to find out what's hot and what's not, and listen to the circle of friends and chums to keep current. They are empowered by the new do-it-yourself, and don't need to pay to get expert advice. When it comes to a fashion decision, a home decorating dilemma, or a travel question, they have the power in their hands to get the right answer.

For marketers that want to hang their hats on an affluent and young clientele, the only problem—and it's a big one—is that there will be relatively few of them until the close of the decade. Not that there won't be lots of opportunity for those brands that find traction in this space, but it will be a slippery slope for brands that make any misstep that makes them "uncool." Marketers who target this customer segment have to give up a measure of control over their brands. This customer will be in the driver's seat, pushing the brand into the future, but that future may not always be the place where the brand's managers want to go.

Marketers who want to succeed in this space must be masters of the social media universe and all things high-tech. They will need an army of 20-somethings monitoring the web and feeding it with meaningful content to excite the fan base and generate buzz. They need to listen carefully to young customers and engage them in dialogue. In this world of social media, brand marketers must let their customers school them in what they want and need from the brand. Frankly, it will be a scary place for many luxury brand managers to venture into. It will take quite an adjustment, to give over so much power to the customer. But that is a price you will have to pay to target this young, affluent customer.

There are dangers inherent in taking this tactic beyond how quickly young people's tastes change. Both Peter Francese and Derrick Palmer alluded to the fact that the younger generation often turns away from brands favored by the older generation. The younger generation wants new brands to call their own, not their parents' or grandparents' brands. So heritage brands must reinvent themselves in the image that suits a younger consumer. Clearly the long-standing heritage brands have been able to do this as the generations shifted during the 20th century, but the rate at which heritage brands must reinvent themselves in the 21st century may be entirely too fast for an older generation of brand managers.

The essential qualities that luxury marketers must master if they choose to target the high-income young person is adaptability and willingness to change—qualities that are inconsistent with the corporate culture many heritage luxury brands have built.

Lower Income/Young Age craves the best for less

If there is a demographic segment that can be generalized as "aspirational," knowing my caution in using this term, this is it. In general, young people have a heady appetite for luxury living, but usually they don't have the money to pay for it, so they can rightly be called aspirational. They express that aspiration by working harder, striving to grow professionally and monetarily to achieve a lifestyle that gives them the luxuries they crave. With their champagne tastes but beer budgets, they use all the tools at their disposal to find the best for less. They are smart shoppers who know how to work the system and have figured out how to stretch their dollars to live a couple of rungs up the income ladder.

As customers, they are going to push for a bargain, wait for the sale, and hold out until the price is right for them to buy. The flash-sale sites that have exploded in the past year will continue to grow as an avenue to reach this type of customer. These bargain-hunting young people will also favor brands like H&M, Zara, and Uniqlo that embody their "best for less" sensibility, and discount retailers with an upscale vibe, like Neiman Marcus' Last Call and Last Call Studio, Saks' Off Fifth Avenue, and Nordstrom's Nordstrom Rack. This aspirational young consumer is the prime target for dispersion brands, i.e., those more affordable brands make up the extended family of luxury labels like KORS Michael Kors, and MICHAEL Michael Kors brand. Such lines give admirers a way to participate in the Michael Kors' design sensibility without paying the ready-to-wear Michael Kors price. Other examples are DKNY, the lower-priced version of Donna Karan, or Simply Vera Vera Wang for the discount store shopper. Coach's Poppy line is another example of how a venerable, mature, high-end brand can prosper by meeting this younger, not yet affluent, but aspirational type of customer in his or her world.

As we look across the landscape of dispersion brands like Coach's Poppy or MICHAEL Michael Kors, the strategy is to build a connection with youthful customers. As these young people mature into affluence, hopefully, they will transfer that loyalty to the higher-end brand. However, this is where marketers may be making a mistake. If a consumer is happy and content wearing her MICHAEL Michael Kors outfits, you can't assume that she will trade up to the high-end Michael Kors line just because she gets a little more money in her pocketbook. This is a shopper that takes great pride in being smart. She is skilled at finding good value and getting more for less. If MICHAEL Michael Kors satisfies her now, it is likely to satisfy her later. Further, with rising affluence, she may well reject those brands she associated with in her in more aspirational days and pursue new luxe brands that haven't been created yet.

Two Younger Generations with Different Tastes and Sensibilities

You need to think about the responsibility you have when you buy something. You're buying the manufacturing process, the resources, the energy, the shipping cost. Don't talk to me about global warming and corporations, because every time you buy an item, you're [having an] impact on the planet.

—Peter Walsh, *Clean Sweep*, TLC's clutter-busting reality show

It is important to remember when targeting affluents under age 45, that we are talking about two different and distinct generations who grew up in different times and with different experiences. Today, the largest share of young affluents is from the cohort called Generation X, born from 1965 to 1979 and today aged 31 to 46. As the decade progresses, Millennials, born from 1980 to 1995, will become a more important cohort in the luxury space. Overall, both younger generations will demand lower price points and leading-edge internet strategies that include both social and mobile media. They will be citizens of the world and a global perspective. Both are highly educated and expert at using high-tech tools to power their lives. As a whole they are keen on sustainability and the environment.

But Millennials, in particular, look with distrust on consumption and the having-and-getting-more lifestyle. Therefore, marketers must recognize that these young consumers come from two very different generations who have different experiences and will have different expectations once they reach affluence.

Finally, I am not altogether sure Millennials will be as materialistic as Baby Boomers were when they hit their peak levels of earnings. Today's young people inhabit a virtual universe powered by the internet and their imaginations. As long as they have the latest and greatest high-tech tools for access to that virtual world, they may not need to be grounded in the material world, as had every generation before them. Who needs to own a $2,000 Michael Kors dress, a $1,200 Chanel bag, and $800 Manolo Blahnik shoes to wear to a party, when you can rent them for less than 10 percent of the price from RentTheRunway.com?

Since happiness doesn't come through material things anyway, these smart young people may well see that the value of ownership is overrated; they won't need to own something fine to enjoy using it or wearing it part time. Surely not all in this younger cohort are going to pursue a post-materialistic, virtual-luxury lifestyle. But if a critical mass of Millennials opt out of ownership and accumulation, many marketers and their brands banking on attracting that critical mass in the future could be left high and dry. People will argue that no generation before has rejected materialism, but then, no generation before has had so many ways to inhabit a virtual world. I think it is wrong to draw hard and fast conclusions about what members of the younger generation will do with their money once they reach affluence. Rather, we should err on the side of caution and figure that, on principle, they will reject following the same path their parents took.

• • • • •

High income/mature age marks the consumer who can have it all, and probably does

The good news for luxury marketers is that this segment can absolutely afford to buy the best of the best, but the bad news is that high income mature consumers don't feel the need to spend to that level. As they reach age 55 and start thinking about retirement, they have probably accumulated enough stuff, and their lifestyles revolve more around downsizing their lives than getting more. Time becomes more of a luxury, whereas money is fungible and they will trade off money for time. They simply don't need or want so much of what many traditional marketers, especially those offering luxury goods, have to sell. They will trade up to luxury occasionally, rather than regularly, such as on a major home remodeling project or for a special event that calls for a new outfit.

They will trade up only when it really matters, and when it really matters most is on their experiences.

• • • • •

Beat Steiner's Bella Coola Heli Sports Offers Luxurious Non-traditional Luxury

To our higher-end clients, it's really not about the money, even if they are spending $67,000. It's about the time.

—Beat Steiner, Bella Coola Heli Sports

Beat Steiner, founder along with partner Swede Mattsson of Bella Coola Heli Sports, says they are, very simply, "ski bums." He says, "We came to Whistler (in Canada) fresh out of university because we wanted to ski as much as possible. Then we got involved in ski-mountaineering programs and expeditions. In 1989, we made a snowboard movie that hit when snowboarding was just coming into the market and people were starting to buy VHS tapes. It did quite well. Burton Snowboards saw it, liked it, and started sponsoring us, which led to bigger and bigger productions. While I was doing documentaries for other companies, we just kept coming back to Bella Coola because the snow was so good for skiing and filming. All we wanted to do was spend the rest of our days filming in Bella Coola, but we knew that soon somebody would catch on and do heli-skiing here and tie up the helicopter. In 2002, we applied to operate a heli-skiing company to lock it up so we could continue filming. Because of our years in the ski industry, we put the word out to our contacts that we were open for heli-skiing. The first year we had 40 people come ski with us. Word-of-mouth spread the news, and the next year we had 50 percent growth, then 100 percent, and it just took off. Now we don't do filming any more; I'm running this heli-skiing business."

Beat and Swede found the basic pieces on which to build a heli-skiing business in place in the valley, including a classic wilderness lodge built in 1929, an airport close by, a hospital, and helicopter bases. He says, "All the infrastructure was in place to make it happen without actually having to invest a lot of money. But what's most important is the skiing experience. People fly from Europe and all over the United States to get the powder experience we can give them. That is the 'Holy Grail' of skiing. The only way to get that is to use a helicopter to reach the nice deep powder snow. People are willing to pay the premium."

Beat explains this experience is perfect for the more mature skier who doesn't want to be jostled around by the young people at traditional ski resorts. "The deep powder cushions, so you don't get the groomed snow, even ice, that's hard on older knees. You actually are floating on snow and that is one of those magical experiences. Powder skiing is the best skiing experience. Add in the helicopter, which is a great and exciting way to travel and you have this pristine, wilderness environment." While Beat doesn't use the term "luxury" to describe it, clearly the experience is the ultimate luxury for his clientele, many of whom pay dearly to experience Bella Coola Heli Sports.

> *"People, especially Baby Boomers, have done the Four Seasons. They've been pampered, they've done the spa, fine dining. But what they are looking for now is a memory, a unique experience that impacts them personally."*

For Bella Coola Heli Sports the primary customers are wealthy individuals in their forties who have done the traditional luxury vacations. His customers want a unique experience. "After they have done all the pampering stuff, they want a truly unique experience that impacts them personally. You're not going to remember your spa treatment, but you are going to remember the perfect four or five thousand foot descents on new snow. Yes, people still want a nice dinner and a fine bottle of wine at night, but during the day they want to experience something. I've literally skied every corner of the planet, including lots of different heli-skiing locations, and what we found here in Bella Coola, we knew was magic. The value for our clients comes down to the skiing experience."

Beat concludes, "I personally have always believed that time and experiences are the most valuable commodities. It's not about owning. All of our high-end business clients work hard and have very little time, and they are going to run out of it. Everybody knows that you never know how much money you might make in life, but you are damn well going to run out of time. We offer our clients a unique opportunity, a very special experience."

• • • • •

Lower income/mature age face an uncertain future

While this segment, with incomes from $100,000–$249,999, lives better than 78 percent of all American households, they feel increasingly poor. They look at their low levels of savings, having traded off spending for saving when they were younger, and the potential insolvency of Social Security and Medicare, and they are afraid of the future. They are opting to put more money aside now and forego excesses in which they might once have indulged. On a day-to-day basis they live a frugal lifestyle, with occasional luxurious purchases, and most of those are tied to experiences or luxury goods that deliver an experience.

As with the younger, less affluent consumer segment, these consumers will turn often toward best-for-less types of retailers. On an individual basis this segment seems to offer little opportunity to luxury marketers, but collectively they represent a strong potential market. They may not have much discretionary money, but they actually have a lot more than those who are lower on the income scale. They will continue to work after the normal retirement age of 65. As a group, they have a younger sensibility and they really believe that 50 is the new 30. It is this core belief to which luxury brands can market.

• • • • •

Help Aging Baby Boomers Capture
the Vibrancy of Their Youth

The thing the sixties did was to show us the possibilities and the responsibility that we all had. It wasn't the answer. It just gave us a glimpse of the possibility.

—John Lennon

There is still a lot of work that marketers can do with maturing Baby Boomers and the first thing is to recognize that they are still in their prime. While the first of the boomer cohort turned age 65 this year, they are an extremely young 65, much younger than what age 65 was for previous generations. They have a good 15 to 20 years of life left in them and will reward with loyalty marketers who make them feel young and vital. Hollywood, which never had much use for the actress over age 45, except in mother or grandmother character parts, has finally discovered the power of the maturing woman. Stars like Helen Mirren, Goldie Hawn, Meryl Steep, Susan Sarandon, Michelle Pfeiffer, and Glenn Close represent a totally youthful and vibrant image of the Baby Boom woman.

Today we are seeing more marketers thinking seriously about tapping this potential maturing, but not-yet-old consumer market. Talbots has brought back 1960s super-model Linda Evangelista and Chico's recently tapped Boomer model-icon Lauren Hutton for a catalog campaign. Such choices should be expected from these two apparel companies since their core demographic is a more mature woman.

I see an opportunity for higher-end premium brands to target older, but younger-thinking consumers. The key will be to focus on value and affordability with experiential brands that help them recapture their youth. A good example of a brand that does just that is Lucky Brand Jeans. Its boutiques are a time capsule from the 1960s. The Lucky boutique connects with Boomers who want a bit of nostalgia, and it connects with Millennials who are fascinated by the period, the music, and the vibe. Critical for Lucky Brand Jeans' continued success and advice to other brands that want to tap the potential of the maturing Boomer generation will be providing solutions that fit Boomers' lifestyles. For fashion brands like Lucky that will mean adapting sizing to the realities of a 50-something figure, and printing price and sizing labels so reading glasses aren't required. How about providing seating in the store and changing rooms so customers can take a load off?

* * * * *

chapter 16

Rainmaking in the Luxury Drought
#3 Create Great Expectations to Support Price Premiums

What is a cynic? A man who knows the price of everything and the value of nothing.

—Oscar Wilde

Getting the price right for today's luxury consumer is a delicate balancing act. Marketers must work competing psychological factors to keep perceived prices low enough to make sales, yet high enough to enhance the luxury allure of the brand. You have to find the right price that enhances the luxe value, but at the same time makes it affordable to a wide enough base of customers to maximize profits.

We have already talked about the psychology of setting an extremely high price for a brand's best-of-the-best offerings to bolster and support a strong price for its better lines. The high price ultimately determines the range of customers who can afford your best-of-the-best range. Hermès, by setting its prices extremely high—its Birken bag starts around $5,000 and ranges up to $50,000—defines the demographic segment it aims to attract: the very rich and super wealthy. However, while Hermès sets the standard for high prices in its class of leather goods, it bows to the financially less well endowed by offering scarves, key chains, small leather goods, and fragrances at relatively more affordable prices. Yet even these lower-priced offerings are priced at the very top of the range for these product categories. For example, scarves are available for far less than the $500 to $700 that the

Hermès brand commands, but by offering these prices, Hermès can attract a much wider range of affluents to participate in the brand. Whereas few can actually afford a $5,000 Birken bag, many more can own an authentic Hermès scarf if they are willing to spend $500, even when $500 is a steep price to pay.

Right pricing your luxury product or service for the next decade will take a combination of art and science. The art is to set prices high enough that the brand is made more desirable. The science is about studying the impact of price on demand and adjusting accordingly. In my days in direct marketing where price testing was the norm, it often happened that a higher price won over a lower one in terms of maximizing response rates. A recent study of the effect of pricing on wine explains how a higher price can build greater expectation of value and ultimate satisfaction. In the study people were given tastes of wine from a bottle they were told cost $45 and from a bottle that cost $5 and asked to rate the quality of the wine. What they weren't told was that everybody was served the same wine from the $5 bottle. Not only did the subjects rate the higher priced wine better, but the researchers even wired up the brains of the subjects and found that pleasure centers in the brain were stimulated more when they were drinking what they believed was the higher-priced wine. Commenting on the study, researcher Baba Shiv, an associate professor at the Stanford Graduate School of Business, said, "We have known for a long time that people's perceptions are affected by marketing, but now we know that the brain itself is modulated by price. Marketers are now going to think twice about reducing the price."

Direct marketing also proved that simple response rates alone weren't the most important factor in setting the final optimum price point. Rather, the best price was determined by which price maximized profitability, not only response. It sometimes happened that the price that got the highest response rate didn't win when measuring profitability. In other words, you can't always make up lost profits by increasing volume alone. In the wine example above, I'd guess that many more people would buy a bottle of wine priced at $5 than at $45; but if that same wine could be sold at $45 and produce a much higher profit margin for each bottle sold, maybe the optimum price point to maximize profits would be to sell fewer bottles at

$45, even if more money had to be invested in marketing that $45 bottle of wine.

People's perception of quality and value and what they are willing to pay for a particular luxury good or service is very much influenced by what they expect to receive. It is often the context in which a purchase is made that sets up expectations, which then influence how customers measure quality, value, and ultimately price. Another important study related to how people's expectations ultimately influence how they perceive value comes out of Cornell University's Food and Brand Lab, headed up by Dr. Brian Wansink. Dr. Wansink invented the dieter-friendly 100-calorie snack packs and as a result of his research, he discovered that people eat fewer calories if their meals are served on smaller, rather than larger, plates.

To study how people's expectations affect their actual perceptions, his team of researchers set up a dining experiment. They went to the local warehouse market and bought frozen fish, green beans, scalloped potatoes, salad fixings, and chocolate cake. One group was served the food on paper plates in a no-frills restaurant setting with a plain menu description of the meal (i.e., fish fillet). A second group was served the same food but in a fine dining setting with white tablecloths, candles, and floral centerpieces, and china and crystal place settings. The diners were presented a menu with a fine dining description of the food, (i.e., panko-crusted Mediterranean sea bass fillet). The only difference in the two meals was that more attention was given to the food's presentation for the second group, but the actual food was exactly the same. Each group of diners was asked to rate their meal on a scale from 1 to 10. The no-frills group rated their meal 3.4 points, while the fine dining group rated their meal an average of 8 points. The experiment showed that people's expectations strongly influenced their overall experience. The no-frills dining group had low expectations of their meal and that is just what they experienced. The fine dining group expected a better quality meal and that is just what they got. Wansink explains, "Anything that raises expectations will make people like it more."

Ultimately, finding the right price for luxury goods or services is less about money, and more about meaning. The meaning is the sum of the expectations built in the minds of consumers. Raising expectations of quality, value, superior performance, better workmanship, fine fabrication or materials, design excellence, or engineering will allow brands to stretch their prices upwards, and push customers to pay more for luxuries.

• • • • •

In Marketing, Perception Is Reality

You can powerfully influence how your customers perceive quality and value by simply changing their expectations. To raise those expectations, you must pay careful attention to the cues and clues that communicate luxury quality, which will ultimately result in greater customer satisfaction and value. What these scientific studies show is that marketers can't fear building high expectations in their customers' minds; rather they should be afraid of not building expectations high enough if they want their customers to experience the high quality and superior performance they strive to deliver. I don't mean to say that the actual quality of your luxury product or service doesn't matter, but creating the perception of high quality is certainly just as important as actually creating the quality in the first place. Marketing creates the value perception in the customer's mind, which is money in the bank for any luxury brand.

You must influence consumers to perceive your brand, product, or service as offering better quality, both objectively and subjectively. The objective criteria are facts and figures about the product, how it is made, and from what materials. The subjective criteria include expert ratings, peer or customer reviews, brand icons, and heritage stories.

When we talk about pricing, we can't ignore discounting. Many retailers and marketers responded to the recession by offering frequent sales and deep discounts. In a Unity Marketing research study conducted in Beverly Hills, ground zero for the conspicuous consumption lifestyle, we asked highly affluent luxury shoppers if the kind of discounts offered in the luxury market during the recession would ultimately hurt those brands. The good news is, our research shows discounting doesn't have to do long-term damage to the brand. As one Beverly Hills shopper said, "What changes the perception [of the luxury brand] is when the quality starts to drop."

Discounting isn't necessarily putting a nail in a luxury brand's coffin, but it can create a perception that the brand isn't worth the full asking price.

That is why brands like Louis Vuitton and Hermès, which didn't resort to discounting in the recession, came out ahead. They heightened consumers' expectations by the very fact that they didn't discount and made news because they were not discounting.

• • • • •

How Ilori Commands $25,000 for a Pair of Sunglasses

We've all noticed that sunglasses, those $10 plain-Jane functional specs we pop on in summer along with our $5 flip-flops, have gone seriously up market and fashion forward. One of the primary companies behind the luxury sunglass trend is Luxottica Group and its new Ilori sunglass boutiques. It has flagship stores on Rodeo Drive and in New York's Soho district, and boutiques in more than 10 states plus Puerto Rico. I sat down with Michael Hansen, vice president and general manager of Luxottica's Luxury Retail Group, to talk about how the company created a luxury eyewear model in Ilori.

"Ilori started in 2007 as a plain old sunglass retail model, but has now moved into the luxury arena with glasses for all occasions, including by prescription. Ilori still sells sunglasses at the entry price point of Ray-Ban, around $200, but this year we sold a special limited edition priced at $25,000. Today we carry a wide range of designer brands, including Chanel, Tiffany, Bulgari, Prada, Versace, Oakley, Ferragamo, as well as up-and-coming designers like Derek Lam, John Varvatos, Thierry Lasry, and Jason Wu."

Mike explains that Luxottica studied luxury handbags as a model of how to transform the sunglass category from a purely functional necessity product into a luxury fashion statement. "We spent two years in research before we launched Ilori. We studied a lot of different categories, but handbags were the closest. Twelve to fifteen years ago, a high-end company would introduce one style a year in multiple colors with price points in the $200 to $500 range. That changed as companies started to launch handbag collections similar to ready-to-wear, at least twice a year and using new styling and better materials. They discovered how far the styling, exclusive materials, and the story lines could take them in terms of price. Hermès found that its Birkin bag could be priced over $10,000 and have a waiting list to buy it. That was when companies realized that there's no ceiling for the true luxury consumer."

Mike continues, "In order to move the sunglass category to where the luxury handbag or shoe or watch category is, we had to treat our products as fashion accessories, not just as a functional item. The fact is when you meet people for the first time you look into their eyes. That is the first thing you see, before you see their shoes or their handbag. And we saw that people weren't really dressing their eyes. We did interviews and asked women about how many pairs of shoes were in their closet and they'd have 30 to 50 or even 100 pairs of high-end shoes. But if I asked about sunglasses, they'd have only one or two and mostly in black, brown, or tortoise. We saw the opportunity to enhance people's looks by moving sunglasses out of the functional area into a fashion accessory, as has been done with shoes, handbags, or jeans."

As the company moved its sunglass brands into a new space, it found that the competition became fiercer. Now it was competing in the trendy world of fashion, not in a commodity or purely functional category. "We are all competing for the same dollars and the competition has increased. You have to ask how you are going to win, when you have so many stores selling so many products and a lot of it at discount. It all comes down to the experience. If you are going to win competing with Neiman Marcus for the luxury fashion customer's dollar, for example, you've got to offer a unique experience. You've got to give people a reason to buy so they feel like it is worth it to pay a higher price in your store. You have to create an experience that makes them feel a level of engagement and a commitment to your brand. Ultimately it is not only about product, but also about the relationship with the sales associate and the experience in the store," Mike explained.

In effect, Ilori delivers a luxury experience to its customers through the designer brands it carries, the service it provides, and the access it gives its customers to the latest fashion trends. "Ilori is an African word that means 'special treasure.' We built the brand around that meaning, so our stores are designed like an art gallery with each style displayed like a piece of art. At least 10 percent of our product is exclusive or limited edition, so it's a place that designers can launch new collections. We tell stories so we are constantly helping the customer understand the latest trends and the new story lines in sun wear. We personalize everything, from the sunglasses to the service. We make a ritual of how we present the eyewear to the customer, in an Asian fashion, using two hands underneath the product. As part of the celebration process, we offer the customer a signature chocolate made by a French chocolatier, branded for Ilori and packaged as part of the experience. Each of these things on a stand-alone basis is not unique, but done consistently it makes a difference. Gracious service is what we do and it is not something I can honestly say is a part of the typical brand."

In closing Mike advises other luxury brands to focus on the service experience. "People are walking away from the typical stodgy luxury environment that is so ostentatious and not customer-friendly. In today's environment you have to deliver a personalized experience. Brands have to turn up their service; I think overall service levels are not where they need to be to be successful long term. There are always going to be luxury customers who want something better, with greater meaning. Luxury becomes experientially based, not product-based. As marketers we have to find ways to offer that exceptional service more efficiently."

● ● ● ● ●

Rainmaking in the Luxury Drought
#4 Speak the New Language of Value

To be successful today, you must touch base with reality. And the only reality that counts is what's already in the prospect's mind.

—Al Ries and Jack Trout, *Positioning: The Battle for Your Mind*

To heighten expectations around your brands, you need to talk to your customers in the new language of luxury value. It's all about aligning what the consumer values with your brand values and communicating that effectively. The right words communicate with your customer, but more importantly the right words inspire your customers and move them to action.

What "luxury" means to affluents

Let's start with the most important word, "luxury." It's a foggy term and like other foggy terms—quality and value come immediately to mind—luxury can mean totally different things to different people. It is emotionally charged as well, so it can turn people off. Luxury is defined by WordNet (a large lexical database of English words and usage maintained by the Cognitive Sciences Laboratory at Princeton University), as:

> something that is an indulgence rather than a necessity, lavishness, luxuriousness, opulence, sumptuousness (wealth as evidenced by sumptuous living).

Implicit in each definition is a personal, subjective judgment of what luxury means to the individual, specifically—

- What distinguishes an indulgence from a necessity for each individual?
- What is excessively expensive vs. just plain high priced?
- What is sumptuous living and how do you measure wealth by it?

There is no valid, widely accepted, objective definition of luxury. We asked highly engaged affluent consumers in focus groups to tell us what they believe luxury means in terms of their lifestyles. We found the definition of luxury varies widely, but it tends to be associated with higher quality, more expensive, more exclusive and special, more customized to the individual, and more personalized goods or services.

Luxury marketers need to drill deeply to understand customers' definitions of luxury in their product or service category in general and their brand specifically. They must learn what values and attributes best define and describe the luxury inherent in their product and brand. A one-size-fits-all description, like the term luxury, doesn't work any longer. Focus groups and one-on-one interviews are research tools that marketers must exploit to hear how consumers describe value and luxury. Then marketers need to feed back customers' words and phrases in their marketing communications, website descriptions, point-of-purchase materials, advertisements, and training materials.

• • • • •

Luxury Is Not Only What You Sell, But How You Sell It—Higher Levels of Service Are Expected with Luxury Purchases

Person-to-person communication is a critical component of the new language of value. Exceptional personalized service sets luxury apart from the ordinary shopping experience. Special service, more attentive and personalized service greatly enhances people's expectation of quality related to whatever they are buying. It makes customers feel special and makes them feel special toward the purchase. One luxury shopper in focus groups described the feeling of a luxury experience this way, "A higher standard of service.

Whether you go to the store, or your vacation spot, or go out for dinner. You are pampered a little bit, and you feel good."

The ability to personalize the luxury product or experience emerged as another key aspect of what transforms the ordinary to the extraordinary. The term "bespoke" was used in the focus groups. Traditionally bespoke was applied to custom-tailored clothing, but the term has been extended to a broader range of product and service categories. The emphasis in bespoke luxury is personalization of both the product and the service experience. As a result of that personalization, it is exclusive to the individual; it is something that not everyone can have, not that everyone would want it because it is created exclusively and personally for the individual.

The sales staff needs to understand how to communicate and deliver outstanding service. It isn't enough to say, "Good morning, may I help you?" It means taking time to observe customers, take cues from their dress, their appearance, the bags they are carrying, or any other focal point to make a personal connection. For example, a sales associate might say, "What great shoes you are wearing. I can see you like styles that are [classic, right on trend, comfortable, fill-in-the-blank]. Would you like me to show you something that would look great with that outfit or that would match your style?" Extraordinary service inspires confidence and trust. It is the foundation upon which brands create extraordinary expectations, which lead to an extraordinary experience.

• • • • •

Practice Subtlety in Logo and Branding

In a high-end vintage shop I recently saw a white Chanel jacket in great shape and in my size, priced at $500, so what stopped me? The prominent logo CC buttons. I won't wear anything with the label on the outside. For me, a prominent logo signals lack of confidence and a desperate need for status. Frankly, anyone in the know would recognize the look and cut of a Chanel jacket. I don't need to shine the spotlight on the fact, so I turned away.

I am not alone. According to research by Joseph Nunes and Xavier Dreze, professors at USC Marshall School of Business, and doctoral student Young Jee Han, published in the *Journal of Marketing*, "a significant segment of the population does not want to be branded, preferring to be understated . . . and is willing to pay a premium to have 'quiet' goods without a brand mark." I've heard it expressed by people in focus groups. They refuse to wear anybody else's initials on their clothes or they don't want to be a walking advertisement for a brand.

> *I love the t-shirt as an anti-status symbol, putting rich and poor in the same level in a sheath of white cotton that cancels the distinctions of caste.*
>
> —Giorgio Armani

Status is a bit of a sacred cow in luxury marketing, yet many luxury consumers in discussions rejected traditional forms of status in favor of an "anti-status," or "quiet status" perspective. Anti-status, as expressed by Giorgio Armani's appreciation of the white t-shirt, is the counter trend to status. It rejects external status and confidence gained by what one owns. Rather, true status comes from the inside and who one really is.

The new language of value demands subtle, anti-status branding messages. Think of the iconic bamboo handle on a Gucci bag or the Gucci horse-bit design rather than the loud GG; or the Chanel quilted leather bag (but without the gaudy CCs) or the totally discreet Bottega Veneta label. It is about finding ways to whisper luxury, rather than scream it.

• • • • •

Jim Sweet Carefully Picks Clients to Deliver the Right Value Proposition

Jim Sweet is owner and creative director for Terrace Views, an outdoor living design firm based in Denver, Colorado. His firm has enjoyed great success, as his affluent homeowner clients have wanted to add special outdoor features to their homes. "What's happening with the landscape industry right now is that every landscape job these days includes an outdoor room, an outdoor kitchen, water feature, fireplace, or fire pit. People are cooking outside, entertaining outside, relaxing, and even sometimes working at a desk outside. It has become a room without walls and everything you can do indoors you now can do outdoors," Jim explains.

With the rising popularity of outdoor living, combined with more people being able to afford multimillion-dollar homes, Jim's business faced a crossroads. "Most of our homeowners have homes in the $2 million range. We are facing a situation right now with a customer in a home like that who is using the internet to shop and he wants us to match that price. We are a design firm. We add value by helping homeowners make sure they don't make mistakes in their backyard, and by finding special products, fabrics, designs, and doing space planning. But all this homeowner wants is a deal. The other trend we see is do-it-yourself. The affluent, who used to rely on service providers to help them make decisions, are now doing it on their own. They are shopping online, shopping more locally to save. It's a bit of a game for them. We had a customer building a 12,000 square foot house who just resigned as chairman of the board of a major company, with multi-millions in net worth. He's beating everyone up on price. Everything is beginning to feel like a commodity. Luxury used to be a relationship business, but now people want something else."

The solution for Jim is to carefully vet his customers, picking those who value the customized solutions his firm provides. "We are trying to analyze and evaluate the customer. We have magnificently loyal customers, typically a little older and affluent, who value time as much as money. They don't necessarily have the time to shop all over. They want to be informed but they also value the service and the relationship. They value the follow-through after the sale that we deliver to them. We are looking to do fewer deals, but bigger ones with the right customers who have a compelling need," he says.

His warning to marketers, "If this trend continues with the affluent customer empowered and using that power as leverage, if they don't want to form a relationship, if they don't value design, and if they want to treat everything as a commodity and try to get the best deal, then it's going to be a tough time for luxury." That is why companies must either adapt to the new environment or find ways to attract the right clientele who value the luxuries you have to offer them.

"Our marketing and advertising model is very direct," Jim explains. "Our customers have to have a love of outdoor living. They have to have a sense of style and like good quality things. They have to have financial means, plus a compelling need, like 'our backyard is a mess,' or 'we're building a new home,' or 'we are renovating.' We track that through building permits and work with our trade partners. If we find a home that is going through a renovation, we jump in with direct marketing, phone calls, drop offs. Mass advertising doesn't work for us because if you attract mass it comes down to price points. We are narrowly targeted to those with a compelling need. There is a lot of competition out there. But you have to separate yourself by doing something that no one else can deliver and then find the right customer who needs that, wants that, and appreciates that."

Jim's final advice is straightforward. Luxury has to avoid becoming a commodity traded mostly on price. "We have to differentiate ourselves through relationships, through service, through products that are unique. The key is to give up the idea of bringing in huge droves. The key to surviving is clearly framing how you define your brand and your customers. That's why we developed an Internet Outdoor Living Design process, where landscape architects and interior designers work side-by-side. We bring the two together to create something wonderful for the client because we understand the complexities and how to integrate all these different elements."

• • • • •

chapter 18

Rainmaking in the Luxury Drought
#5 Master 21st-Century Technology Tools

Strong marketing campaigns in the 21st century are built on pithy statements of what a brand represents, rather than flashy technology, a rush to social media, or glib sloganeering.

—Jack Trout

By now I think the myth that luxury shoppers don't want to shop online has been debunked, yet I know that many corporate executives in charge of luxury brands still believe that the primary purpose of their websites and social media activities is to drive shoppers to the store. They also believe that luxury shoppers get a better overall brand experience in the store. Nothing could be further from the truth. Luxury shoppers are extremely busy people with demanding jobs and family responsibilities. For many, going to the store is a luxury they simply can't afford. What do they do when they need a new outfit, a new pair of shoes, or refill of their favorite skin care treatment? Go online, of course.

⤵ **Figure 18.1 Online vs. In-store Shopping**

Please think about how shopping online compares with shopping in-store. Do you . . .?

Enjoy shopping online more than in-store — 44%

Enjoy shopping online about the same as in-store — 45%

Enjoy shopping online less than in-store — 11%

Source: Unity Marketing

In a Unity Marketing survey among 1,237 luxury shoppers, 90 percent of those surveyed said they like online shopping at least as much as in-store (45 percent) or more than in-store (44 percent), leaving only about 10 percent who favor in-store shopping. If that doesn't make a luxury brand's online tools and applications a priority, nothing will.

Our findings show luxury consumers who were most active online shoppers were also people who spent more on luxury during the study period, including through any medium. Luxury marketers' best potential customers are those who also shop online. Therefore, marketers need to allow their best potential customers to do more than "window shop" online. But brands like Patek Philippe and Chanel, among many others, fear that selling their exclusive brands online will diminish the image of the brand. They are also concerned about counterfeiting.

What these luxury brands should fear more is making their goods inaccessible to affluent customers who choose to shop online or haven't the time to go to the store. All the research shows that the internet attracts the kind of high-value customers that luxury brands need. In the luxury drought, high-end brands can't afford to cut themselves off from an online revenue stream.

Social media has reached critical mass among affluents

As far as luxury brands are concerned, the case is closed on the question of whether to sell over the brand website, but more guidance is needed when it comes to social media or mobile strategies. First, let's look at the data. More than 80 percent of luxury customers surveyed have one or more social media profiles, with Facebook being by far affluents' social media destination of choice. But when it comes to their social media activities, connecting to or friending brands in the social media sphere is relatively low on their priority list.

Affluents' primary use of social media, by order of ranking:
1. hear what friends and family are doing,
2. share news with friends and family,
3. reconnect with old friends and classmates,
4. share photos, and
5. fun.

While many luxury brands are focused on social media as the next big thing, the fact is social media is not yet an important medium for affluents to use for shopping. Shopping-related uses, such as looking for coupons or exclusive offers, conducting pre-purchase research purchases, are used by fewer than 15 percent of affluent social media users. As of now, social media is currently not thought of often or frequently for shopping.

• • • • •

Social Media Is Used by Affluents Socially, Not Commercially—Luxury Brands Need to Go Undercover and Use Stealth to Connect

The race is on to social media. We all need to participate in it at some level for learning alone, but the strategies of how companies and brands can most effectively use social media to build their customer bases are still not clear. What luxury consumers say to me in focus groups is summed up by the comments of this woman, "Why should I use Facebook to buy a product or learn about a brand? I'd just go to the website." That, in a nutshell, expresses how people segment the online world: Websites are to buy and social media is to socialize. Brands that want to maximize their investments in social media to potentially build their customer bases need to use social media for stealth marketing, rather than direct marketing. Here are a couple of ideas.

Mobilize your fan base to spread your brand message to their friends

Friend-get-a-friend promotions are an excellent way to deploy the power of social media to build brand awareness and potentially convert lookers to buyers. People pay attention to news and views that come from their friends. A message sent to a friend is much more likely to be read than an advertisement, an email, or other marketing communication from a company. This recommendation is backed up by research: In Unity's study we found that the number one reason affluents connect with or friend brands on social-media sites like Facebook or Twitter is because they learned something interesting about the brand or company through one of their social media contacts.

Consider Audi. It used its Super Bowl advertising spot in 2011 to drive social media buzz through a contest. Social media activists were asked to mobilize their communities of followers to win $25,000 for the charity of their choice. They were asked to use the a Twitter hashtag tool to tweet a 140-character definition of "progress." The result: Audi's contest mobilized hundreds of thousands of social media mentions of Audi through Twitter, Facebook, and YouTube. Audi was one of the first luxury brands to use traditional advertising to generate social media buzz.

Create compelling and meaningful content about things in which your customers are interested

Brian Halligan, CEO of HubSpot, a software firm that specializes in inbound marketing techniques, has advice to brands that want to use social media to generate business: "The people who win will be thinking more like a content publisher, than as an advertiser." The key is using a brand's social media platform to deliver news that its customers can use, especially information that makes them smarter, better-informed shoppers.

The main reason why affluents "friend" a brand through social media is to gain access to discounts, coupons, and special offers. They also are highly motivated to friend a brand to learn about new products, interact with a community of like-minded people, and to access special exclusive content. Coupons may seem too down-market for some luxury brands, but giving customers access to exclusive products or content is very much in keeping with luxury lure. For example, Louis Vuitton celebrated its Twitter launch by introducing an exclusive Totally Monogram tote bag available only through the company website. This also marked the first time the company introduced a design online, as opposed to in stores. Its air of exclusivity was its greatest appeal to loyal Louis Vuitton customers.

A luxury brand's loyal followers can also use information about new designs, which many fashion brands are showcasing online through exclusive insider, behind-the-scenes views of fashion shows. A|X Armani Exchange is venturing into new areas with an A|X TV network spinning off the company's website with social media content. The network features fashion shows and a look at how the brand develops advertising campaigns. In the spirit of providing its customers with news they can use, the television channel also has a "How to Wear It" section to provide style advice and trend tips, and highlights ways its fashionista followers can build their wardrobes around key pieces. Essential to the implementation of the A|X video content is that it can be shared among friends. This brand is one of the first to innovate with the concept of seamless online shopping combined with social media video content.

Explaining the new concept, Patrick Doddy, SVP and brand director for A|X Armani Exchange, said about the young customers the brand attracts, "Shopping online and offline is still very much a 'social experience,' so giving our customers a chance to see new trends, get style tips from industry experts, and share this information with their friends is an easy and natural extension of their online behavior."

• • • • •

Social media is about building relationships, not selling products

⮑ Figure 18.2 Most Popular Facebook Brand Friends

Ann Taylor	Groupon	Microsoft	Silk
Apple	Gucci	RJ Nabisco	Sony
Audi	Harry & David	Neiman Marcus	Southwest Airlines
Bare Essentials	HP	Nike	Starbucks
Body & Bath Works	IBM	Nordstrom	Steve Madden
Borders	iTunes	Olay	Target
Chik-fil-A	J.Crew	Old Navy	Tide
Coach	Kohls	Oreo	Toyota
Cola-Cola	Kraft Foods	Pepsi	United Airlines
COVERGIRL	Lands' End	Philosophy	Victoria's Secret
Dell	L'Oréal	Pillsbury	Virgin America
Disney	Lowe's	Planter's Peanuts	Weight Watchers
Dove	M&M Mars	Ralph Lauren	Wendy's
Dunkin' Donuts	Macy's	Samsung	Whole Foods
Einstein Bros. Bagels	Marriott	Sears	Williams-Sonoma
Gap	Marshalls	Sephora	World Market
Google	Mercedes-Benz	Shutterfly	Yahoo

Source: Unity Marketing

As luxury brands develop a social media strategy, they need to keep their focus on their customers and their needs, rather than on the brand and its goals. When we looked in our latest survey at the brands that affluent shoppers have friended, the list was heavy on consumer packaged goods brands, technology, retail, sports, travel, beauty, and food. Only a few luxury brands were listed (i.e., Audi, Gucci, Mercedes-Benz, Coach, Neiman Marcus, Nordstrom, Ralph Lauren). Luxury brands should study the strategies of these most successful mass-market brands among affluent customers to get inspiration for their own social media efforts.

For mobile, think global, but act local

Finally we can't end our discussion of using high-tech tools to put the luxe back in your luxury brand without mentioning mobile applications. Mobile apps are the next frontier in the high tech landscape. Unity Marketing's January 2011 survey reported nearly two-thirds (60 percent) of affluents use a smart phone, such as an iPhone or Blackberry, and most of those users have also downloaded special apps to enhance their use. To date, weather, games, and social media apps top the list of their favorites. As with social media, the younger and the more affluent the customer, the more likely luxury brands are going to find them using mobile devices. Therefore, luxury brands that want to find and attract their best long-term prospects need to be on the forefront of creating mobile apps.

The greatest opportunity for marketers to use mobile is to catch people when they are out and about in their local community. For example, Point Inside offers an interesting mobile app for location-based advertising. Its shopping center application provides shoppers with interactive directories of mall interiors, level by level, and shows the locations of stores, restrooms, elevators, ATMs, and parking lots. Its Indoor Mobile Ad Platform lets retailers send information to shoppers while they are in the mall. Nordstrom uses Point Inside to promote its local store special events, such as the St. John Spring fashion show.

While marketers should focus mobile apps on enhancing the experience of their shoppers in their communities, brands also must think globally to extend these applications into all local points of contact with their shoppers. Nordstrom, with its 187 stores, is on the forefront of mobile technology as it implements a "think global, but act local" strategy. Nordstrom invested early to have all stores wi-fi enabled and now the company is deploying that technology to serve its customers better. By the end of 2011 the company will equip its sales staff with mobile devices. Customers in dressing rooms will be able to text or call employees to get a different-sized clothing item. No doubt, as Nordstrom deploys the technology, new ways of using it to enhance the customer shopping experience will be discovered.

In thinking globally about their mobile strategies, luxury brands must also integrate their mobile and internet strategies effectively. Most importantly that means optimizing the message for the smaller mobile phone screen. Chanel is a marketer to study. It recently launched a mobile-optimized website. Visitors who access the Chanel website from mobile phones are directly rerouted to a mobile-optimized site where they can search and browse through fragrance, makeup, and skin care products, as well as special offers and a store locator. Via mobile, Chanel users have all the same features from the original website maximized for the smaller screen, including being able to enter their email address to sign-up for Chanel's news and updates.

As a final thought, luxury brands need to incorporate their mobile channel story in all outbound marketing and communications to make customers aware of their brand-specific apps. That means including information about their mobile commerce on the company e-commerce site, in catalogs, in-store and point-of-purchase, and through advertising and social media like Facebook and Twitter.

• • • • •

How Saks Serves Customers Online

There has definitely been a mind shift in the country. People are thinking more about how they are spending their time, their money, thinking more about everything. That helps us because our customers are smart and they want to be smart about what they are investing in.

—Denise Incandela, president, Saks Direct

The recession was hard for most public companies in the luxury market, so when you find bright spots, like the consistently positive quarter-after-quarter postings from Saks Direct, people take notice. That's why I appreciated sitting down with Saks Direct's president Denise Incandela to talk about how her group achieved success in the face of the recession's headwinds.

Saks was one of the early adopters of the internet, going online in 2000. Its then company chairman and chief executive predicted in the *New York Times* that profit and sales from e-commerce would surpass that of the Saks Fifth Avenue store within five years. While it hasn't yet reached that level, Denise says that it has been the chain's number two producer for the last three years. She says, "We have been growing at 20 to 50 percent since we launched the website. We've taken some interesting twists and turns along the way to understand what the right e-commerce model should be and what the right organizational model should be. And we continue to think about how we should evolve over time. The industry overall has grown at a very fast pace and Saks.com has worked hard to stay at the forefront of the industry. We continue to evolve and change to ensure that we are offering the best product, the best customer experience, the best usability, and all the other components that make a successful website."

While the website is right behind the flagship store in sales, the Saks.com business is very different from operating a retail store. Denise explains, "Online we have a much younger, fashion-forward customer who is more item-driven than the store customer. The number one reason why people shop online is convenience, so you may shop in the store today and shop online at night."

Another key difference between the online universe and retail operations is how fast changes must be processed in each world. "Internet time is very different from store time. The internet changes very quickly, so we need to change our website every six months. We are continually reinventing ourselves," Denise says. "Shopping in a Saks Fifth Avenue store is a high-touch experience, whereas it's a self-serve experience online. It's a completely different paradigm. But we have to incorporate that customer service touch online, too, with our sales associates who are on the phone, emailing or live chatting, then there is the touch of the fulfillment experience, plus the usability of the site. So we have spent a lot of time testing different features and functionality to measure and track that, so when we roll out a feature, we are not shooting blind, but we actually know it is going to work."

The extremely fast pace in the online sphere keeps Denise and her team on their toes. "What happened five years ago is literally irrelevant today.

Everything has changed; portals have changed; search has changed; now we have affiliate marketing and comparison-shopping. Our marketing budgets and how we allocate dollars has dramatically changed. Right now we are having a hard time monetizing social media, but I expect that to change a year or even six months from now. What we love about this space is that it changes so dramatically in a very short period of time. The onus is on us to be willing to change our game and our approach constantly to get better," she says.

One of the recent innovations introduced online is a flash-sale concept called "Fashion Fix." Similar to Rue La La and HauteLook, Fashion Fix offers designer fashions at deep discounts on sale for only a day. Saks.com is also looking to significantly grow its mobile and international opportunities. In fall 2010, Saks.com rolled out product reviews and Denise has been very pleased with the feedback from both her customers and brand vendors. While she was initially concerned about how their brands might react, everyone now agrees that the value added has been tremendous. "Times are changing quickly," Denise says. "I remember in 2001 when European brands didn't want to come online because they didn't believe in it. And then they didn't believe in globalization. Now we are shipping to 91 countries. The world is changing and we are going to constantly be nudging our partners along with us to change as the world changes."

Denise sees her future customer as very savvy and discerning. Denise plans to keep up with her by reinventing, reimagining, reconfiguring the Saks.com business. "I think there has been a mind shift in the country. People are thinking more about how they spend their time, their money, thinking more about everything. That helps us because our customer is smart, and she wants to be smart about what she is investing in. So when you are talking about apparel shopping, that becomes, 'I want to invest in pieces that are going to last a long time, that are good quality. I want to buy an updated jacket that I can wear with three other things in my closet. And I want this new boot of the season that is going to make all of my skirts look even more fashionable.' Those are smart choices to be making, and I think our customer is going to stay smart," Denise concludes.

• • • • •

chapter 19

Rainmaking in the Luxury Drought
#6 Raise Corporate Social Responsibility

The world's leading brands are rightly judged today not just on the quality of their products and services, but also on the way they act in the community and toward the environment.

—Patrizio di Marco, CEO, Gucci

A well-developed sense of social responsibility and consciousness runs deep among affluent consumers. Whether this is out of a sense of guilt or more benevolent motives, the fact is affluent consumers account for the lion's share of the $277.4 billion charitable gifts attributed to individual contributions in 2009 by Giving USA. Further, in 2009 Americans increased their support of causes such as human services and emergency aid, health, international aid and relief, and environment and animal-related causes. In their giving, affluents are putting their money where their hearts are, marking a profound shift away from "me-first" to a "we-together" approach, to a new enlightened mindset of caring, sharing, and conserving. Affluent consumers' goals have shifted to a drive to enhance the quality of life, not acquire more stuff.

It is in consumers' desire to do good that luxury marketers can find a new, more meaningful and substantive platform upon which to connect with their customers. Everywhere you look, you find luxury brands supporting charities, getting behind causes, and instituting giving programs. Companies should not approach these efforts as marketing strategies and as a means to grow their businesses, but as ends in themselves. Affluents aren't going to buy your products or shop in your stores because your company supports a cause that they also support. However, these efforts do make the affluent customer feel good about making that purchase or shopping in your store, which is a good thing and ultimately contributes to the bottom line.

• • • • •

Ten Thousand Villages Makes Its Customers Feel Good Even as They Splurge on Themselves

[Sales] is the reason we exist as an organization—to try to generate income and jobs for our artisans.

—Craig Schloneger, Chief Executive, Ten Thousand Villages

Forbes magazine recently profiled feel-good, do-good retailer Ten Thousand Villages that has a footprint in over 70 upscale shopping areas. Ten Thousand Villages is a fair-trade business that exclusively sells artisan-made goods imported from underdeveloped countries. The secret of its success is people feel good about shopping at a Ten Thousand Villages store. The company fulfills its mission to promote economic development through crafts by giving back on average 21 cents on the sales dollar to its artisan partners, compared with the usual 1 to 5 cents of the retail dollar from other commercial channels.

Ten Thousand Villages has successfully tapped a profound change in affluent consumer psychology and as a result attracts a clientele made up largely of women who are highly educated and concerned about social issues. Luxury marketers today and in the future need to be attuned to this rising social consciousness and think about highly visible as well as more subtle ways that they can support their customers' desire to be socially responsible consumers.

• • • • •

Unity Marketing's research backs up the growing importance of social consciousness. More than 80 percent of 1,168 luxury consumers surveyed reported some level of charitable giving in the past year, including making a monetary donation, buying a product where a portion of the proceeds are donated, volunteering time, or attending a charitable event. Overwhelmingly they give to causes that they personally care about, with health causes such as the American Cancer Society and religious causes, such as Salvation Army and local churches and synagogues, at the top of their list. Charities working in the local community, such as United Way and local animal shelters, and children's causes, notably Make-a-Wish Foundation were also among those noted. Another cause growing in importance, especially among the affluent, is environmental and green issues.

Green is the new black—as in green marketing

Many corporate executives feel that "environmentalism" is little more than a fad that is not destined to last. They give lip service to green marketing and environmental issues, but they don't really take it too seriously. However, my advice now and into the future is to take it very seriously.

Affluent consumers, as the most educated people in the culture, are keenly attuned to environmental issues. They know that the typical American lifestyle that centers on personal consumption negatively affects our quality of life and that of generations to come. This awareness translates into the purchase decisions they make. While affluents still may hesitate to consistently trade off convenience or higher price for living a more fully realized green life, they frequently are willing to opt for the greener, more environmentally friendly alternative. I believe this tendency will grow in the future, which is why brands need to bring green marketing into their frame of reference.

A Unity Marketing survey among more than 1,200 luxury consumers found that three-fourths said that a company or brand's concern with the environment influences which products they buy. More than two-thirds said a company's green practices influence where they decide to shop. It's a trend toward responsible consumerism, not an over-the-top green lifestyle, but one where environmental concerns are increasingly entering into the purchase equation. Following fuel and energy shortages, the most important green issues for luxury consumers are renewable energy sources, protecting the environment, and water pollution.

Our survey also revealed that women represent the environmental consciousness in the household. Women rated nearly every one of the environmental and green issues surveyed as higher in overall importance than did men. This finding has powerful implications for luxury goods marketers targeting women. They buy the bulk of the household's consumables and are key in most other family shopping decisions. Luxury marketers across many different categories from fashion and beauty to home furnishings, electronics, and autos must build their green consciousness and implement green efforts. They need to recognize and reach out to their female consumers with focused, authentic, and responsible green efforts to stay relevant to this rapidly growing trend.

· · · · ·

The New Lincoln Hybrid Delivers Luxury Wrapped in a Green Package

We tend to think of customizing as adding things, but the modern form of customization is simplifying, getting rid of stuff that is irrelevant or not pertinent at the moment.

—Sheryl Connelly, Ford Motor Company

I recently helped Ford Motor Company launch the new Lincoln Hybrid by sharing with the press the importance of green issues among affluent consumers. Afterward I talked with Sheryl Connelly, manager of the company's global consumer trends and futuring, about why Ford felt now is the time to innovate with a luxury version for the Lincoln brand. Sheryl explained, "My job is to identify consumer trends and to understand how social and political shifts and technological advances are shaping the products consumers will want in the future."

The Lincoln MKZ is targeted to a luxury consumer who values substance over status. Everybody knows that using less gasoline is a good thing, but in the past when consumers were asked to pay more for more fuel-efficient models, they tended to opt for the lower-priced gasoline engine. In introducing the Lincoln Hybrid, Ford innovated by taking money—the traditionally higher cost for the hybrid model—out of the equation.

Sheryl explains, "One of the things about the launch of this new vehicle is we priced the gas and the hybrid vehicle at the same price point so consumers don't have to make that choice based on price. Hybrids came on strong when gas prices were volatile, but the point of pay off when it was cheaper to go hybrid vs. gas was hard to decipher. In this premium market it isn't about pinching pennies, it is about values and lifestyles and priorities. If price doesn't determine it, which would you choose? All things being equal, people are more likely to choose the green option, so that is what we are trying to do with the hybrid, take out that obstacle."

Sheryl explains that environmental responsibility is a core component of the Ford brand, ever since the days of its founder Henry Ford. "It is consistent with Ford's heritage. Henry Ford was a farmer; he was constantly looking for ways to do things in a sustainable fashion. It was Bill Ford, his great-grandson, who insisted that the company invent a hybrid vehicle. In the early days it was hard to build a business case for it. It is very expensive technology and we weren't sure whether the consumer would pay for it. But Bill said, 'I still want it done.' It was that leap of faith that put hybrid on the map for us. Then we decided we needed to offer hybrids across our portfolio; now we are moving it into our luxury segment."

Important to the overall success of Ford Motor Company is that it keeps reimagining its role in society. "Our CEO Alan Mulwally often describes Ford Motor Company as no longer a car company, but an electronics company. In fact our company will be a keynote speaker at an electronics conference two years running. It is changing people's minds about what a car can do for you, so we make investments into our SYNC platform that seamlessly integrates people's vital hand-held devices into the driving experience. You will hear us talk about performance and fuel efficiency; that is just the price of entry. But customers want to know what else a car can do. The real difference is in customized instrument panels. They engage the driver in ways that they haven't seen before. It reignites the customer's love affair with the car, a relationship that had grown tired. By the way, we tend to think of customizing as adding things, but the modern form of customization is simplifying, getting rid of stuff that is irrelevant or not pertinent at the moment."

Sheryl defines Lincoln's focus on the interior of the car and the over-all driving experience as discreet chic, which is in keeping consumers' new value-oriented mindset. "Luxury has morphed. Luxury used to be a statement of wealth, but today when you spend $90,000 for a car, a lot of people don't admire you; they think it is a foolish way to spend your money. When I think about marketing for the Cadillac Escalade, it is very in your face, aggressive, ostentatious. Some would say a vulgar display of wealth. Compare that with the Lincoln, which is about discretion, discreet chic, understated elegance. It is more confident. The luxury consumer today isn't buying to impress people, but they are buying what is right for me, what is uniquely suited to me."

In Sheryl's trend watching, she agrees with me that a new age of post-materialism is emerging where consumers give up the idea of owning more stuff in favor of new experiences. "I wholeheartedly agree we are going from being a culture of consuming materials to a culture of consuming experi-ences. Look at when videos came out and people collected whole movie libraries. That was material consumption at its best. Contrast that with today where owning a lot of stuff means baggage and clutter. Today you don't have to own, as long as you have access. Netflix gives you access without the issue of owning, maintaining, storing, or insuring. It is simplified. Or take Bag Borrow or Steal, or Rent The Runway, which are 'Netflix' for dresses and accessories. People recognize it doesn't make sense to spend $400 on a dress you are only going to wear once. It doesn't seem smart to spend $500 on a bag, if you only carry it a couple of times a year. It is not a good use of resources, both financial resources and physical space. You can rent those things when you need them. It is in keeping with a sustainable lifestyle. It means you don't have to produce as much with more people sharing a single item. It is a compelling business proposition," she concludes.

• • • • •

chapter 20

Rainmaking in the Luxury Drought
#7 Look to Emerging Markets

Our prospects would look grim without China and the other fast-emerging economies.

—Guy Salter, deputy chairman, Walpole British Luxury;
chair, China Luxury Summit 2011

The race is on to the developing markets: China, India, Russia, and Brazil. These markets are starting to see some real money being accumulated by those at the very top of the food chain. Underneath the very wealthy populations in each market is a burgeoning middle class, setting out on the road to material consumerism that the American middle class experienced in the post-war years.

A few years ago Unity Marketing did a study of seven global luxury consumer markets, including China, Japan, the United States, France, the UK, Germany, and Italy. We found, as have many other researchers, that affluent Chinese consumers are distinctly different in outlook and priorities than those in the States and the European markets. They are far more materialistically oriented and status conscious. Westerners have pretty much given up on the idea of conspicuous consumption, but it is alive and well in China and other developing markets where the wealthy want to distance themselves from the *hoi polloi*.

That is why it was no surprise to me that professor Joseph Nunes and his colleagues' research found that during 2008–2009 luxury branded logos gained more prominence as they worked to build share in developing markets. To reach consumers in places like China, India, Brazil, and Russia, where wealth is new and all the trappings of a truly luxurious lifestyle mean something, luxury brand marketers will need strategies and tactics different than those used in developed markets.

To understand the unique challenges and opportunities for luxury in developing markets, I talked with Amit Dutta, founder of Luxury Hues Consultancy Services (India). He was formerly vice president of marketing at American Express, where he led the transformation of the consumer card business in India. He also heads up the Luxury Marketing Council in India, which brings together the major players in the local luxury scene. Better than anyone else, Amit knows the Indian consumer mindset and helps luxury brands find traction as they enter this burgeoning and exotic market, which despite its growth potential is still fraught with challenges.

With a total population exceeding 1.2 billion and projections to surpass China as the most populous country by 2025, India offers tremendous opportunities for luxury brands seeking to tap the affluent segment. I asked Amit about households with incomes comparable to $250,000 and above in the United States. He said that there are a mere 220,000 ultra-affluent, or high-net-worth (HNW) households in India, compared with 2.4 million in the U.S., but that the ultra-affluent segment is growing at about 15 percent per year. If growth rates continue apace, the total number of ultra-affluent households will top 1 million by about 2020.

Underneath the ultra-affluent segment is a larger super-affluent segment of some 900,000 households with incomes ranging from $125,000–$250,000 U.S. which is growing at about 18 percent per year. By 2020 that segment of modestly affluent households will be just shy of 5 million. This segment is more easily targeted because these newly affluent consumers have a heady appetite for indulgence, are concentrated in a few major cities, and are socially and financially less diverse than the more stratified U.S. affluent segment. Of the super-affluent, Amit says, "These super-affluent are getting access to a more exclusive luxury lifestyle, and often their lifestyles imitate the HNWs in terms of the holidays they take, the education they are giving their children, and the sort of lifestyle pursuits to which they aspire."

In India, indigenous alternatives for luxury have always existed,

—Ritu Kumar, fashion designer

Amit advises that many affluents in India are not waiting with bated breath for luxury brands to appear in a local shop. Affluent Indians may not recognize your brand and what it means. Amit explains, "Luxury brands are all about creating that emotional connection with customers. A lot of luxury brands that come into India assume that customers know about the emotional allure of their brand and will buy it. But a lot of Indians who can afford to buy luxury brands haven't spent their childhood knowing about Prada or Zegna. There's a strong need to educate consumers about a luxury brand and why it is worth so much. The challenge you often have in India is that customers question why they should be paying those prices for luxury brands. They've not been steeped in the entire halo of that brand, and that needs enrichment, in creating the allure of the brand. Some luxury retail brands may struggle in this country, because while they've been very popular in their native country, the brands may be known by only a very small section of Indians. The brands have not invested in creating that brand equity."

Just as in Western markets, traditional advertising is less effective in portraying the value inherent in a luxury brand. "The role of traditional media has diminished," Amit advises. "You can't create buzz and excitement around the brand through advertising. What's important is having your brand associated with the right people, which is where the role of celebrities and socialites carries a fair amount of value. If you see people in the right social circles wearing the brand, who talk about the brand, that is what has meaning. In India the high-net-worth individuals have their own clusters; they're very connected to each other. Word-of-mouth has become increasingly important, as has social media through Facebook and Twitter. You have certain socialites who put their comments on Twitter, and it's getting picked up and listened, too. That is increasingly important to build and create a brand myth in India."

A second word of advice for marketers venturing into the Indian marketplace is to make no mistakes because affluent Indian consumers are unforgiving. Since they are so well connected with each other, one misstep will spread virally and cast a kind of shame on your brand that will be very hard to overcome. He says, "HNW Indian consumers are very conscious of their purchasing power. They realize they can demand the best in the world. One of the challenges for international brands is they can't afford to have flaws in the product quality, in the craftsmanship or in the service. Brands need to be very careful about how they provide end-to-end customer service delivery and not have any slip-ups. This is what brands have to be very careful about, especially if they launch in a hurry. They have to make sure there is not room for mistakes, because a customer in India is very unforgiving and intolerant to errors that may crop up."

High-net-worth individuals in India expect a store to send its salesperson to their home for personal shopping. Internet shopping hasn't caught on in India, because affluents want super-personal service. Amit says, "Indians want to look and touch and feel and that is an important requisite in buying luxury goods. They want to be pampered and will ring up the store and ask them to send a person over with their latest luxury collection so that they can have a look and then buy."

One thing HNW customers do once the luxury goods are hand-carried to their homes is check the stitching and examine the details. "In India the customer has a very keen eye for craftsmanship. It is difficult to fool the best customer just by passing off something as luxury if the quality and craftsmanship doesn't match," Amit warns.

As for the future of luxury in India, Amit shares his projections. "The economy in India is growing about 8 percent per year and that kind of economic growth is going to lead to much higher disposable income which can be spent on luxury goods and services. For the future, I see much higher consumption of luxury goods and services. In the past, one of the biggest constraints on luxury retail was the lack of space. Most luxury retail was housed in very expensive five-star hotels. But that is changing with the growth of 'High Street'–style luxury malls, which will attract a much larger group of customers. And we are going to see a change in the luxury consumer mindset with a change from savings to more conspicuous consumption. Younger Indian customers who may not be able to buy expensive luxe cars will be able to afford smaller luxuries and brands like Coach and Calvin Klein that are more premium than luxe. I foresee a boom for a lot of luxury and premium brands that will lead to exponential growth as the Indian economy continues to grow."

But Amit reminds marketers that marketing luxury brands in India is more than just making sure product is available. Luxury marketers have to deliver the kind of personalized, exceptional service that consumers in this culture have come to expect. "Increasingly, delivering exceptional services is going to be a priority for luxury brands. While many of these brands have products that are very good, there is a realization that service quality could be better. People will walk into a luxury retail store and show a lot of fascination about the product. However, the entire luxury shopping experience, which includes customer service, will have to improve. This is an area that brands have to watch out for. At times it seems like they believe that because they have a great product, they can knock off a little on their service standards. But Indian customers are unforgiving and they can't get away with low service standards."

That is a critically important message for luxury brands both at home and abroad. The affluent consumer with means expects exemplary standards of customer service. Putting the luxe into luxury is not just about making great product, but delivering it with supreme caring and concern for the wishes and desires of the customer.

Rainmaking in the Luxury Drought
#8 Evolve Your Luxe Brand or Risk Extinction

The best approach to take in our over-communicated society is the oversimplified message.

—Al Ries and Jack Trout, *Positioning: The Battle for Your Mind*

As we wrap our discussion of the steps you must take to make rain in the luxury drought, it all comes back to branding. Branding is the tool luxury marketers use to build expectations, enhance value, justify price, communicate the message, and deliver the experience to the ultimate customer. The key to putting the luxe back in luxury is to recreate, reimagine, and redefine the qualities of your product or service according to the luxury values the customer wants and desires. All that is done through branding; It is the very essence of luxury marketing.

While business libraries are chock full of books on branding, it isn't often you come across something that brings a different perspective, and new ways to approach the hard work of branding. That is why I was thrilled to discover the work of Andrea Syverson in *BrandAbout: A Seriously Playful Approach for Passionate Brand-Builders and Merchants,* her "how to" book on branding.

Andrea's inspiration for her BrandAbout methodology is the Aussie tradition of walkabouts, the famed rite of passage where an Australian Aborigine adolescent boy leaves his tribe to live on his own in the wilderness and after a time returns a man. Andrea describes her branding process as a "business walkabout ... a pause in the daily and weekly hubbub to stop and get not only a sense of how the brand and all its components are evolving, but also time to think about any course corrections that might be warranted."

The first question I asked of Andrea was whether different rules apply to luxury brands than to any other brand. Her answer, "No. Good branding, whether for a $5 product or $5,000 outdoor grill, involves respecting your customers, engaging them in an emotional way, telling your story, involving them in your story, and constantly having an aspect of wonder. It's the same for all brand disciplines even though the story, the price point, and the heritage are all different. Underneath it all, the foundation of brand building is the same."

But while the disciplines of branding are the same, luxury marketers seem to be particularly vulnerable to thinking that they operate in a special universe where the normal rules don't apply. Andrea explains, "Luxury brands tend to be insulated. They can be staid and sometimes they are slow to evolve, to innovate. Brands that target a mass audience recognize that their customers are constantly changing and so they need to change with them. Luxury brands tend not to embrace change, but change they must. The fact is luxury brands can reinvent themselves based on their heritage. Just look at Burberry. The company has evolved its heritage brand to make it relevant to today's and tomorrow's customer. Luxury brands need to keep reinventing, reimagining their brand. They need to tell new stories, or write new chapters of their old story, but tell it in new ways. Those that do that will continue to thrive and survive. When luxury brand leaders say our story has been told and we aren't changing it, this is where elitism and snobbery creeps in. There is no room for change or growth."

Innovating the brand and changing it as the customer changes is key. I asked Andrea about innovation. "It brings a sense of newness and wonder to an existing brand, product, or service. It is company executives putting their minds to their business in new and different ways. It's about thinking of ways to improve customers' lives in ways that they haven't thought of. The best way to make a real difference for customers is to be very curious about your customers and the world around them. That is where relevancy comes from. For example, Procter & Gamble brand managers spend twelve hours per month getting face time with their customers, listening and observing them, being an anthropologist to see if they can find new and better ways of delivering to the customer. And many technology companies, like Google and Microsoft, let their staff devote a certain portion of their time to pursuing their own independent projects. Innovation comes from getting outside of the day-to-day corporate structure. Luxury companies should foster that kind of environment of discovery."

Her advice to luxury brands is to stay inquisitive and find inspiration for innovation by studying their customers, their needs, their desires, their aspirations, their longings, and their expectations. Luxury brands need to be careful not to fall into the trap of believing that the normal branding rules don't apply. They need to keep changing and evolving with their current customers with an eye toward their future customers. Change in the consumer landscape is coming on faster and more furiously than ever before. Luxury brands are warned to change with the times, rather than let the times change them. The choice ultimately is brand evolution or brand extinction.

• • • • •

Ten Values on Which to Build Your Luxury Brand

People no longer buy a specific product just because of a brand (name). They want to know more about the story behind the product.

—Lutz Bethge, CEO, Montblanc

Atelier London, a design firm that specializes in bespoke bridal and party planning services, published a *Luxury Trend Report* based on insights from a panel of experts including Fiona Sanderson of The Luxury Channel, Georgie Coleridge-Cole of Sheerluxe, Fran Page of Liberty, and Pippa Isbell of Orient-Express. The report laid out ten key stories that a luxury brand has to tell. I have adapted their report into ten specific luxury values that you can use to craft brands that will inspire the ultimate customer.

The foundation of the Montblanc branding story is mythic, "Soulmakers for 100 years." The website tells the story: "In days gone by, people believed that if they touched an object, that object would form a bond with a part of their soul. Today such a thought seems almost absurd . . . until you enter the realm of Montblanc's master craftsmen." This brand myth transmits a quality story, but also it magically creates a connection with its products and the customer's soul. Let's look at how a venerable luxury brand like Montblanc uses each of these values to tell the story of its brand.

⊃ **Figure 21.1 Ten Brand Values**

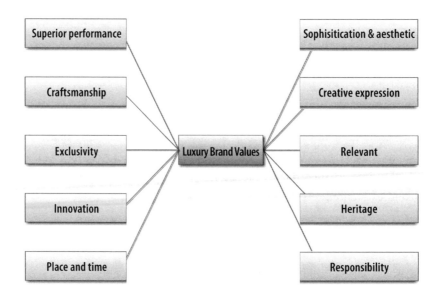

Source: Unity Marketing & Atelier London

Superior performance

A luxury brand connects with its customers by being at the top of its class, the best in its field. Montblanc has been renowned for fountain pens. The Meisterstück is Montblanc's classic fountain pen, which was first produced in 1924.

Craftsmanship

Luxury brands connect with customers by presenting the highest quality and craftsmanship. The connection is intimate and personal, like the touch of the hand. The Montblanc website celebrates the traditional craftsmanship and artistry that goes into every pen. To certify high quality, every pen is capped with a nib made from a band of 18K gold.

Exclusivity

Luxury brands connect with customers by making them feel special through the presentation of a unique experience. A Montblanc pen isn't just a pen; it is a fine writing instrument designed to be collected and cherished. It's far from ordinary or even premium; it's only for those who truly value its unique and innate qualities.

Innovation

Luxury brands connect with customers by presenting new visions and new ideas. Montblanc has used its heritage, craftsmanship, and expertise in fine materials to expand its product range to jewelry, watches, and leather goods. These products are new, but totally in keeping with the core brand heritage.

Sense of place and time

Luxury brands connect by being both timely, grounded in the here and now, and timeless, transcending time from the past to the future. Montblanc presents a profound understanding of its place and time, from the past with the brand named after the highest European mountain peak, to the present, offering old-fashioned writing instruments to special customers who crave an alternative to the fast pace of contemporary life.

Sophistication and design aesthetic

Luxury brands connect with their customers with an appreciation of customers' sophistication, and a celebration of the brand's unique design aesthetic. A Montblanc writing instrument is a work of art with every feature carefully designed to enhance the customer's writing experience.

Creative expression

Luxury brands connect through the spark of artistic creativity through a designer or visionary. Montblanc honors the writing craft by offering a line of "Writer Edition" pens to celebrate literary achievement. Inspiration for this line includes Ernest Hemingway, Agatha Christie, Edgar Allan Poe, and Oscar Wilde to name few.

Relevancy

Luxury brands connect by being relevant to their customers' lives and lifestyles. Relevancy makes the brand special and bespoke for the individual. For its Baby Boomer collectors, Montblanc introduced a John Lennon Edition to honor what would have been his seventieth birthday in 2010. The writing instruments came in three models: a $900 standard edition with a gold nib; a more premium "1940" edition engraved with the word "Imagine" and limited to only 1,940 pieces; and an ultra-luxe special limited edition of 70 called the "70s" made of white gold and set with sapphires and diamonds, priced for $27,000.

Heritage

Luxury brands connect with their customers through the story of their lineage and provenance. When customers buy a Montblanc pen, they are becoming part of and celebrating a 100-year heritage.

Responsibility

Luxury brands connect with their customers on a platform of social responsibility, giving back and doing good. Montblanc supports the arts and UNICEF. Of note, sales of the John Lennon edition pen support The John Lennon Educational Tour Bus, which provides students with the opportunity to compose, play, record, and produce songs and videos.

Invest

If past history was all there was to the game, the richest people would be librarians.

—Warren Buffett

Invest: That's the final word which is important for both you, luxury marketers, brand builders and retailers, and your customers. As marketers, you must invest resources—time, money, but most importantly, attention—to get ready for a new environment in the luxury market. You must invest in order to:

- **Integrate** new understandings about your customers, their lives, their challenges, their priorities and their values into your marketing strategies. You must transform your businesses around the concept of consumer-centricity for a prosperous future. You must reject old notions of product-centric marketing and organizational structure. You have to recognize that in this day when products are abundant and perfectly acceptable product substitutes can be found at all price points that product alone or even mostly won't set your brand apart. What will set your brand above the rest, makes it unique and unsubstitutable is the experience it delivers to the customer. That experience is defined by the values that your brand delivers to the customer. All this requires commitment to invest in understanding that customer through market research, CRM data and other customer tracking methodologies. But collecting customer data is not enough. You must use that data to discover new insights, new connections, new opportunities and new ways of delivering value to the customer.

- **Innovate** throughout the organization including the products and services you deliver to the customer and the way you deliver those products and services to the customer. It is through innovation that you will differentiate your brand's unique experience. Innovation requires being change. You must innovate to adapt to the new realities that you will face in the years to come as the demographics of the luxury market change and as their psychographics shift to express less materialistic values in their behavior as consumers. Further you must innovate as new ways of shopping and buying transform the retailing culture. Surely that will include internet shopping, mobile and social media, but with the rapid pace of change in technology, I expect that shoppers will have other new ways of shopping and buying in 2020 than we can even envision today.

- **Inspire** first yourself, your colleagues, your management as well as those you manage. In order to integrate consumer insights into your business and to innovate through new concepts, new processes, and new products and services you must engage the formidable imaginative and creative power that resides in the organization's staff from the lowest to the highest in the hierarchy. That is the only way to be successful in the business of luxury in the next decade as you confront powerful competitors both the ones you know and the new ones that will arise from unexpected places. The challenges of the future can't be met by people just doing their jobs by rote or just putting in their time; they have to be imaginatively and creatively engaged. After inspiring those in the organization, you must inspire those outside the organization: your customers and target customers. You will inspire them by showing them you understand their issues and priorities by delivering the experiences they value most through the products and services that you sell. Inspiration helps build desire, which creates an environment where a transaction can be happily to both parties' mutual benefit executed.

Invest is a key word for your customers of the future. As the luxury economy becomes more values based, customers are viewing their indulgences in luxury as an investment, rather than an expense. With an eye toward investment, that is maximizing the benefits or return they get from the money they spend, customers are willing to spend what it takes to create a relationship or execute a transaction with your company.

Today's smart affluent shoppers don't look at buying luxury goods and services as simply an expense; they treat the purchase of luxury as an investment in an improved quality of life. So they look at that potential purchase of a Tiffany bracelet, or that Hermès handbag, that Chanel jacket, that Patek Philippe watch, that four-day stay in the Ritz-Carlton Grand Cayman or that ten-day Mediterranean cruise on the Seabourn Odyssey as an investment toward greater happiness, greater satisfaction, greater self expression and realization.

Yet this savvy consumer-investor is able to immediately recognize that sometimes, maybe often or mostly, they don't need to invest as much as Tiffany charges when they want to enjoy a bracelet experience; or invest as much as Hermès commands for a handbag experience; and so on. As soon as you recognize that your brand is ultimately replaceable in the consumer's investor mindset, then you can start to build up the values in your brand to justify the customer's investment.

Investing is the new way that your luxury customers view their purchases and their interaction with your luxury brand.

About the *author*

Pamela N. Danziger is an internationally recognized expert specializing in consumer insights, especially for marketers and retailers that sell luxury goods and experiences to the masses or the "classes." She is president of Unity Marketing, a marketing consulting firm she founded in 1992.

Advising such clients as PPR, Polo Ralph Lauren, Diageo, Constellation Wines, Tempur-Pedic, Google, Darden, Swarovski, GM, Ford Motor Company, Orient-Express Hotels, *Marie Claire* magazine, Italian Trade Commission, Japan Brands, The World Gold Council, and The Conference Board, Danziger taps consumer psychology to help clients navigate and master the changing luxury consumer marketplace.

In recognition of her groundbreaking work in the luxury consumer market, Pam received the Global Luxury Award presented by *Harper's Bazaar* for top luxury industry achievers in 2007.

Pam is a member of "The League of Extraordinary Minds"—a panel made up of over 50 marketing and business experts, including such noted authorities as Al Reis, Jack Trout, Jay Conrad Levinson, Serigo Zyman, and Stephen Covey to name a few. Visit ExtraordinaryMinds.com.

Her other books include *Shopping: Why We Love It and How Retailers Can Create the Ultimate Customer Experience* (Kaplan Publishing, 2006); *Let Them Eat Cake: Marketing Luxury to the Masses—as well as the Classes,* (Dearborn Trade Publishing, 2005), and *Why People Buy Things They Don't Need: Understanding and Predicting Consumer Behavior* (Dearborn Trade Publishing, 2004).

Learn more about Pam and her work at UnityMarketingOnline.com.